CD BWK 061

MODERN
ECONOMIC PROBLEMS

PRENTICE-HALL ECONOMICS SERIES

E. A. J. JOHNSON, EDITOR

PREDECESSORS OF ADAM SMITH, *by* E. A. J. Johnson, Ph. D.

PLANNED SOCIETY, *edited by* Findlay MacKenzie, Ph. D.

MODERN BANKING, *by* Rollin G. Thomas, Ph. D.

ELEMENTS OF MODERN ECONOMICS, *by* Albert L. Meyers, Ph. D.

THE THEORY OF PRICES, *by* Arthur W. Marget, Ph. D.

LABOR PROBLEMS AND LABOR LAW, *by* Albion G. Taylor, Ph. D.

A HISTORY OF ECONOMIC THOUGHT, *by* Erich Roll.

MODERN ECONOMIC PROBLEMS, *by* Albert L. Meyers, Ph. D.

MODERN
ECONOMIC PROBLEMS

by

ALBERT L. MEYERS

Senior Economist
United States Department
of Agriculture

New York
PRENTICE-HALL, INC.
1940

COPYRIGHT, 1939, BY

PRENTICE-HALL, INC.

70 FIFTH AVENUE, NEW YORK

ALL RIGHTS RESERVED. NO PART OF THIS BOOK MAY
BE REPRODUCED IN ANY FORM, BY MIMEOGRAPH OR
ANY OTHER MEANS, WITHOUT PERMISSION IN
WRITING FROM THE PUBLISHERS.

First printing .... October, 1939
Second printing .... November, 1939
Third printing .... June, 1940

PRINTED IN THE UNITED STATES OF AMERICA

To

Professor Fritz Machlup

Preface

ALTHOUGH this book has been written as a companion volume to *Elements of Modern Economics,* it may well be used independently. The reader is assumed to be familiar merely with the modern theory of value and distribution and with the principles of monopolistic competition.

I wish to express my thanks to Dr. G. B. L. Arner and Dr. Theodore Norman, who read various chapters and made valuable suggestions. My debt to Professor Machlup is so great that nothing short of dedicating the book to him can properly express my appreciation.

It is to be distinctly understood that all expressions of opinion are my own and in no way reflect the official attitude of the United States Department of Agriculture.

ALBERT L. MEYERS

Table of Contents

CONTENTS

MODERN
ECONOMIC PROBLEMS

CHAPTER I

The State and Economic Policy

WHAT role the state should play in economic activity is one of the most difficult questions for the average individual to approach with an open mind. Most of us have simply accepted by absorption the ideas of the particular family or social group to which we happen to belong, without taking the trouble to examine or question these ideas on their own merits. This attitude is apt to be equally true whether we are the children of mineowners or mineworkers; of sweatshop owners or members of the Amalgamated Clothing Workers; of steamship owners or seamen; of chain store operators or of small independent retailers.

It is not the purpose of the author to advocate any particular cause or "ism." The minute that the economist indulges in such advocacy, he ceases to be an economist and becomes a politician or a moralist.[1] *As an economist,* all that he can do is to advise the politician, the moralist, or the social reformer as to the *economic* causes and consequences involved in their proposals. The economist may, therefore, say to the politician: "You desire to achieve a certain result for the people, but the plan you propose will not bring about the result you desire because of such and such economic principles." Or: "You desire to achieve two different results, but these two results are

---

[1] See Robbins, Lionel, *The Nature and Significance of Economic Science,* The Macmillan Co., New York, 1932.

1

not consistent with each other. If you attain one it will prevent you from attaining the other. Consequently you must choose between them." Or: "You desire to attain a certain result. It can be done, but only at such and such costs. Is the result worth the cost?" Or: "You desire to achieve a certain result. It can be done by any one of the following methods, each of which has such and such a cost. This is the one which will cost the least."

It will be noticed that the economist, *as an economist,* passes no judgment on the merits of the desired result itself. For instance, economics cannot prove whether or not this country would actually be a better place if everyone had absolutely equal wealth and absolutely equal income. (It may be doubted whether any other science could settle this question either, since the desirability of economic equality is disputed and hence there are no absolute criteria on which to base judgment.) Granted, however, that it is desired to bring about a situation in which all wealth shall be equally distributed, economics can show what would be the probable results of attempting to achieve such an end by taxation, by direct expropriation of wealth, or by whatever other means may be proposed. Economics can show further the probable changes in total expenditures by the people after wealth was so divided. It can also show (since people with smaller incomes ordinarily spend a greater percentage on consumer's goods than people with larger incomes) that, with equal incomes, total savings and total investment in capital goods would decline if saving were still to be a matter of individual choice. Perhaps our present rate of material "progress" is too rapid. Who knows? Nevertheless, we do see that rapid expansion of capital equipment is not consistent with equal incomes and voluntary saving. To meet this problem in Russia, the state has taken over the function of saving and investment by forcibly directing a certain amount of the labor and resources of the country to the production of capital goods, rather than consumer's goods. Whether the Russian worker is better off under successive Five-Year Plans than the American laborer under "exploitation" can partly be answered by budgetary studies, but must remain partly a matter of opinion.

It is not the intention of the author to influence opinion on questions such as these. He will be entirely satisfied if the reader has the same opinion after he has finished this book that he had before he started it. He will be more than pleased, however, if the book contributes in some measure to the formation of an opinion, based on reasoned judgment, instead of prejudice, on the questions which will be discussed.

The sphere of influence of national governments in the economic life of their individual citizens is widening greatly and is apt to continue to increase, regardless of the political form of government adopted, and even regardless of the avowed politico-economic philosophy of the parties in power. The fundamental structure of our economic life has become so complicated through specialization and through the interdependence of individual economic activity that we are confronted with a strange paradox. Even the advocates of laissez faire and the people who advocate "less government in business" are forced to devise laws to put their aims into effect or to attempt to achieve the ends they desire.[2]

Man's economic life has always been a struggle to obtain means for the satisfaction of his wants. Strange as it may seem, however, many of the most perplexing problems of governments of modern times arise out of the increasing command over natural forces which scientific discovery has given to man. There was no electric power problem until he discovered and harnessed electricity; no railroad problem until railroads were invented; no farm problem in the modern sense

[2] See Simons, Henry C., *A Positive Program for Laissez Faire,* University of Chicago Press, 1934.

until agronomy and mechanization had increased agricultural yields and until modern transportation fostered production for a world market; and no problem of labor and capital in the modern sense until the invention of tools and machines, too expensive for the individual workman to own, prevented the individual laborer from being his own capitalist.

It must not be assumed, however, that control by the state over the economic life of the individual is anything novel or startling.[3] It would be hard to imagine a more "regimented" form of "economic planning" than existed in the prescribed system of agricultural life on the medieval Manor, even as the control over the individual in the ancient city-state of Sparta probably still leaves something at which Mussolini and Stalin may shoot. The hereditary caste system of occupations in India might be cited as another example, although not one that resulted from conscious planning. The very existence of the state is a restriction on the individual, regardless of the benefits which may flow to the individual from such existence.

It may be doubted whether any state has ever existed that did not exercise some form of control over property. The question in dispute over governmental policy, however, is seldom the fact of such control. What we dispute about is: What constitutes property? Who shall own the property (individuals, groups or the state)? How shall property be acquired or disposed of? If property is privately owned, how much and in what manner shall it be taxed?

In spite of what we have said about the antiquity of government control over economic life, there are many aspects of the problem of government and business which have a distinctly modern flavor. Most of the ancient states were confronted with the relatively simple problem of crystallizing into laws

---

[3] See Mackenzie, Findlay, *Planned Society: Yesterday, Today, Tomorrow,* pp. 3-156, Prentice-Hall, Inc., New York, 1937.

the customs of an agrarian or pastoral people which had been developed and tested over long periods of time. The modern state, however, is confronted with the problem of changing its laws to conform to the much more rapid rate of technological and economic development which exists today. Furthermore, the modern state, in a greater or lesser degree, is attempting to direct consciously and actively the course of such development to particular ends. Both the ends to be achieved and the means by which such ends are to be attained are matters about which there are many grounds for legitimate differences of opinion.

In considering the role of the state in economic activity, we will be wise if we forget the old phrase, "natural rights." This phrase is really an unfortunate heritage from a pre-revolutionary school of French philosophers who contributed much that was otherwise valuable in early economic writings—writers so impressed with the "natural laws" that were then being discovered in the physical and biological sciences that they believed that anything which was "natural" was right. In consequence, when attempting to defend or to attack existing or proposed economic institutions, they devoted most of their time and effort in trying to prove whether the particular institution was "natural" or not, rather than endeavoring to ascertain whether the institution was expedient or whether it brought about results which they considered desirable. (In this attempt to prove the "naturalness" of institutions, they often demonstrated their ignorance of history and anthropology as well as their limited economic understanding.)

A single example may serve to show us how the phrase "natural rights" leads us into slipshod thinking. Private property is considered as a right under the laws of most countries today. Is it a "natural right"? Not at all! Without strong governments, capable of enforcing laws, property can be held only by those who are strong enough to prevent their neighbors from taking it. A very good case can be made for the institution of private property as a stimulus to economic activity, but the person who calls private property a "natural" right is simply weakening his case by giving his opponent an easy straw man to knock down. If capitalism is to survive under democratic government, its defenders must be active and intelligent rather than merely complacent.

We shall have more to say about the functions of government in connection with the specific problems discussed in the following chapters. It may help us, however, to review briefly at this time the more general functions of government in relation to economic activity.

Establishment of Definitions

One function of government is that of providing standard definitions so that people may know that they are talking about the same thing when they make an agreement. Thus, government defines what is to be considered property, what is a valid transfer of property, what is a claim of debt, and how such a claim may arise. It also establishes weights and measures, such as the pound, the quart, the foot, and the bushel. It defines what is to be considered as legal money. It may define grades for certain products such as corn or cotton.[4] This list of definitions made by government might be extended to some length, and their establishment is a tremendous help, without which modern business could be conducted only with extreme difficulty. Most of these definitions were established through the insistence of businessmen themselves. (The still faulty nature of some of the definitions provides lucrative employment for lawyers.)

---

[4] In some cases, the government simply takes grades or weights and measures already in use by the trade and gives them legal status. In other cases the government may actually establish standard grades where none have been in use before.

The Regulatory Function

A second, and extremely important, function of government is the establishment of regulations governing the economic conduct both of individuals and of business firms. Some of these regulations are designed to prohibit certain activities entirely (for example, laws against the purchase of stolen goods), while others may place very sharp limitations upon the field of business (laws prohibiting the sale of narcotic drugs without a doctor's prescription). Most of the regulations are designed to prevent certain specific abuses, either of one individual against another, of one business firm against another, of business firms against their employees or the public, or of individual actions against what is deemed to be the public welfare. Merely to list all of the regulations by Federal, state, and local governments that affect the economic life of individuals or businesses would require many volumes the size of this book. This large number of laws is due not only to a developing social conscience which tends to outlaw many old practices formerly considered permissible, but also to the fact that modern technology and modern economic development bring about many situations which the old laws fail to cover. (Old and useless laws of course tend to survive in our system unless they are systematically eradicated from time to time.)

For regulations to be passed by the legislatures and sustained by the courts it must be shown that they are in the interests of the "public welfare." At least in English-speaking countries, the presumption is in favor of individual liberties and private property. When a measure is proposed which will infringe on individual liberty or impair rights in private property, it must be shown that the "welfare of the community" will be increased sufficiently to justify the infringement on the rights of the individual. There are, to be sure, no absolute objective standards of what constitutes the "welfare of the community." In a people of diverse economic interests, diverse education, diverse religious beliefs, and diverse racial backgrounds, there will be wide differences of opinion as to what sort of measures will "improve the welfare of the community." We find laws proposed to prohibit the sale of intoxicating liquors, to prevent the use of animals in experimental medicine and biology, to prohibit railroad trains from running on Sunday, and to prohibit teaching that the earth is round. The sponsors of these laws all claim (and no doubt most of them sincerely believe) that they are in the interests of human welfare. In the absence of absolute standards, our legislature and judges operate on the theory that the people themselves are the best judges of what is for their own good, so that, when a sufficiently large majority is in favor of a measure, it is adopted and sustained by the courts. Thus we are dependent for our regulations upon the collective intelligence, or the collective ignorance, of the community.

Public Ownership

Ownership and/or operation of productive units to provide certain services for the people represents a third type of governmental economic activity. Here the question at issue is not only the matter of public welfare, but also the question of whether public welfare will be better served by public or private provision of the service in question. In some cases there is little doubt: public health, for example, is undoubtedly better protected in large cities by the municipal collection and disposal of garbage without charge than if the people were left to hire their own garbagemen. We could, of course, simply pass laws regarding the disposal of waste matter, but the cost of enforcing them (in the absence of free garbage collection) might be equal to or greater than the cost of free collection. Certainly the degree of sanitation achieved would be apt to be much lower. In connection with the rendering of some other services, light and power for example, the question of the relative efficiency (and other benefits) of public and private operation is much more in dispute.

Establishment of Monopolies

A fourth economic function of government is the establishment of monopolies. It is somewhat startling to reflect that a supposedly anti-monopolistic government establishes hundreds of thousands of monopolies for every one that it breaks. There are, of course, many kinds of monopolies. First, there are those that are called "natural monopolies," which may consist of the ownership of resources sharply limited by nature as, for example, a case in which there is only one single deposit of a certain valuable ore. The term has also been used to describe a situation in which the public is better served by allowing a single company to perform the service, rather than to allow competition in the field. For example, the streets of a large city would be a hopeless mass of confusion if anyone who wished to do so were allowed to lay street car tracks and run a street car line. Equally obvious difficulties exist in the competitive provision of electric power, gas, and water services. In the case of telephone service, there is clear advantage to the customer if the service is provided by a monopoly: he requires only one telephone in order to be able to talk to everyone else who subscribes to the same service, instead of two or three different telephones which would be necessary if the service were provided by two or three different companies, each with its own group of subscribers. In the services we have mentioned above, there is also a vast saving in cost, both to the companies themselves and to society in general, when the service is provided by a monopoly rather than by competitive companies with needless duplication of transmission lines, plant and equipment.

In the field of "natural monopolies," an appropriate governmental department grants the exclusive right to one company to render the service. The legal instrument which grants this right is called variously a license, a franchise, or a charter. The attempt is then made to obtain the benefits of lower cost of monopoly operation for the people, in the form of lower prices, rather than to allow the monopoly to absorb them as profits. This gives rise to the problem of rate regulation which will be considered in subsequent chapters. (Regardless of whether the lowest possible rates are achieved, we should not ignore the saving in real wealth for society which these forms of monopoly give by avoiding the waste of labor and resources resulting from the needless duplication of plant by competition.)

By the issuance of patents, government also creates monopolies. For a limited period of years, the inventor who receives a patent is given an exclusive right to use or dispose of his invention on the theory that the prospect of making a monopoly profit will act as a stimulus for invention. Undoubtedly it does so for many people. It should be noted, however, that physicians, surgeons, and many other research workers in the fields of pure science, ordinarily do not patent their discoveries but publish them instead for the world's benefit. These men seem to feel amply repaid simply by the respect and admiration of their fellow workers.

Copyrights for books and songs come under much the same general economic classification as patent monopolies. Of course we had both authors and composers before we had copyright laws. The ingratitude of public memory which has remembered the songs but forgotten their composers has ill-rewarded the creators of the folk ballads. Regardless of the motives of the creative workers, there is one argument that may be advanced in favor of the monopolies which are granted in books, songs, plays, and inventions. If it were not for the opportunity of sharing in monopoly profits, it is doubtful if

businessmen would be as willing as they are today to assume
the risk of placing a new product on the market. While we
can all think of many of these kinds of products which we
would prefer not to be marketed (perhaps this book is one of
them), we can have no assurance that the absence of monopoly
profits would eliminate them.

Trade-marks registered by the government are another form
of government-sponsored monopoly. The argument usually
advanced in favor of government protection of trade-marks is
that it allows the customer to identify the goods and to be
sure that substitution is not being practiced on him. This is
only partially true. All that trade-mark registration does is to
assure that the goods are being sold by the owner of the trade-
mark. A firm that builds up good will for its brand of coffee
by starting out with No. 1 Santos Coffee may gradually reduce
the grade to No. 4 or 5, while still retaining the same brand
name. Moreover, any owner of a trade-mark who has built up
a reputation for the quality of his product, may sell the trade-
mark, and the buyer may then sell whatever grade of product
he pleases under the old brand name. Clearly then, a trade-
mark protects the consumer only so long as its owner is interested in maintaining the quality of his product. As soon as
either the original owner or a second owner of the trade-mark
attempts to make a quick profit by deteriorating the product,
the brand name becomes a snare and a delusion instead of a
protection to the consumer. Even where quality is maintained,
blind adherence to trade-marks by consumers tends to render
price competition ineffective and so prevents the consumers
from obtaining the most for their money. There is no objection to maintaining the identity of goods by trade-mark. It
may be argued that the manufacturer who consistently maintains a high standard for his product should be allowed to
benefit somewhat from the resultant good will. But if what is
desired is protection for the consumer, trade-marks are not

enough. The establishment of Federal grades, plus the requirement that these grades be printed on the label *and in the advertising,* plus periodic inspection to prevent false statements, would be a far better protection to the consumer. As consumers are given objective standards by which to judge the quality of products, price competition becomes more effective and competitive increases of selling costs lose their attractiveness. The benefit of government protection of trade-marks accrues primarily and certainly to the owner alone. Such benefit as accrues to the consumer is incidental and is dependent upon the desire of the trade-mark owner to maintain his "good will" over a long period of time.

We have seen (1) that the government provides definitions and regulations for the conduct of economic activity, (2) that it engages in the provision of some economic services directly, and (3) that it grants monopolies to encourage the performance of some other kinds of services. We have by no means, however, exhausted all the economic implications of governmental activity. Many whole books have been written on the subject and many more will be written in the future. But a start has been made in developing a basis for consideration of the various possible positions the government may take in respect to the specific problems that we shall discuss in the following chapters.

CHAPTER II

Principles of Taxation

FROM the standpoint of their general economic significance, taxation and public expenditure should not be treated separately but should be considered rather as separate parts of one subject. For taxation is merely a means of raising revenue to meet the general or specific expenditures of the state. Economically, taxation involves taking money from some people and giving it to others to spend, but the net effect is that the tax-gathered money is spent differently than it would have been had people been allowed to use this money as they saw fit. The ordinary justification of this process of taxation and expenditure is that the collection of taxes from some people and the expenditure of the proceeds by the government results in a greater well-being than would have occurred had the individuals been allowed to make their own decisions as to the use of their money.

The Budget

A statement of anticipated income and anticipated expenditures drawn up by a government for some fiscal period (usually a year) is called the government's budget. If income and expenditure are equal, the budget is said to be balanced; if income exceeds expenditure, we call the excess a surplus; if expenditure exceeds income, the difference is called a deficit. Surpluses and deficits may occur either as the result of delib-

13

erate planning or as the result of circumstances which were unforeseen when the budget was drawn up. The government, for example, may plan its expenditures to be less than its income in order to have the surplus usable as a sort of reserve for emergencies which may arise, to repay old debts, or for any other purpose; or the surplus may arise simply because the income proves to be greater or the expenditures less at the end of the period than was anticipated when the budget was drafted. Thus an unforeseen deficit will occur whenever revenues fall below anticipations or when expenditures are undertaken which were not allowed for in the budget. A planned deficit arises when the government decides that certain expenditures are so desirable that they should be undertaken regardless of the fact that it is impossible (or politically inexpedient) to pay for them out of current tax revenue. In this event, it must borrow to meet the excess expenditures.

Government borrowing raises so many other questions that we shall consider the subject in another chapter. For the purposes of this chapter, we shall assume that the budget is balanced. For the time being, we shall also make the further assumption that all the government expenditures are desirable. We are thus left free to concentrate on the economic aspects of taxation itself.

Theories of Taxation

Several theories have been developed concerning the manner in which taxes should be levied by the states. Of these the principal ones which merit attention are called the ability theory, the benefit theory, the diffusion theory, and the economy theory. As we shall discover later, it is not always possible to devise a tax which will conform to all of these theories. But before beginning the discussion, some attention must be paid to different types of taxes. The following table will indicate the three fundamental types:

TABLE I

EXAMPLE	$1,000 INCOME		$10,000 INCOME		$100,000 INCOME		TYPE OF TAX
	Tax in dollars	Tax as per cent of income	Tax in dollars	Tax as per cent of income	Tax in dollars	Tax as per cent of income	
Poll Tax $10.	10	1.0	10	0.1	10	0.01	Regressive tax
Tax 1% of Income	10	1.0	100	1.0	1,000	1.0	Proportional tax
Graduated Income Tax	5	0.5	250	2.5	12,500	12.5	Progressive Tax

A regressive tax is one which declines *as a percent of income* as incomes become larger. In the example we have assumed a flat tax per head—constant in *amount* for all incomes. Note, however, that even a tax which increases in amount for higher incomes but does not increase in full proportion to the increase in income will still be regressive as a percentage. For example, suppose a tax of $10, $90, and $800 for the three income groups listed in the table. The tax as percent of income would then be 1.0 percent, 0.9 percent, and 0.8 percent respectively—still regressive taxation.

A proportional tax absorbs an equal *percentage* of income from all income groups.

The progressive tax is higher both absolutely and as a percentage as income increases. Sometimes (as in our Federal personal income tax), a part of this progression is achieved by exempting a certain minimum amount of income from the tax as well as by imposing higher percentages on the higher income brackets.

The Ability Theory

The ability theory states that a tax should bear most heavily on those who are best able to pay it. At one time the possession of property was regarded as a good indication of the ability to pay taxes. This was probably true, in a rough degree, in the days when real estate constituted not only the principal form of wealth, but also the principal form of income-producing property. Moreover, the existence of real estate is obvious to the naked eye and it is comparatively easy (economy theory!) to locate the owner for the purpose of collecting taxes from him. It is these two considerations which undoubtedly account for the survival of the real estate tax as such an important part of our state and local systems of taxation. Very early in its history, however, the real estate tax was found to be inequitable and many attempts were made to improve upon it in order to make it to conform more closely to the ability theory. Obviously, a flat tax of so much per acre on all farm land, good and bad alike, would not result in a just tax burden as between different land owners. To meet this problem, the tax on farm land was changed from a flat tax per acre to a tax based on assessed valuation, which supposedly took into account the earning power of the land.

In the case of urban dwellings, the application of the ability theory to real property in a misguided manner resulted in many curious taxes, some of them having exceedingly unfortunate results. For example, in England at one time houses were taxed according to the number of windows they possessed. The attempt to evade this tax by decreasing the number of windows resulted in a great number of badly lighted and ill-ventilated homes. The bricking-in of windows and the building of houses with fewer windows greatly reduced the amount of revenue which accrued to the state. Many other curious and unwise tax laws can be found in the old statute books. Even today, however, the regular practice of the assessors of raising the assessed valuation of a piece of property when painting and modernization are done probably accounts at least in part, for the squalor of many of our tenements.

In recent years we have come more and more to consider the income of an individual, rather than the property which he possesses, as the proper measure of his ability to pay taxes. This brings us to the question of graduated *versus* proportional taxation. A proportional tax would levy the same percentage rates on all incomes regardless of size. A graduated tax levies a *higher* rate of tax on higher incomes.

A little reflection will show that the progressive (or graduated) tax conforms far better to the ability theory than the proportional tax. It must be obvious that a tax of 40 percent, or $400,000, on a person with a $1,000,000 income would impose a far less strain upon his ability to pay than a tax of 10 percent, or $100.00, on a person with an income of only $1,000. It is also argued that the progressive tax imposes a more equal sacrifice upon all taxpayers. The measurement of such psychic sacrifice is, however, highly conjectural.

Some opponents of the graduated income tax have complained that it discourages initiative and decreases investment. Thus baldly stated, this argument is utter nonsense. As long as the tax is so graduated that an individual will receive a higher net income after taxes are paid on a higher income than he will after they are paid on a lower income, there is no discouragement for him to attempt to earn the higher income. I am sure that you and I would both rather be in the position to pay a tax of 50 percent on a million dollar income than we would to pay a tax of 30 percent on a $100,000 income.

There is an element of truth in the argument that a graduated tax discourages investment. If the graduated tax imposes a sufficiently serious burden, the person with a very large income may choose to invest all or a very large part of it in tax-exempt government bonds. The answer to this, however, is not to repeal the graduated income tax, but to remove the income tax exemption privilege from all forms of government bonds.

The risk element must also be considered. Investments that promise the most profits usually involve the greatest risk of the principal invested. As higher income taxes cut down the possible net return which may be realized from such investment, they tend to discourage the undertaking of risks. We may see this more clearly by considering it as the odds of a bet. Suppose there is a proposition with equal chances of success or failure that requires $50,000, but which will double my money if successful, and there is no income tax. This is an even-money bet. Now suppose that the government will tax my income 50 percent if the speculation is successful. I must then invest $50,000 in order to make $25,000 (after tax is paid). In other words, I have to give two-to-one odds on an even-chance bet. The limitation on possible profits is thus a deterrent to risk-taking.

An objection to the removal of the tax exemption privilege on government bonds has been made on the grounds that it would force the government to pay higher interest rates. This is not, however, so serious an objection as would appear at first sight. A comparison of the rate of yield on tax-exempt government bonds with the yields on industrial bonds which receive a triple A rating by *Moody's Manual* shows only a slight difference over a period of time. So long as safety of investments is the prime requisite in the minds of many investors, the bonds of a solvent government will continue to command high favor. This is evidenced by the fact that many charitable foundations whose entire income is untaxable nevertheless retain large portions of their funds invested in government securities. Furthermore, in times when a "strike of capital" is alleged, the removal of the tax exemption privilege from government securities might encourage more people to invest in private business, thus tending to create more employment and saving the government the necessity of borrowing more money for relief purposes.

The presence of the tax-exempt privilege on government securities in our income tax structure is certainly a contradiction of the ability theory. The person who draws an income of $50,000 a year in interest on government securities is obviously as fully able to pay a tax as an individual who draws a similar income as a salary for services to an industrial corporation. Indeed, the bond holder is really in a better position to pay a tax, since the business executive will lose his income whenever he is unable to perform his services or whenever the company decides to discharge him; the bond holder's income, in contrast, will go on regardless of other considerations so long as the government remains solvent.

The Benefit Theory

The benefit theory of taxation argues that taxes should be proportioned among different individuals in accordance with the benefits received from governmental activities. In its narrowest construction, this theory relates specific taxes to specific government expenditures. For example, the cost of laying water mains by a municipality is often assessed directly against the property owners whose property connects with the main. In the case of some improvements, such as new streets, the strict application of the benefit theory is apt to prove difficult. For instance, since all the citizens are free to use the new streets, it is obvious that the full benefit of the construction does not accrue to the adjoining property owners alone. This problem quite often receives a rough rule of thumb solution by simply assessing half of the cost of the streets to the adjoining property owners and the other half to the general taxation fund of the municipality. However, this solution still does not conform strictly to the benefit theory. Those property owners in the next block or in the immediate surrounding neighborhood will obviously derive more benefit in the use of the new streets and in the enhanced value of their property than

will accrue to property owners located in more distant parts of
the city. Some communities have attempted to meet this
problem by assessing the cost in inverse proportion to the distance from the improvement. Regardless of the method of
assessment adopted, it will be difficult to prove that it is in exact
accordance with the benefit theory.

Another tax that is in rough conformity to the benefit theory
of taxation is the tax on gasoline, to the extent that all the receipts are spent on public roads and none are diverted to the
general revenue of the state. However, since the damage done
to roads by trucks is probably greater in proportion than the
damage done by pleasure vehicles when compared to their
respective rates of gasoline consumption, the benefit theory is
not strictly applied by a flat tax per gallon on gasoline. This
deficiency is made up in part by charging the trucks a higher
license tag fee than is charged for pleasure cars. Since different
trucks travel different mileages over the public roads, a license
tag fee, even though based upon the weight of the truck, is not
strictly equitable. Diversion of gasoline taxes to uses other
than roads violates the theory entirely.

In the case of some services performed by the government, it
is simply impossible to apply the benefit theory of taxation.
For example, take the public health service of a municipality.
It is impossible to determine who would and who would not
have contracted smallpox in the absence of free and compulsory
vaccination, or who would or who would not have contracted
diphtheria in the absence of quarantine laws. Consider public
playgrounds as another area where the benefit theory cannot be
applied. People who live in the near neighborhood and have
children feel that they derive a great benefit from the existence
of the playground. On the other hand, people who live immediately adjacent to or across from the playground may feel
that the noise made by the children detracts from the value
of their property. The reader can think of many other kinds

of services in which it is difficult or impossible to apportion
the cost of the service in proportion to the benefit conferred.

A much more liberal interpretation of the benefit theory is
advanced by some authors and disavowed by others. This interpretation advances the thesis that in contrast with those with
smaller incomes or smaller amounts of property, those with the
greatest incomes or the greatest amount of property derive
much more benefit from governmental laws protecting private
property and enforcing contracts, and from the efforts of the
police force and of the army and navy in protecting the actual
holding of private property. This interpretation of the benefit
theory is then made an additional argument to the ability
theory in advocating a graduated system of taxation. A very
plausible argument can be made along these lines. However,
when we come to consider the activity of the police force and
the army and navy in protecting human lives as well as property, the application of the benefit theory becomes difficult
and doubtful. It would seem that the ability theory alone
would constitute an adequate defense for a graduated system
of taxation without having recourse to a somewhat doubtful
interpretation of the benefit theory.

Before turning to another subject, it may be well to point
out that there are some charges made by governments for
services rendered which cannot properly be called taxes at all.
Such, for example, are the charges made for registering deeds.
Where the charge simply covers the cost of the service rendered, such a charge is not a tax but a fee. No one is required
to register a deed to property, but the registration of the deed
makes it easier to prove the legal ownership. The county
usually performs this service and charges a fee for it which
covers its cost. Similarly, when a municipality furnishes the
water supply and charges in proportion to the cost of the
service rendered, such a charge is not a tax but a fee. In many
other cases this distinction may be more difficult to draw.

The Diffusion Theory

The diffusion theory (sometimes called the principle of the broad base) postulates that the tax burden should be spread over as many people as possible. The implication behind this is that the taxation of more people will mean that more people will take an interest in the government activity and will attempt to curb government extravagance. To the extent that this implication is true, the wide diffusion of the tax burden is particularly desirable in states which have universal suffrage. If each individual is made to realize that he must bear a share of the cost of government, he may be more hesitant to vote for foolish expenditures or to vote for legislators who propose foolish expenditures. In order to make this principle effective, however, the taxes must be levied in such a way that the individual realizes the full burden of the tax that he is actually paying. Indirect taxes which are concealed in the price of the product have no merit in this respect. It is even difficult for trained economists to determine exactly how much of a real estate tax is being paid by the landlord himself and how much is being passed on to the tenant in the form of higher rental. Consequently, many renters of dwelling space may vote for municipal expenditure without realizing what proportion of such costs they themselves will actually have to pay in the form of higher rents.

The Economy Theory

The economy theory of taxation postulates that as little as possible of the proceeds of a tax should be expended in actually collecting the tax and as much as possible should be available for the general revenues of the state. In the case of some types of taxes, the economy theory and the diffusion theory will be found to be in contradiction to each other. Ordinarily, the fewer the sources from which a tax must be collected, the less will be the cost of the collection in proportion to the total receipts. Thus, in the case of a tax on a manufactured article, the cost will be less if it is collected at the factory than if it is collected from wholesalers, and much less than if it is collected from retailers. It is sometimes claimed in such a case that diffusion is achieved by passing the tax all along the line to the consumer in the form of a higher price for the finished product. We shall discuss later under what circumstances and to what extent tax shifting may take place. For the moment let us grant that a full shift of the tax does take place and that the final consumer does pay the full amount of the tax. If under these circumstances the tax is concealed in the price of the product, the end sought by the diffusion theory is still not fulfilled, for if the consumer is in ignorance of the amount of tax he is paying, he will not thereby be motivated to demand governmental economy. For example, the federal revenue stamp on a package of cigarettes bears merely the picture of DeWitt Clinton and the words "twenty cigarettes" but states no amount of tax, so that an individual would have to look up the U. S. Internal Revenue laws in order to realize that if he smokes a package of cigarettes a day, he is paying about $30 a year to the federal government.

The income tax is another example of a tax in which the economy theory and the diffusion theory may conflict. At present, only a minority of our citizens pay this tax. However, if the exemptions under the income tax were drastically lowered, say to $500 for a single man and $800 for a married man, and at the same time the rate of tax imposed on these new taxpayers were made much lower than that paid by present taxpayers (to conform to the ability theory), it would be found that there would be large numbers of people paying income taxes of 25 or 30 cents apiece. Against this we would have to set the fact that the probable cost of sending out income tax blanks, receiving the returns, auditing them, and checking for possible violations would likely be in the neighborhood of 50 cents for each taxpayer. There still is one way out of this dilemma: we might repeal all or a large number of indirect taxes, such as those at present imposed on cigarettes, oleomargarine, cosmetics, beer and other articles bought in large volume by the poorer class. The revenue lost by the removal of these taxes might then be assessed on the poorer classes in the form of an income tax. If all of the federal taxes which an individual with a low income now pays without being aware of it were presented to him as a single lump sum income tax which he might see, the effect might be salutary. It might even prove to be the case that Congressmen could no longer make themselves popular by pointing with pride to the fact that they secured an (unnecessary) post office for the community or rushed through a bill to make Goose Creek navigable. Or it might be simply that people would vote for Congressmen who would promise to repeal their taxes and "soak-the-rich."

Although it is probably safe to say that a majority of the expenditures of government are for socially desirable purposes, even at present people with small incomes are paying a considerable proportion of the total cost of government directly or indirectly whether they realize it or not. Further expenditures of government will tend to be borne more and more by the lower salaried group. Remember that we are still assuming a balanced budget. The sooner the average individual is made to realize that services performed by the government are not a free gift, are not something for nothing, the sooner will he be prepared to take an active and intelligent interest in honest and efficient government.

Steady Government Income

In addition to the theories which have already been explained, there are certain other principles which are said to be essential for a sound policy of taxation. The first of these is that the revenue from a tax should remain fairly steady from year to year, or that it should be such that it can be counted upon fairly certainly at least a year or two in advance. If the revenue which a tax yields is fluctuating and uncertain, the government is apt to make expenditures, counting on estimated receipts from a tax, and then find that the returns are less than anticipated, thus giving rise to unforeseen deficits. The duties on imports furnish us with examples both of some of the steadiest and some of the most violently fluctuating forms of tax revenue return. The degree of stability of returns from import taxes varies both with nature of the product taxed itself and with taxing policy of the government. In general, the steadiest return from import taxes will be yielded by those commodities whose consumption is a matter of habit, or varies little from year to year, and which are not produced domestically. For example, the import tax on tea has been the steadiest form of revenue for the United Kingdom throughout its history. Taxes on sugar, coffee, and similar products are likewise steady producers of revenue. On the other hand, commodities whose purchase is a matter of fad or fancy are subject to wildly fluctuating degrees of revenue return—an import tax on batik shawls or mahjong sets might yield a fabulous return one year and shrink to zero the next.

For import taxes to constitute reliable sources of revenue, the government must so design the tax that it will be a revenue producer. This means that the government must give up all idea of a protective tariff in connection with its revenue policy, for the greater the degree of protection afforded by a tariff, the fewer goods will be imported and the less the revenue will be.

The principles to be followed by a government in designing a tariff to raise revenue are quite similar to those to be followed by a monopolist in determining his best monopoly price. In seeking the greatest return, the government will set its tax at such a point that the tax per unit times the total number of units imported would yield the greatest total revenue. Too low a tax will mean that the government is sacrificing some of the revenue which it possibly might have obtained from a commodity. Too high a tax will discourage imports either by decreasing domestic consumption or by encouraging domestic manufacture of the product and so will decrease the total revenue accruing to the government. The analogy to monopoly net return is practically perfect. In the days when England's tariff was designed primarily to produce revenue, a very simple device was adopted to avoid fluctuations in the returns due to domestic manufacture. Whenever a tax was placed upon the importation of a certain product, a similar tax was likewise placed upon its domestic manufacture. Thus, the government received its return regardless of whether the products were imported or manufactured at home. The problem then was simply the one outlined above, that of placing the tax rate at the point of greatest possible return. It should be noted that the imposition of a tax on domestic manufacture equal to the import tax on an article is a complete negation of any idea of protection; as far as the tariff is concerned, the foreign and the domestic producer are placed upon the same competitive basis.

The income tax, although conforming well to many other theories of taxation, is not reliable as a steady producer of revenue. The returns from this tax tend to fluctuate upwards and downwards with the movements of national income in the business cycle. It is not always possible or desirable for a government to expand and contract its expenditures in accordance with its receipts from the income tax. Indeed, if government expenditure is to be used as a means of alleviating business depression, it must be adjusted upwards and downwards exactly opposite to the fluctuation of the business cycle and of the private national income. This leads to the suggestion of government borrowing in periods of depression and repayment of government debts in periods of prosperity, which is considered in Chapter IV.

Simplicity of Tax Computation

Another requirement of a good tax is that it should be fairly easy for the average individual to determine the amount of the tax that he should pay. This requirement of simplicity offers many advantages: a tax which is simple to compute is more apt to be considered a fair tax and hence the motives to evade it are less; simplicity of computation reduces the number of suits which are brought in the court on interpretations of the tax law, consequently reducing the expenses of litigation both to the government and to private individuals; a simply drawn tax law is always far less expensive to administer than a complicated one.

The relative complexity of the American income tax structure arises from the fact that it is a tax on net income, and from the fact that no standard methods of accounting procedure are universally used by all individuals and corporations. Hence the Treasury is driven to the necessity of laying down more or less arbitrary rules of what does or does not constitute a legitimate expense or loss which may be deducted from gross income in order to determine net income. These rules must be applicable both to the proprietor of a corner candy store and to the president of a large steel corporation. The inclusion under the definition of income of increase in value of unsold property, and the allowance of deductions for losses in value on unsold property, further complicate the problem. Even professional accountants are apt to differ widely in their estimates of the value of a given piece of property and of the change in value which has taken place during a fiscal year. The attempt of the Treasury to lay arbitrary rulings for the computation of such values results in a complicated tax form. However, so long as capital gains and losses are a part of the law, the Treasury must of necessity make such rulings. It cannot simply leave the problem up to the individual and say, "Let your conscience be your guide."

Regulatory Taxes

A tax is sometimes used as a means of regulation for certain activities, either with no regard for revenue or with revenue as a second consideration. This use of the taxing power is generally resorted to by the legislatures to accomplish regulation which lies beyond their powers as defined by the constitution. It has long been recognized that Chief Justice Marshall was right when he said, "The power to tax is the power to destroy." If there is any business which the legislature wishes to wipe out, all that it has to do is to place a sufficiently high tax on it to render its operation extremely unprofitable. Yet this is really an abuse of the taxing power. In a dictatorship such a procedure is unnecessary; all that a dictator has to do is to publish an edict forbidding the practice of a certain kind of business, and the enforcement of this edict will accomplish the end. In a democracy the use of the taxing power for regulatory purposes generally means that the legislature is exceeding the authority entrusted to it by the people. If the people desire to give the legislature more power, this can be done by constitutional amendments. Such an amendment may be drawn either so as to confer more general power on the legislature or to empower them to act with respect to the particular evil under consideration. If the people do not wish to entrust the legislature with such power, the power should not be exercised by indirect means through this use of the taxing power.

Unless there is external evidence, it is sometimes not easy to tell whether a particular tax is designed as a revenue producer or as a means of regulation. Sometimes, either through ignorance or through unforeseen circumstances, a tax which was designed in all good faith as a means of raising revenue may prove to be a weapon that drives an industry out of business. However, when specific regulations are laid down in the tax bill and the tax is then levied on those who do not conform, the intent of the legislature is clear. In such cases, if the regulation is beyond that entrusted to the legislature or the constitution, the courts will not hesitate to throw the law out. Such was the fate of one of the child labor laws passed by Congress. It may be regretted that this and many other socially desirable laws may be likewise declared unconstitutional. However, we cannot overlook the fact that if legislatures are given free rein with the taxing power, they may pass many socially undesirable laws as well as many socially desirable laws. For example, a lobby of potato growers might be able to bring sufficient pressure to bear upon Congress to jam through a law putting a tax of $2 a pound upon spaghetti; or an anti-vaccination society might succeed in getting a state legislature to put a tax of $50 a gram on smallpox vaccine.

Sometimes the regulatory tax is designed merely as a discouragement rather than as an outright prohibition of a particular practice. For example, some people advocate high taxes on cigarettes and alcoholic liquors in the hope that this will decrease their consumption. Such laws are usually upheld by the courts, since the revenue that is raised is clear and the regulatory aims are not stated in the act. Nevertheless, the same objections apply to them as to taxes that are outright confiscatory or prohibitive.

CHAPTER III
Shifting and Incidence of Taxation

WE NOW come to one of the most difficult and involved subjects in the field of economics—the question of who actually bears the burden of the taxes that are levied by the various agencies of the government, and the question of who will actually bear any new taxes that are imposed.

By the "shifting" of a tax we mean the passing of the burden of paying the tax from the person or firm on whom it was originally levied to someone else. If, for example, a tax of 3 cents per unit is levied on the manufacture of a certain article, and if the manufacturer should then find it expedient (that is, that it gives greatest net return after the tax is paid) to raise the price of the article by 3 cents as he sells it to the wholesaler, we should then say that the manufacturer had shifted the tax to the wholesaler. If the wholesaler in turn finds that he fares best by raising his selling price by 3 cents, he will shift the tax to the retailer. The retailer might then raise his selling price by the same amount and so shift the tax to the consumer.

Before going any further we must note that, in the actual world, the mere fact that the price of a product rises by the amount of the tax is not sufficient evidence that a tax has been shifted. In the example above, if, at the same time the tax was imposed, the manufacturer's other costs had risen by 2 cents, then the raising of the price by 3 cents would shift only

1 cent, or one-third, of the total tax burden and the manufacturer would himself be paying two-thirds of the tax. If the other costs had risen by 3 cents, an increase in price of only 3 cents would leave the manufacturer paying the entire tax and not shifting any of it.

Contrariwise, the mere fact that the price of a product does not rise after a tax is imposed is insufficient evidence that the tax has not been shifted. The manufacturer may find that he is able to force the producers of his raw materials to accept lower prices, or that he is able to force his workmen to accept lower wages, as a result of the tax. Taxes may be shifted backward as well as forward in the production process. Note, however, that before we say that the tax has been shifted backward in any case, it must be shown that the tax was the occasion for the decline in raw material prices or wages. If such declines would have occurred without the tax (and no decline in selling price would have taken place), then the manufacturer is himself paying the tax out of what would otherwise have been increased profits.

By the "incidence" of a tax we mean the place where the tax burden actually falls. The incidence of a tax falls on the person who is unable to shift the burden to someone else, that is, the one out of whose pocket the tax finally comes. It does not matter who turns the tax money over to the government. If a tax is levied on a manufacturer, he will be the one to turn the money over to the government. However, if through higher prices the tax has been shifted all along the line to the consumer, he is the one upon whom the incidence of the tax actually falls. In some ways the manufacturer and the other dealers may be said to be acting as agents in collecting the tax for the government.

So long as the government receives the money, it might, at first sight, appear to be a matter of indifference on whom the incidence of the tax falls. Many taxes are indeed levied in this careless fashion with little heed as to what group of people is actually going to bear the tax. Nevertheless, difficult as the problem of determining incidence may be, it cannot be ignored if we are concerned with equalizing the burden of taxation or apportioning it according to any of the theories (ability, benefit, and so forth) outlined in the previous chapter. We may say, for instance: "Here is an industry which can well afford to pay a tax." However, unless we are extremely careful of the manner in which the tax is levied, we may find that the tax is finally paid not by the industry on which it was levied but by a group of people who were already overtaxed.

Even from the point of view of raising revenue, however, the incidence of a proposed tax must be taken into consideration. If the burden of paying a new tax falls on a group of people who are already buying other taxed articles, the purchase of which they now reduce, then the loss of taxes on these goods will have to be offset against the receipts from the new tax. Under circumstances which are not at all improbable, the imposing of an unwise new tax may even decrease the total revenue which accrues to the state. Let us suppose, for example, that there is already a tax on women's silk stockings but that this tax is actually being borne by the manufacturer and not passed on to the consumer. Now let us suppose further that a new and extremely heavy tax is placed on lipsticks and that this tax is shifted to the consumers (by the consumers I mean the women who buy the lipsticks—not the men who absorb them incidentally). It is entirely possible that many women might then be willing to go bare-legged rather than refrain from painting their lips. The loss in revenue from the tax on silk stockings, which are no longer sold, might then be greater than the returns from the new tax on lipsticks, and the total revenue to the state would have declined because of the imposition of the new tax.

Factors Affecting the Incidence of Taxation

We shall now attempt to analyze the conditions which either force the persons or firms on which a tax is levied to bear the tax themselves, or which enable them to shift the incidence of the tax to others. Except for a few rare individuals, anyone on whom a tax is levied will cheerfully attempt to pass the tax on to someone else if he is able to do so, rather than pay the tax himself. We must look for the conditions under which people are able to shift all or part of a tax to others. We may assume, with a fair degree of accuracy, that a tax which is capable of being shifted will be shifted.

Let us consider the question of incidence first in connection with what we may call business taxes (taxes which are levied on the manufacture or sale of a product, on the use of capital goods or productive factors, or on the income of business firms). There are several factors which we shall have to consider in connection with these taxes: (1) the type of tax which is imposed; (2) the nature of the total demand for the product; (3) the degree of competition in the market where the industry sells its products (monopoly, oligopoly, monopolistic competition, pure competition); (4) the technical cost conditions in the industry (shape of the technical cost curves); (5) the nature of the total supply of the means of production to the industry; (6) the degree of competition in the market where the industry buys its means of production (monoposony, oligopsony, pure competition among buyers). Unfortunately we shall not be able simply to take each of these elements and generalize upon it, but we must take them in various combinations according to the special problems which are presented by them.

Taxes as Business Costs

Any tax which is imposed on a business must be considered first as an addition to cost. The question then arises as to whether it is advisable for the firm to alter its scale of output as a result of this change. If output is decreased by a monopoly, the smaller output can be sold at a higher price. The difference between the higher price and the former price will then represent the amount of tax per unit of product which is being shifted to the buyer. This difference, multiplied by the total number of units sold, is the amount of the total tax which is shifted to the buyers. (As we shall see later, the price rise may exceed the tax under certain conditions.) We must note carefully, however, the different results which are occasioned by different types of taxes. A tax which is in the nature of a lump sum (that is, which does not vary in amount with output or sales) will be in the nature of an addition to fixed cost. Such a tax will not change either marginal cost or average variable cost and hence will occasion no change in output by the monopoly. On the other hand, a tax of a certain sum per unit of output, or a tax expressed as a percent of gross sales, will be an addition to average variable cost and to marginal cost and will thus occasion a change in output to the point where the new marginal cost (including tax) and marginal revenue are again equal.

Tax as Fixed Cost

Under monopoly, any tax which is in the nature of a lump sum tax will be paid entirely by the monopolist and not passed on to the buyer. A lump sum tax is really a fixed cost. A fixed cost, it will be remembered, is one which remains constant as a total and does not vary with changes in output, regardless of the number of units produced. Since marginal cost is defined as the additional cost necessary to produce one more unit of output, it obviously contains no element of fixed costs. This is the case with any tax assessed as a fixed amount on a monopoly. Such a tax makes no change in the marginal cost curve of the firm, and so the point of greatest monopoly profit is at exactly the same output as before. Monopoly profits will, of course, be decreased by the amount of the tax, but there will be no other point of output at which net monopoly profits will be any greater than at the old output and the old price. This statement is based on the assumption that the monopolist was already charging the full monopoly price for his product before the tax was imposed. If this is not the case, the imposition of a tax may cause him to re-examine his price policy with a view to charging the full monopoly price. In such an event some part, or all, of the tax may be passed on to the buyer. However, we have no assurance that the monopolist would not have sooner or later discovered the error in his pricing policy even without the imposition of the tax. Thus, under these circumstances, the tax is the immediate occasion rather than the ultimate cause of the higher price to the buyer.

A lump sum tax might be imposed in the nature of a license fee or franchise tax, a tax as a percent of net income, or, in the short run, a tax stated as a percent of the assessed value of capital or real estate. While we have said that a tax of this sort on a monopoly cannot be passed on to the buyer (if the monopolist has previously been charging the full monopoly price), there are some circumstances under which the tax may be evaded. If the monopoly is not dependent upon location, the firm may move out of the jurisdiction of the government which imposes the tax. The burden of heavy taxes has been the cause of movement from one city or state to another by many manufacturing firms which were highly competitive, as well as by firms which possessed a greater degree of monopoly power.

If a tax burden absorbs all or a great part of the net income of a monopoly firm which is unable to move, other expedients may be adopted. Maintenance expenditures may be discontinued or greatly reduced in an effort to recover some part of the money capital invested. To the extent that the capital goods of the firm are not specialized to the particular business, they may be sold or invested in other lines not so heavily burdened by taxes. It is a nice question to be determined how much a monopoly can be taxed without being taxed out of existence.[1]

Tax as Constant Variable Cost

A variable cost is a cost which changes *as a total* with changes in output. When we speak of a tax as a constant variable cost, we mean one which is constant *per unit of output* but which increases *as a total* when output increases, because the tax must be paid on more units of output.

When a tax is levied on a per unit of output basis on a monopoly, the tax becomes an addition to marginal cost at each possible output. The point of intersection of the marginal cost and marginal revenue curves is thus shifted to the left. That is, the point of greatest monopoly profits after the tax is included as a cost will be at a lower output than before the tax was imposed. The assumption is again made that the monopolist has been charging the full monopoly price before the tax was imposed, and that the conditions of production other than the tax and the conditions of demand are unchanged. Part of a tax per unit of output on a monopoly will be passed on to the buyer. There are several circumstances which will govern the proportion of the tax which is so shifted:

(1) The closer to horizontal the slope of the demand curve, the greater the proportion of the tax that will be paid by the seller; and, conversely, the steeper the slope of the demand curve, the greater the proportion of the tax that will be paid by the buyer.

(2) (a) If the point of greatest monopoly profit was on the declining part of the marginal cost curve before the tax was

---

[1] If the invested capital is mostly borrowed, the firm may, of course, be taxed into bankruptcy long before the operating unit is taxed out of existence. However, so long as any positive rate of return is being earned on invested capital, it is most likely that the firm will continue to be operated either by the original owners or by the creditors rather than an attempt made to withdraw capital in the manner outlined. All monopoly profits might be absorbed by the discussed type of taxation without causing the business unit to discontinue.

imposed, the greater the slope of the marginal cost curve, the greater the proportion of the tax that will be shifted to the buyer; and, conversely, the less the slope of the marginal cost curve, the greater the proportion of the tax that will be borne by the seller.   (b) If the point of greatest monopoly profit was on the rising part of the marginal cost curve before the tax was imposed, the greater the slope of the marginal cost curve, the greater the proportion of the tax that will be borne by the seller; and conversely, the less the slope of the marginal cost curve, the greater the proportion of the tax that will be shifted to the buyer.   (c) In general, a greater proportion of the tax will be shifted if the point of greatest monopoly profits was on a declining phase of the marginal cost curve than if the point was on a rising phase of the marginal cost curve before the tax was imposed.

Diagram 1 illustrates the effect of the imposition of a tax per unit of output on a monopoly under one set of demand and cost conditions.   Note the following results:

	Before Tax Was Imposed	After Tax of $5.00 Per Unit of Output Was Imposed	
Selling Price.......	$ 22.00	$ 25.00	Increase in price to buyers.......... $ 3.00
Average Total Unit Cost	12.50	19.00	
Profit per Unit.....	9.50	6.00	Decrease in seller's profit per unit..... $ 3.50
Total Revenue.....	528.00	500.00	
Total Cost........	300.00	380.00	
Net Profit.........	228.00	120.00	Decline in seller's profits $108.00

Consumers lose 4 units of goods formerly
worth $22.00 each—total $88.00, but
spend $28.00 less, leaving a net loss to
consumers of[a]...   60.00

Total loss to consumers and seller............ $168.00
Revenue to government $5.00 on 20 units, total
tax revenue............................   100.00

Apparent net loss to the community........... $ 68.00

[a] The $28.00 is now spent for other goods, but these other goods presumably yield less satisfaction or the consumers would have bought them before they were induced to do so by the price change occasioned by the tax. Consequently, the total loss to the consumers may exceed the money loss of $60.00.

A TAX AS A CONSTANT

VARIABLE COST

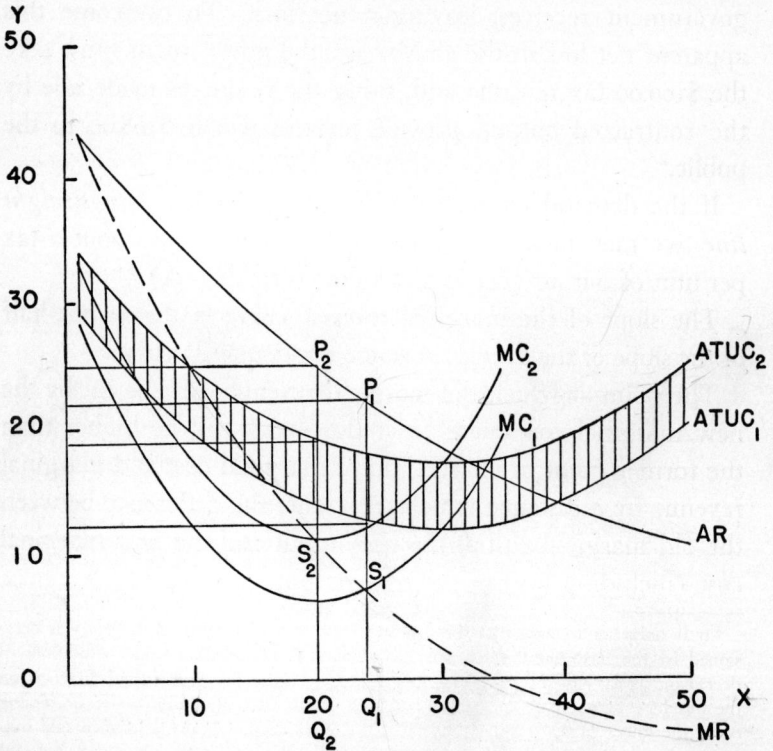

DIAGRAM 1

AR is average revenue (that is, demand curve)
MR is marginal revenue
$ATUC_1$ is average total unit cost before the tax
$ATUC_2$ is average total unit cost including the tax
MC_1 is marginal cost before the tax
MC_2 is marginal cost including the tax
S_1 is the point of intersection of marginal cost and marginal revenue before the tax
S_2 is the point of intersection of marginal cost and marginal revenue after the tax
P_1Q_1 is the price before the tax
P_2Q_2 is the price after the tax
OQ_1 is the monopoly output before the tax
OQ_2 is the monopoly output after the tax

It will be noted that there is sometimes a sort of "dry loss" possible in taxation—that is, a loss in value to the seller and consumers combined which is greater than the revenue the government receives, leaving a net loss. To overcome this apparent net loss in the above case, the government must take the $100.00 tax revenue and, using the resources made idle by the contracted output, provide services worth $168.00 to the public.[2]

If the demand curve for a monopoly product is a *straight line,* we may make the following generalizations about a tax per unit of output (tax as a constant variable cost):[3]

The slope of the marginal revenue curve is always one-half of the slope of the average revenue (or demand) curve.

The point at which the marginal revenue curve is cut by the new marginal cost curve (including tax) will be higher than the former point of intersection of marginal cost and marginal revenue by a distance which represents the difference between the old marginal cost at the old output and the new marginal cost (including tax) at the new output.[4]

---

[2] It is only fair to note that the loss in excess of the amount of the tax was occasioned by the fact that the tax was placed on a firm operating under conditions of decreasing costs. If the government should spend the tax proceeds of $100.00 on the purchase of goods from some other firm or industry operating under decreasing costs, the lower prices to other buyers of this second good (caused by increased output at lower cost) might offset the "dry loss." We neglected, of course, the cost to the government of collecting the tax.

[3] See Robinson, Joan, *Economics of Imperfect Competition,* Ch. 5, Macmillan & Co., Ltd., London, 1934, for a fuller explanation of this subject.

[4] These rather lengthy statements are necessary to avoid ambiguity. I had experienced some difficulty in reading Joan Robinson, but it was Professor Machlup who pointed out to me that this is an example in the use of the phrase "change in cost" exactly analogous to the ambiguities we have suffered from the use of the terms "change in supply" and "change in demand" both as point changes and as schedule changes. Whenever Mrs. Robinson uses the expression "change in marginal cost," one must be careful to note from the context whether she means: (1) A change from one point to another on the same curve, (2) a change from one

Therefore, with a straight line demand curve, the rise in price due to the tax is always equal to one-half the difference between the old marginal cost at the old output and the new marginal cost (including tax) at the new output. This may be seen from Diagram 2.

TAX AS CONSTANT VARIABLE COST
STRAIGHT LINE DEMAND CURVE

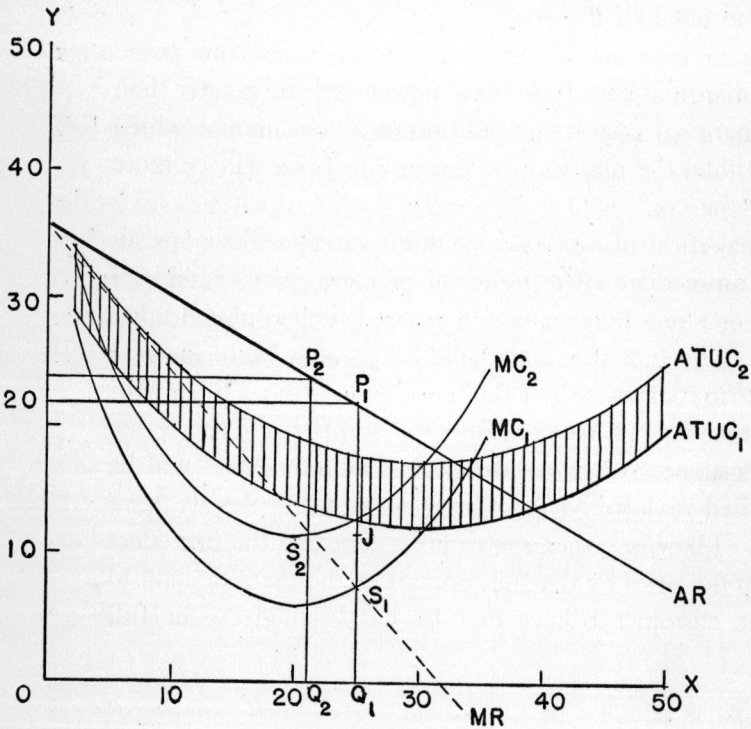

DIAGRAM 2

Point S_1 is marginal cost at old output
Point S_2 is marginal cost including tax at new output
On the line P_1Q_1 point J is measured equal in height to point S_2
The distance JS_1 then represents the change between marginal costs at the old and the new output
P_2 is above P_1 by one-half the distance JS_1

---

cost curve to another, or (3) a change from one point on one cost curve to another point on another curve. Until our economic vocabulary is enriched by words which sharply distinguish these meanings, we shall have to suffer from circumlocutions for the sake of clarity.

If marginal costs are constant, the increase in marginal cost will be equal to the tax and the increase in price will be equal to one-half the tax.

If marginal costs are rising at the former equilibrium output, the difference between the marginal cost at the new equilibrium point on the new marginal cost curve (including tax), and the old marginal cost at the old output, will be less than the amount of the tax. Therefore, the increase in price will be less than one-half the tax.

If marginal costs are falling at the former equilibrium point, the new marginal cost at the new output will be greater than the old marginal cost at the old output by an amount which is greater than the tax, and the increase in price will be more than half the tax.[5]

The final effect of a tax as a constant variable cost is not always the immediate effect in actual practice. For example, a new tax, or a tax increase, of 1 cent per gallon is placed upon gasoline. The first reaction of the sellers may be to increase their price to consumers by 1 cent in order to impress them with the idea that the tax has been imposed and that the rise is due to the tax alone. Later on, the price (including tax) will be either raised or lowered according to the principles we have outlined. Likewise, when such a tax is repealed, the first effect is to drop the price by the full amount of the tax reduction to make the customer believe that he has been given the full

---

[5] In this case, if the slope of the old marginal cost curve is equal to the slope of the average revenue curve, the price will increase by the full amount of the tax. If the slope of the marginal cost curve is greater than the slope of the average revenue curve, the price will increase by more than the tax. If the demand curve is concave, the effect upon price by the tax will be greater the greater the concavity of the demand curve.

Most of the ideas in this section on taxes on monopoly as constant variable costs are the result of Mrs. Robinson's efforts to examine further the proposals of Marshall and Pigou to tax increasing cost industries and to give a bounty to decreasing cost industries. Whatever improvement in statement I have made in Mrs. Robinson's propositions is due to the help of Professor Machlup.

benefit of the reduction. Later the price will return to the most profitable point (not including this tax or part of tax).

Tax as a Changing Variable Cost

By a changing variable cost we mean a cost which changes both *per unit of output* and *as a total* when output is changed.

A TAX AS A CHANGING

VARIABLE COST

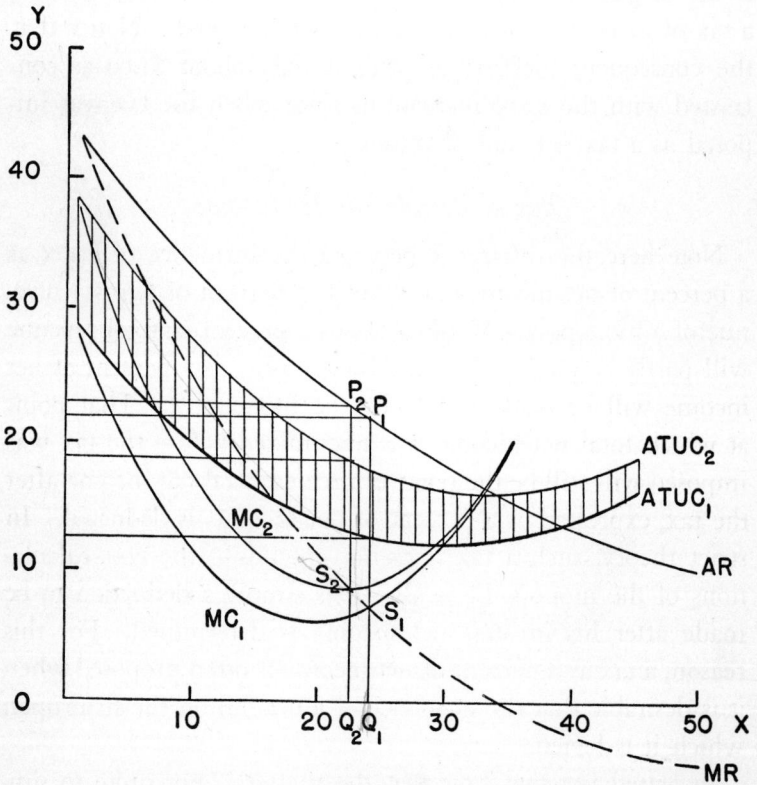

DIAGRAM 3

A good example of such a tax is a Gross Sales Tax. Such a tax is simply a tax expressed as a percent of total revenue. The marginal cost of such a tax will be the same percent of marginal revenue as the tax is of total revenue. It follows from this that a tax expressed as a percent of total revenue will occasion much less reduction of output and much less increase in price than a tax of a similar amount levied as a tax per unit of output. The demand curve and the cost curves, before the tax was imposed, in Diagram 3 are exactly the same as in Diagram 1. In Diagram 1 the tax was assumed to be $5.00 per unit. This is slightly less than 23 percent of $22.00 which is the original monopoly price in both cases. In Diagram 3 a tax of 23 percent of total revenue was imposed. Notice that the consequent increase in price is only about $1.00 as contrasted with the $3.00 increase in price when the tax was imposed as a tax per unit of output.

Tax as Percent of Net Income

Note here the difference between the incidence of a tax as a percent of net income and a tax as a percent of (gross) revenue of a monopoly. While a tax as a percent of total revenue will partly be passed on to the buyer, a tax as a percent of net income will be paid entirely by the monopolist. That point at which total net income was maximized before the tax was imposed will still be the point of greatest total net income after the tax, expressed as a percent of net income, is deducted. In strict theory, such a tax does not enter into the cost calculations of the monopolist at all. It is simply a deduction to be made after his greatest net income is determined. For this reason, a tax as a percent of net income is often proposed when it is desirable that the incidence of a tax fall on the firm upon which it is levied.

In actual practice, however, the matter is not quite so simple. Although the tax cannot be shifted, it is one of the types most subject to evasion as there is no commonly accepted definition of what constitutes net income. It is true, of course, that net income is generally defined as gross receipts minus the costs of production. This, however, does not help us much, for it only gives rise to the question of what are the legitimate costs of production which may be deducted in computing net income for tax purposes. For instance, a man may own all, or the majority control of a certain company. He then may decide to pay himself $50,000 or $100,000 a year, alleging that this sum represents his wages of management and should be allowed as a cost deduction in figuring net income for the firm. Such a sum may, in many cases, be obviously much greater than his services are worth, but who is capable of saying with exactitude that the man's services are worth exactly so much and no more to the firm? Under such circumstances, the Treasury (or other tax collection agency) is forced to make arbitrary rulings and even then every individual firm's tax return may be subject to review by the courts. Such a process is costly and uncertain both for the taxpayer and the government. Moreover, the manager's salary is not the only element of cost which may be a subject of tax evasion or a matter of legitimate doubt. For this reason, a tax as a percent of gross sales may sometimes be preferred to a tax as a percent of net income because, although some part of the sales tax may be shifted, it is much less subject to evasion than the tax on net business income. The incentive to tax evasion is present, of course, in all taxes; the difference is one of degree.

Taxes on Industries Operating Under Conditions of Monopolistic Competition

The probable incidence of taxes on industries operating under monopolistic competition is even less certain than their incidence on perfect monopolies. Under the heading of perfect monopolies, we were free to assume that the demand curve of the firm would remain unchanged after the tax was imposed and to devote our entire attention to the effect of the tax upon marginal cost. Under monopolistic competition, however, the demand curves as well as the cost curves of the individual firms may be altered by the tax, and we shall have to take this circumstance into account. A tax that is applied generally to all or to a large part of articles consumers buy will have some effect on the demand curve for a monopoly product, due to changes in relative prices of other goods and to changes in income distribution occasioned by the tax. However, since by definition there are no close substitutes for monopoly products, the results on the demand curve are largely indeterminate and we have neglected them. On the other hand, firms operating under conditions of monopolistic competition are, by definition, selling products which are closely competing substitutes for each other. Therefore, we shall try to consider the effects resulting from their competitors' reaction to the imposition of a tax on the demand curves of the individual firms.

Tax as Fixed Cost

For a group of firms operating in an industry under conditions of monopolistic competition, the effect of a lump sum tax upon the *cost* of each individual firm will be exactly the same as the effect of the same type of tax under monopoly. That is, the tax represents an increase in fixed costs but has no effect upon marginal cost, and hence there is no tendency *on the cost side* to reduce output of the individual firm in order to shift the tax to the buyer. On the demand side, however, several circumstances may occur:

(1) The burden of the tax may be such as to force some of the competing firms out of business. In this case, the customers of the defunct firms will be distributed among the firms that remain in business, increasing the demand for their products, but we have no reason to presume that the increased demand will be distributed equally among the re-

maining firms. Some firms may obtain the lion's share of the old firms' customers; some may obtain very few, and some may obtain none at all. In this event, the firms receiving the greatest increase in demand may find it most expedient to raise their prices sufficiently to shift the entire burden of the tax on to the buyers. (It may even be that their net profits are greater after the tax is imposed than before.) Some firms will be able to shift a part of the tax to the buyers, while others may have to absorb the entire cost themselves.

Under certain circumstances, the prices charged by all firms that remain in business may be even less than before the tax was imposed: (a) If, before the tax was imposed, there were a large number of firms each operating at less than optimum capacity, and (b) if, after some firms are forced out of business, the demand curves of those which remain become more elastic (since the new customers they acquire may be somewhat indifferent as to their special services). For example, suppose that there is an excessive number of gasoline stations in a large city. A license fee of $500 per year per station might cut the number of stations in half, and the remaining stations might then find that by cutting their price and operating at capacity, their net profits, even after paying the tax, are greater than before the tax was imposed. This situation will apply only in certain cases of diminution from a great number of firms to a number which is still fairly large. It will not be applicable in the case of a small oligopoly.

(2) It may be that no firms are forced out of business by the fixed cost tax. In this event, it is still remotely possible that a considerable proportion of the tax may be shifted to the buyers. This is most likely to apply in the case of an oligopoly (a small number of firms which do take account of rival prices in determining their own price policy). When a tax is imposed, if all firms raise their prices simultaneously

in an effort to shift the tax to the buyer, any single firm will lose much less business than if it attempted to raise its price alone. Nevertheless, even under these circumstances, we cannot assume that the full burden of the tax will be shifted to the buyer; as all firms raise their prices simultaneously, some of the customers of each firm may cease to buy the product entirely. The extent to which the tax can be shifted is thus dependent upon the elasticity of demand for the product in general, rather than on the elasticity of demand for the product as sold by the individual firm. It may be argued, however, that the possibility of shifting the tax to the buyer is not very great, because if conditions of total demand are such that all firms can raise their prices together (without encountering a serious decline in the amount sold), it seems reasonable to suppose that they would have done this without the impetus of a tax.

Tax as a Constant Variable Cost

A tax per unit of output on the firms operating in an industry under conditions of monopolistic competition constitutes an addition to marginal cost. Here again, however, we must consider the most likely changes in demand as well as the change in cost, so that the analysis that we made for this type of tax on perfect monopoly is no longer applicable. All we can say definitely is that because the individual firm's demand curves will be shifted somewhat (as all firms attempt to raise prices to shift the tax), the proportion of the tax shifted will tend to be somewhat greater than it would be in the case of a perfect monopoly. We cannot assume, however, that each firm's demand curve will be shifted by the amount of the tax, particularly if the competing products sold at different prices before the tax was imposed. Suppose, for example, that a new tax of $100 each is imposed on the manufacture of automobiles. If, then, the tax were simply passed on to the buyer, it would mean that car *A,* which formerly sold for $900, would now sell for $1,000, and car *B,* which used to sell for $1,000, now sells for $1,100. But a great many of the former buyers of car *B* may feel that $1,000 is all that they care to pay for a car. In that case they will now buy car *A* at $1,000 (including tax) rather than car *B* at $1,100. The manufacturer of car *B* may then find that, in order to retain some of these customers, he will have to price the car at $1,050 or $1,025, thus paying one-half or three-quarters of the tax himself.

A tax per unit of output may be the means of forcing some of the competing firms out of business, which we found to be the case under a lump sum tax. Similarly, depending upon the circumstances, the prices charged by the various firms may be either higher or lower than before the tax was imposed.

Tax as a Changing Variable Cost

The effects upon the cost curves of the various firms will be the same as those indicated for the gross sales tax under perfect monopoly. If the tax is applied to one industry alone, there will be less tendency to shift it than there was in the case of the tax per unit of output. However, if the tax is applied to all goods and services, the tendency to shift it is much greater than if it were applied to one industry alone, since all the alternative uses for the buyers' money are likewise subject to the tax. Nevertheless, it must be obvious that if a 3 percent sales tax is imposed, buyers with total incomes unchanged cannot pay 3 percent more for all goods which they buy and continue to purchase the same quantity. Furthermore, people obviously will not purchase three percent less of all kinds of goods but will rather give up first those kinds of goods whose denial represents least sacrifice to them. To the extent that popular tastes (or needs) are similar, this will tend to concentrate the decrease in demand in particular lines of goods.[6] In these lines, even if the sellers pay the tax themselves, it is highly improbable that they could recover the full volume of their former sales since it is not merely the tax on these particular goods, but the necessity of paying three percent more for nearly all other goods, which is causing the curtailed purchases. The tendency of a general sales tax is thus to increase the price of some goods and to decrease the price of others, but it is more likely that the tax will be shifted in the case of necessities and goods of inelastic demand than in the case of goods for which the demand is elastic.

Tax as a Percent of Net Income

This tax will not force any firms out of business in any single industry to which it is applied. Those firms which are just breaking even (making no net income) will not have to pay any tax. Other firms will have to pay only a certain percent of their net income so that there is no compelling motive for them to cease business. It is extremely unlikely that this type of tax will be shifted; should those firms making the greatest profits (and therefore paying the greatest taxes) attempt to increase their prices, it would be to the advantage of other firms to keep their prices low and to take away business from the firms which raise prices. The increased tax that the low-priced firms would have to pay would be only a fraction of their increased net income. It appears, if the tax were 10 percent, that anyone would gladly pay $1,000 in order to secure an additional $10,000 net income, leaving a clear gain of $9,000 even after the tax was paid.

We have already noted that, due to the difficulty or impossibility of shifting this type of tax, it is more subject to evasion than other taxes and is subject to high costs of adminis-

---

[6] If the tax is imposed in a period of unemployment and the proceeds are used for relief, there will also be an increase in demand for other types of goods, perhaps causing their prices to rise by more than the tax.

tration. The tax is also apt to be an uncertain producer of revenue for the government since business profits are subject to wide fluctuations in the business cycle.

Taxes on Industries Operating Under Pure Competition

Since decreasing costs are not, in general, compatible with pure competition, we can ignore this situation and concentrate our attention upon the situations arising when taxes are placed on industries operating under conditions of constant or increasing costs. Furthermore, we do not need to look for situations in which some sellers will shift a tax and others will not, since it is one of the conditions of pure competition that all sellers will sell at the same price.

Under conditions of constant cost: Price is equal to both marginal and minimum average total unit cost for all firms in the industry and there are no pure profits. In the long-run equilibrium, therefore, the full burden of any tax, regardless of the type, will be shifted. In the short run, all firms may operate at a loss until some are forced to leave the industry. The decreased output may then be sold at a price which covers all costs, including the tax. The less the slope of the demand curve, the greater the number of firms that will be forced to close to restore an equilibrium price including the cost of the tax. In some cases it may be possible to shift some of the tax burden back to labor or the suppliers of raw materials, which would occasion a correspondingly smaller decrease in the number of firms and a smaller increase in the price of the product. Nevertheless, we can say definitely that under pure and perfect competition and under conditions of constant costs, all taxes will be shifted eventually.

Under conditions of increasing cost: Price, before the tax is imposed, is equal to marginal cost of all firms and to minimum average cost of the highest priced firms remaining in business under equilibrium conditions. The incidence of taxation will be different under different types of taxes:

Any tax upon the use of scarce factors of production (such as land) will be absorbed by the owner of the factor and will not be shifted. This is true, however, only when the tax is imposed on the economic rent of the factor, regardless of the use to which it is put. For example, if a tax of 20 percent of the economic rent is placed on land used to grow wheat, but no tax is placed on land used for alfalfa, then the price of wheat will have to be sufficiently high so that the returns from growing wheat after the tax is paid are equal to the returns from growing tax-free alfalfa. On the other hand, if a tax of 20 percent of the economic rent is placed on all land, regardless of the use to which it is put, then the relative attractiveness of different uses for the land will not be changed; prices of the various products will remain unaltered and the landlord will have to assume the full burden of the tax.

It is interesting to note that a tax upon economic rent is absorbed once and for all time by the person who owns the land (or other resource of production) at the time when the tax is imposed. For example, suppose there is a piece of land which yields a net income of $1,000 a year. If the going rate of interest is 4 per cent, the land will be worth $25,000 ($1,000 is 4 percent of $25,000). Now, suppose a tax of 20 percent is placed on the rental value. The net return after the tax is paid will be $800. Anyone who now wishes to buy the land and to earn 4 percent on his investment will pay only $20,000 ($800 is 4 percent of $20,000). The original owner thus takes an immediate loss in asset value of $5,000 when the tax is imposed. Subsequent owners will bear no part of the tax burden unless and until the tax rate is increased.

A tax per unit of output (tax as constant variable cost) on

an industry operating under pure competition and increasing cost will be partially shifted to the buyers of the product. The tax will constitute an addition to the marginal and to the average total unit cost curves of all firms. Those firms which were previously so situated that the price was just equal to minimum average total unit cost will be forced out of business, while others will contract output to the point where the new price is just equal to marginal cost, including the tax. As output is contracted, however, a lower point will be reached on the old marginal cost curve. Therefore, the price of the product need not rise by the full amount of the tax in order to equate the new marginal cost, including tax, with the new price. Since we have assumed that under pure competition there are no pure profits, any part of the tax that is not shifted to the buyers will be at the expense of economic rent of the scarce factors of production being used in the industry.

A tax as a percent of gross sales (tax as changing variable cost) will be shifted in a manner quite similar to the tax per unit of output, as outlined in the preceding paragraph. A lump sum tax, or license fee, will likewise be at least partially shifted. To the extent that marginal firms are forced out of business and to the extent that other firms contract output, the decreased output can be sold at a higher price including at least a part of the tax.

Taxes on Personal Property and Personal Income

So far we have been discussing taxes on business enterprises. When we come to the subject of personal taxes the problem is much simpler, as personal property is owned by the individual and is not being produced for sale. Consequently, there is almost no possibility of shifting this tax, or that on personal income.

While there is no possibility of shifting the tax on personal property that is already in the possession of the individual, one form of a shift may take place in connection with property not yet acquired. If the property tax is placed on only a few articles and not on all personal property, a number of people may refrain from buying these particular articles. This decrease in demand may cause the price to be lowered somewhat so that subsequent purchasers do not feel the burden of the tax so heavily. For example, if I have to pay a tax of $10 a year on a piano that sells for $800, I am as well off as if I had to pay $1,000 for a piano when no tax was being charged (assumed rate of interest 5 percent). This is an example of the backward shifting of a tax. The price might even fall below $800, if people are afraid of further higher taxes on this article. It is not likely, however, that the entire burden of a personal property tax will be shifted in this way, since in that event people would buy as much of the article as they did before the tax was imposed and the price would not fall.

Backward Shifting of Taxes

So far we have been giving our attention mainly to the shifting of taxes forward to the buyer of the product. The process of tax shifting often takes place by the shifting of the burden of the tax backwards to the sellers of raw materials or the resources of production. Whether a tax is shifted backwards or not depends, in part, upon the elasticity of supply of the resources of production. The less elastic the supply, the greater will be the possibility of backward shifting of a tax. In other words, as business firms offer lower prices for resources (their means of passing the tax backwards), they will be able to obtain very nearly the same amount of resources if the supply is inelastic. Whereas, if the supply of resources of any kind is very elastic, any attempt to beat down the price will result in greatly curtailed offerings so that the firms will not be able to obtain the desired quantity.

The same type of tax may happen to be shifted forward in one industry and backward in another. We have a good example of this in the case of the processing taxes. In 1933 a tax was placed on the first domestic processing of both cotton and hogs in order to defray the expenses of the Agricultural Adjustment Program. The Treasury Department is apparently of the opinion that the tax on cotton was shifted forward, while the tax on hogs was shifted backward to the farmer. There are several reasons for this difference. The value of raw cotton constitutes only a very small fraction of the price of finished cotton goods, so that the shifting of the tax forward resulted in only a negligible rise in the price of the finished products to be borne either by dealers or by the consumer. On the other hand, the price of live hogs constitutes an important part of the price of pork products and the demand for pork is fairly elastic, so that it apparently was not expedient to shift the tax to the consumer. The short-run (market) supply of hogs is also more inelastic than that of cotton. Cotton which is unsold stands a chance of appreciating in value during the season by an amount which may cover the carrying charges. Hogs, on the other hand, must be fed at considerable cost during the time they are withheld from market and, as the hogs become too heavy, their price per pound is much below that of lighter hogs. Consequently, the farmer could be fairly easily forced to stand the cost of the processing tax if he wished to dispose of his hogs.

Other conditions being equal, a tax upon the use of a single factor of production is apt to be more readily shifted backward than any of the other types of taxes. Consider, for example, the payroll tax for Social Security funds. This tax does not penalize the employer upon his output but upon the amount and value of labor that he uses. Consequently, if he can produce the same output with less labor, he has an added incentive to do so in the reduced payroll tax that he will have to pay. Processes which use more capital and less labor have now become more attractive than they were before the tax was imposed. As workers become unemployed, or are threatened with unemployment, through this process they may be willing to work for lower wages. It may eventually prove to be the case that the workers will bear the full burden of the payroll tax in the form of lower wages.

Conclusions

We have made some attempts to analyze the principles which govern the shifting of taxation. Perhaps we have only discovered more forcibly how difficult it is to determine where the incidence of a tax finally falls. Even this may prove helpful, however, if it tends to make us more cautious in proposing and enacting new taxes.

CHAPTER IV

Government Borrowing and Creation of National Income[1]

IN CHAPTER II a budget deficit was defined as an excess of government expenditures over income and it was pointed out that such a deficit would be financed by government borrowing. It was also noted that such a deficit might be either unanticipated or due to deliberate fiscal policy. If the Treasury officials are astute, however, unexpected deficits will be small as compared with the total budget and negligible as compared with the total national income. Moreover, to the extent that budget deficits are unexpected, they are also unavoidable. We will therefore devote most of our attention to government borrowing as a deliberate fiscal policy.

Funded and Unfunded Debt

The unfunded debt of a government consists of its accounts payable, borrowings from banks, and borrowings on short-term notes. The government may borrow for short periods either: (1) because income receipts do not coincide exactly in time with the dates for making payments (this may be the case even when the budget balances for the entire year); or (2) because the market for government bonds appears to be unfavorable at the moment and is expected to be better in

---

[1] I am indebted to Professor Fritz Machlup for suggesting that this chapter be written, for its outline, and for most of its theoretical content.

the near future; or (3) because the interest rates on short-term securities are much lower than those on long-term securities.

The funded debt of the government consists of interest-bearing bonds with a definite maturity date. Such bonds are always issued for more than one year and generally the maturity date is ten or twenty years or more from the date of issue. Some governments issue bonds without a fixed maturity date. In this case the bonds are redeemable at the option of the government and not at the option of the bond-holder. A funded debt may arise in one of three ways: (1) through the funding of previously unfunded debt, that is, by long-term borrowing to repay short-term obligations, or through borrowing to repay old funded debt as it falls due, called *refunding* (this process is simply a change in the form of debt and need not concern us further *unless a new unfunded debt is contracted* which would then represent a net addition to the total debt); (2) through the decision of the government to reduce taxes and to meet some part of its regular budgetary expenditures by borrowing rather than by taxation (this method has special economic implications which will be considered in the latter part of the chapter); (3) through the decision of the government to undertake additional expenditures and to pay for them by borrowing rather than by additional taxation. It will be observed that categories (2) and (3) are general causes for increase in debt, which may be either funded or unfunded.

For our present purposes, the form of the public debt is not a material question. Our immediate concern is with *net additions to the total public debt* which are undertaken for the purpose of *additional government expenditures*. Our only concern with the length of time of the debt is as follows: Since debt repayment (that is, repayment out of taxes, not simply refunding) will exert an opposite economic effect to government borrowing, we assume, in the discussion which follows, that a debt is not repaid until it has had time to exert its full effect upon incomes.

Sources of Government Borrowing

Government bonds may be sold to individuals, to corporations and business firms, to financial institutions (insurance companies and investment trusts), to government agencies (for social security and other retirement or pension funds), to commercial banks, and (indirectly) to the Federal Reserve Banks. The sale to different buyers has considerably different economic effects, depending upon the source of the funds with which the bonds are purchased.

Individuals who buy government bonds may do so out of several sources of funds, each of which has somewhat different implications for our problem: (a) The bonds may be purchased out of current savings from income which has just been received. In this case if the government spends the money for productive purposes, we might have a mere change in the form of investment (government investment instead of private investment). If the government spends the money on consumption (say, to buy food for relief clients), we have government consumption instead of private investment or spending. In all of these alternatives there is no increase in money flow and no new income has been created. (b) The bonds may be purchased out of idle bank deposits. This will tend to increase the money flow. (c) The bonds may be purchased from hoarded cash. This will increase money flow and may also tend to increase cash reserves somewhere in the banking system. Both (b) and (c) will represent a net increase in total investment or total consumption, depending upon the purpose for which the government spends the borrowed funds.

Business firms may buy government bonds: (a) from current sales receipts instead of replacing inventories or of making maintenance expenditures (disinvestment on the part of the firm). The government may then use the funds for investment or consumption, as we have seen above. This is merely replacement of government investment by private investment and does not increase money flow. (b) The bonds may be purchased from idle bank deposits. (This is called "dishoarding" by some authors.) This practice will increase the money flow in the economy and will create new income.

Government agencies, such as the Social Security Fund, obtain their funds from what we may call *extra budgetary taxation* (payroll taxes, pension deductions from government workers' salaries). Unless these funds are turned over to the Treasury to be spent, the government will actually be hoarding money. If this deflationary influence is to be avoided, the government's expenditures must increase by the amount of the net increase in the Social Security Fund.[2] So the Treasury borrows the money from the Social Security Fund and gives government bonds in exchange for it. Since expenditures are equal to the taxes collected for this purpose, this does not increase money flow.

Commercial banks: (a) may buy bonds as someone happens to repay bank loans (this creates no increase in the money flow); (b) may buy bonds to increase their earning assets (this is called deposit creation, or credit creation, and does increase the money flow). From June, 1933, to December, 1936, member bank holdings of government securities increased by 8 billions of dollars, most of which represented a net increase in created bank deposits.

---

[2] Since it was not deemed advisable to invest in private securities (for one reason there are not enough first- or even second-grade private securities to equal the 40 billion dollars which the fund might reach if the payroll tax schedule of the original law is retained), the Treasury is ordered to issue special 3 percent bonds to the fund. Although the 3 percent interest constitutes an apparent additional income to the Social Security Fund, it is at the same time an additional obligation of the Treasury. Eventually new taxes will have to be raised for the government to pay the interest, or other government expenditures will have to be reduced. (Amendments are now being considered to change this provision.)

Open market purchases of the Federal Reserve banks will be made by created Federal Reserve bank deposits and will increase money flow. To the extent that the bonds are bought from member banks, or their customers, this will mean an increase in member bank deposits with the Federal Reserve banks. Since such deposits constitute the legal reserve of the member banks, they may be in a position to increase their own customers' created deposits by some multiple of the increase in their Federal Reserve bank deposit. It is illegal for the Federal Reserve banks to purchase bonds directly from the government, but they can and often do purchase bonds in the open market (from member banks and others) at the same time that the Treasury is selling bonds.[3]

Financial institutions other than banks—for example, insurance companies and investment trusts—who may purchase government bonds, act mainly as agents for individual savers and therefore simply transfer existing funds. If we wish to inquire further into the source of these funds, we must go back to the individuals (or business firms) who paid them to the financial institution.

We are now prepared to make certain general considerations. Let us first take up those sources of government borrowing which do not increase money flow. The question to be considered is: Would the funds have been invested otherwise had the government not borrowed them? If the funds would not have been invested, then the government borrowing and expenditure prevents the funds from becoming idle and so prevents a deflation of monetary circulation. If the funds would have had another outlet, then we may say that the government has competed with private industry for the funds and private investment has been foregone.

---

[3] To the extent that member banks buy government bonds on their own account and do not resell them to the Federal Reserve banks, the effects on money flow are the same as those outlined for the other commercial banks.

A brief tabulation may help us to summarize the effects upon money flow of these various sources of government borrowing:

Lender	Sources of borrowed funds which represent money flow through different channels	Sources of borrowed funds which represent increased money flow
Individual	Current savings from income just received	Idle bank deposits Idle cash
Business Firm	From current sales receipts instead of maintenance or inventory replacement	Idle bank deposits
Government Agencies	Payroll taxes and other extra budgetary taxation	
Commercial Banks	Replacing loans just repaid	Newly created bank deposits
Federal Reserve Bank		Newly created deposits (which may constitute member bank reserves against which still more deposits may be created for member banks' customers)
Financial Institution	Acts as transfer agent. Effect on money flow depends on source of funds that the institution obtains from individuals or firms. (See above.)	

We have no way of arriving at an arbitrary or definite answer to the question of whether the funds would have been invested had the government not borrowed them. Presumably, if the government had not been competing for funds, the interest rate would have fallen somewhat. This lower rate might then have attracted a large number of borrowers who wished to expand their capital or to undertake new enterprises. The mere fact that the government borrows at a low rate of interest does not mean that private firms could have obtained funds at anywhere near the same rate. The government bonds may have been bought by nervous individuals (or banks or firms) who would otherwise have simply held cash but who buy the government bonds because they consider them the most "liquid" form of asset which still yields them some return.

On the other hand, it may be argued with some degree of plausibility, that mounting government expenditures, by weakening public confidence, may frighten off as much or more investment than is being undertaken by the government. The argument runs in this fashion: Potential investors, who see government debt mounting, start to worry about when and on whom taxes will be levied to pay the interest and to repay the principal. They are afraid that if they invest in some firm, subsequently imposed taxes will prevent them from earning a return on their investment and perhaps even endanger the safety of the principal. Even if taxes are not imposed directly on business firms, their prospects may be impaired by other taxation. Thus, new higher income taxes might impair the market for a firm manufacturing luxury goods, or new sales taxes, by reducing the income of the lower-paid workers, might seriously alter the demand for a firm making low-priced goods.

If there is fear of an immediate inflation, this would result in a heavy volume of investment as people rush to reduce their cash balances and to acquire instead some asset which might give more promise of retaining its value. If, instead, there is simply the vague fear of possible inflation at some undetermined future date, this would be apt to induce the desire to remain extremely liquid in order to be able to take the best advantage of investment opportunities when the time does come. (The fear may be strong enough to preclude investment in fixed interest-bearing securities, but not strong enough to induce purchase of equities or commodities.   Hence, "When in doubt, hold cash.")

During a period of business decline, since other investment opportunities are rare, the presumption is that government spending will act to reduce the extent of deflation. This is accomplished through "facilitating the process of disinvestment." For example, when a WPA worker buys a suit of clothes, the storekeeper (if prices are declining) either will not replace the suit in his stock at all, or will replace it with one which costs him less. Either of these courses will decrease the storekeeper's investment in inventory (the former, of course, represents the greater decline). To the extent that government spending facilitates the orderly disposal or revaluation of inventories in this manner, it may prevent the "dumping of inventories on the market" and the consequent panic prices. In periods of decline as inventories are sold, the tendency is likely to be either to use the proceeds to repay bank loans or to hold idle cash balances (both deflationary measures). The government, by borrowing and spending an equivalent amount of money, may offset this deflationary influence.

In a period of recovery, government borrowing and spending, to the extent that it causes higher interest rates or higher costs of production through competition with private business for resources, may simply be displacing what would otherwise be a similar volume of private investment. If lack of confidence is also a factor, the net effect on total investment may be negative.

The Multiplier Theory

We now turn our attention to those government expenditures financed by borrowing from sources that actually do increase the money flow. As the "new money" is passed on from one person to another in the course of a year, it may create not only one income but perhaps two or more. This brings us to a consideration of Mr. Keynes' famous doctrine of the "investment multiplier." [4]   First of all, Mr. Keynes gives us a new term which he calls the "marginal propensity to consume,"[5] which is the ratio of an increment in consumption to an increment in income. He assumes that, due to certain "psychological propensities," people will not spend all their income on consumption goods and that they will spend a smaller part of income on consumption goods as their income rises. The proportion of additional income that people will spend on consumption goods is used in an attempt to measure the amount of increase in total national income which will result from any given increase in investment (or in government deficit spending). To keep the presentation simple for the non-mathematical reader, I shall try to translate Mr. Keynes' equations into words as far as is possible:

If we call k the multiplier,

$$\text{(Increase in Income)} = k \text{ (Increase in Investment)}$$

k is determined by the marginal propensity to consume, the relationship being expressed by the following equation:

$$\text{(Marginal Propensity to Consume)} = 1 - \frac{1}{k}$$

Or, this may be written:

$$k = \frac{1}{1 - \text{(Marginal Propensity to Consume)}}$$

By substituting various possible assumed or estimated values for the marginal propensity to consume, we arrive at the related value for k, the multiplier. Thus, if at a certain time

[4] Keynes, J. M., *The General Theory of Employment Interest and Money,* Chs. 8, 9, 10, Harcourt, Brace & Co., New York, 1936. I have not hesitated to use non-Keynesian language wherever it appeared to simplify the presentation.

[5] The use of the concept of a "marginal propensity to consume" is a "catch-all" for a large number of assumptions, many of which may raise doubts as to the validity of the multiplier doctrine or at least as to its practical applicability.

people will consume one-half of any additional income they receive, the equation becomes

$$k = \frac{1}{1 - \frac{1}{2}}$$

which is equal to 2. Substituting this value for k in our first equation, we find that a given increase in total investment (or of government deficit spending) of $100 would result in an increase in total income of $200. In a similar way a marginal propensity to consume of 3/4 will give a multiplier of 4, a marginal propensity to consume of 4/5 gives a multiplier of 5, a marginal propensity to consume of 7/8 gives a multiplier of 8, and so on.

The people who first receive the "new money" as a result of investment or government spending are called the *primary income recipients* and their income is called *primary income*. Those who receive the money later on as it is passed from hand to hand are called *secondary income recipients* and their income is called *secondary income*. For our purposes, we may construct a table based largely on non-Keynesian concepts which may give a somewhat different interpretation of the multiplier doctrine. We assume that the government is spending "new money" at the rate of $100 in each successive income period and that the marginal propensity to consume is 4/5, resulting, according to Keynes' equation, in a multiplier of 5.

The first column of the table indicates the successive income periods. The second column is based on the assumption of new government spending (primary income) of $100 per income period. Note that it is not just one expenditure which is then discontinued but that the government is assumed to spend $100 of "new money" each income period. We are now beginning to part company with Mr. Keynes by introducing the concept of an income period. Not only does Mr. Keynes omit the element of time from the multiplier equa-

TABLE II
THE INCOME MULTIPLIER

INCOME PERIOD	GOVERNMENT EXPENDITURE	SECONDARY INCOME — Income Recipients No											TOTAL INCREASE OF INCOME
		2	3	4	5	6	7	8	9	10	11	12	
1	$100												$100.00
2	100	$80											180.00
3	100	80	$64										244.00
4	100	80	64	$51.20									295.20
5	100	80	64	51.20	$40.96								336.16
6	100	80	64	51.20	40.96	$32.77							368.93
7	100	80	64	51.20	40.96	32.77	$26.21						395.14
8	100	80	64	51.20	40.96	32.77	26.21	$20.97					416.11
9	100	80	64	51.20	40.96	32.77	26.21	20.97	$16.78				432.89
10	100	80	64	51.20	40.96	32.77	26.21	20.97	16.78	$13.42			446.31
11	100	80	64	51.20	40.96	32.77	26.21	20.97	16.78	13.42	$10.74		457.05
12	100	80	64	51.20	40.96	32.77	26.21	20.97	16.78	13.42	10.74	$8.59	465.64

tions, but he also specifically disavows it in this connection.[6]

We must first inquire into the nature of and length of time of the income period. The relevant income period for our purpose is what Professor Machlup[7] calls "the income propagation period," which is the length of time necessary for income received by one person to be transformed into net income received by another person. This period will be different from, and may be considerably longer than, the period involved in the "transactions velocity of circulation of money," since many money payment transactions are not net income transactions. An example may help us: Suppose that WPA workers spend part of their pay (primary income) buying suits from a storekeeper who sells them exactly at cost. Thus no part of the money is net income for the storekeeper (this is a non-income transaction). Suppose, then, that the storekeeper uses the money to buy suits from a wholesaler who also sells at cost price (another non-income transaction). Now suppose that the wholesaler uses the money to buy suits from a manufacturer who sells them, out of stocks on hand, at exactly what they cost him to make (still no net income). Finally, suppose that the manufacturer decides to make more suits and hires workers for this purpose with the money he has received from the wholesaler. At last, when the clothing workers receive their pay envelopes, the money spent by the WPA workers becomes net income for a second group. We see that three non-income transactions have intervened between "income paid out" and "net income received."

In our illustration if the storekeeper had sold the suits for

---

[6] Keynes, J. M., *The General Theory of Employment Interest and Money*, p. 122, Harcourt, Brace & Co., New York, 1936: "I have found, however, in discussion that this obvious fact often gives rise to some confusion between the logical theory of the multiplier, which holds good continuously, *without time lag, at all moments of time*, and the consequences of an expansion in the capital-goods industries which take gradual effect, subject to time-lag and only after an interval." (Italics supplied.)

[7] Machlup, Fritz, "Period Analysis and the Multiplier Doctrine," *Quarterly Journal of Economics*, November, 1939.

something above what they cost (to cover his own wage and possibly interest on his own investment), then this part of the money received would constitute net income for him at the moment he received it. The income propagation period for this part of the money is thus considerably shorter than for the remainder, being merely the interval between the time the WPA workers receive their pay and the time they spend it at the clothing store. (That part of the money which represents the cost of the suits is still a non-income transaction as far as the storekeeper is concerned.) In their turn, the wholesaler and the manufacturer may also be selling so as to make a net income and this will shorten the income propagation period on other parts of the money. That part of the money which is paid to the clothing workers, however, will not be net income until it has passed through all previous hands and they receive it.

We see that the average income propagation period depends upon: (1) the length of time that the money is held by the primary income recipients (WPA workers); (2) the number of non-income transactions which may intervene before each part of the money becomes net income; and (3) the length of time that part of the money which represents non-income transactions remains in the cash balance of each person through whose hands it passes. Professor Machlup "guesses" that the average income propagation period for the United States on all income is about three months. Although he points out that the marginal income propagation period (the period involved for a small addition of "new money" to total income) may be either shorter or longer than the average income propagation period, he assumes for his argument that it also is three months and we shall make the same assumption.

Now let us examine the table again. The workers employed by the government in Income Period No. 1 spend 4/5 of their income, according to our assumed marginal

propensity to consume, and after one full income propagation period it appears again as $80 income for the group la-
beled Income Recipients No. 2. These, in their turn, spend
4/5 of their new income, or $64, which is received as income
by Income Recipients No. 3 in the third period and so
on. Meanwhile in Income Period No. 2 another $100 has
been paid out by the government and started on a similar
course. The last column shows the total increase of income
which is being received in each income period. The reader
may observe that, if we continued to expand the table for a
number of periods, the total income figure would approach,
but never quite reach, a full $500 as we continued in each
income period to add 4/5ths of a smaller and smaller amount.
It would require thirty-three income periods (or 8 1/4 years
on our assumption of a three-months' income period) for the
total to reach $499.06.

This is too far into the future for any government to look
for revenue with which to balance its budget. It is idle to
assume that "all other conditions" will remain unchanged for
such a length of time, particularly when these conditions will
very probably be altered by the very fact of government spending alone. So instead of looking at the ultimate theoretical
value of the multiplier, let us find the value for shorter periods
(still assuming for the time being that the theory itself is
valid). Total increase in rate of income at the end of the
first year (assuming a three-months' income period) is $295.20,
of which $100 is the government expenditure, giving a multi-
plier of 2.952, or slightly under 3, as compared with an 8 1/4
year multiplier of 5. At the end of the second year the multiplier is 4.16. At the end of the third year the multiplier is
4.65, still about 7 percent short of the final assumed value.

For short periods the Treasury is more apt to be interested
in aggregate income created rather than the increase in the
rate of income. Total income created for the first year is

found by adding the first four items in the last column of the table, and amounts to $819.20, of which $400 is government expenditure, giving a multiplier of only 2.05. At the end of the second year, total income created for the two-year period is $2,335.54 and total government expenditure is $800, the multiplier being 2.92. At the end of the third year, total created income is $4,137.33, government expenditure is $1,200, and the multiplier is 3.45.

The Leakages

The reader may have already started to wonder why only 4/5 of the new income is spent and what becomes of the amount that is not spent during the period of expanding income. Some of it may be used for debt repayment. In this case it represents no new income to the recipient but merely the return of the principal to the creditor. It will not become income for anyone again unless and until the creditor spends or reinvests it. Some of the money may be absorbed in idle cash balances. To the extent that prices rise as a result of the new money flow, individuals and business firms will find it desirable to carry larger cash balances and will not feel free to spend the full amount of the new income as they receive it.

Note that if at any stage of our table the income recipients should happen to take their income and buy government bonds with it, this would cancel out an equivalent amount of bank deposit creation. To put it simply: To the extent that these income recipients invest in government bonds, the government will not be spending "new money" and so will not be adding to the money flow nor creating new income.

Defects of the Multiplier Theory

If the multiplier theory would actually work without qualification as Mr. Keynes and some of his followers in this country seem to believe, one would hardly venture to argue against the policy of "government spending as the road to prosperity." In addition to the qualifications we have already mentioned, however, there are certain other serious omissions in the theory. In the first place the whole idea neglects the induced fall of private investment due to lack of confidence created by rising government deficits. *We must not forget that "secondary income" can be created as readily by private spending or investment as by government spending or investment.* Therefore, if government spending simply replaces private investment of an equivalent amount, it may do no harm, but it certainly does not increase total national income. In this connection, it was previously stated that the multiplier doctrine was applicable only to those cases in which government borrowing caused an increase in money flow. Mr. Keynes' followers either blithely ignore this point or else tacitly assume that all government funds for increased spending are drawn from sources that will mean an increase in money flow.

If, however, it happens to be the case that government spending "scares off" a greater than equal amount of private investment, then the multiplier may work in reverse. That is, not only will total national income decrease by the difference between the amount of government spending and the amount of private investment which is discouraged, but also all of the secondary income which would have been created by the greater amount of private investment will vanish.

The multiplier theory also neglects the element of discouragement to private investment which may result from high costs of production due to government competition for the resources of production. Such discouragement of private investment may, of course, have similar results to that due to lack of confidence. Costs of productive resources will tend to rise more seriously the more government spending is concentrated on particular lines. Thus, if all government spending were concentrated in the building of concrete roads, the prices of cement, crushed stone, gravel, and reinforcing iron might rise to such an extent as to make their cost to private industry almost prohibitive. So long as there are large numbers of unemployed workers, government competition for labor in general may not cause wage rates to rise sufficiently to prevent workers being employed by private industry, but if the government employs large numbers of workers of particular types of skill, then "bottlenecks" may develop; that is, private industry may be prevented from hiring large numbers of unskilled workers because there is an insufficient number of the right type of skilled workers to go with them to make up the desired production organization. This condition will tend to be the more serious as "prevailing rates of wages" are increasingly paid on government contracts.

On the other hand, the doctrine of the multiplier does not include the possible induced rise in private investment which may be caused by increased consumption. This is the principle of acceleration of derived demand as enunciated by Professor J. M. Clark.[8] If this principle operates, the effect may be much greater than that indicated by the multiplier. Professor Clark points out, however, that the extent of this derived demand will depend very largely upon whether businessmen expect the boom induced by deficit spending to be of long or short duration. If they do not expect "pump-priming" to produce lasting results, they will simply try to make the best possible use of existing capital equipment, and such investment as does take place is likely to be in the form of inventories rather than in long-term capital expenditures.

---

[8] Note, however, Professor Clark's very careful qualifications of this doctrine as applied to government deficit spending in his paper: "An Appraisal of the Workability of Compensatory Devices," *American Economic Review,* Vol. XXIX supplement, March 1939, p. 195 ff.

The Employment Multiplier

So far our discussion refers only to the possibilities of increased money income and increased money expenditures which may or may not be occasioned by deficit spending. However, the arguments of the government spending advocates, who base their case on Mr. Keynes' theories, center almost entirely around their claim that "government spending is the only way to obtain full employment of resources." The only resource for which full employment is economically imperative seems to be that of labor.   Therefore, let us focus our attention on the possibilities of more extensive employment of labor resulting from such increased money income as may happen to result from greater government spending.

Following the terminology of R. F. Kahn,[9] the employment caused directly by the government expenditure (including the employment of those who manufacture the materials the government purchases) may be called *primary employment* and the employment resulting from the spending of those who receive the government funds may be referred to as *secondary employment*. (Note at the start that, unless government spending actually does cause an increase in total spending, there will be no increase in total employment since, as Mr. Kahn himself states, there is just as much secondary employment to be expected from private investment as from public investment.)

The amount of employment resulting from increasing money income depends primarily on two things: (1) wage rates; (2) commodity prices. If wage rates rise at the same rate that income rises, there will be no secondary employment and no more goods produced.

---

[9] Kahn's own views as to the probability of increased employment are somewhat more sanguine than those expressed here. See "The Relation of Home Investment to Unemployment," *Economic Journal,* Vol. XLI, p. 173.

If wage rates remain constant, there will be increased employment resulting from the enlarged income, but technical or institutional conditions under which output would be expanded will determine the extent to which the enlarged income causes increased employment and the extent to which the income is merely absorbed by rising prices for the same output of goods. (Under a system of universal monopoly there might simply be augmented monopoly rent and no more employment.) Therefore, with constant wage rates the increase in employment depends finally on the elasticity of supply of various commodities that the income recipients attempt to purchase. Increased employment might be proportional to the increase in income. This, however, is very unlikely even in the midst of a depression with the existing unemployed resources. When plants are being operated at depression levels, only the most efficient machines and the most efficient workmen are being put to work. Raw materials may be temporarily selling at less than replacement cost. It follows that any increase in demand which causes serious reductions in inventories will meet with rising supply prices for many lines of goods. Due to rising supply curves, the ratio of non-wage income to wage income will increase.

Government Investment to Prevent Secular Stagnation

According to Keynes, Hansen,[10] and others, wealthy countries have a high propensity to save. At the same time they have a large stock of capital which has a low marginal productivity. These authors also claim that rates of interest cannot fall sufficiently low to induce enough investment to be undertaken to absorb savings because at low rates people prefer to carry their funds liquid. (Liquidity preference curve becomes infinitely elastic.) In previous periods one

---

[10] See Hansen, A. H., "Progress and Declining Population," *American Economic Review,* Vol. XXIX, No. 1, March 1939, pp. 1-15.

could count on new investment opportunities to develop through: (a) the rate of population growth, (b) opening of new areas within the country and abroad, (c) new inventions requiring large amounts of capital. The authors claim that these avenues of investment opportunity are now closing so as to cause secular (long-run) stagnation and hence they believe that government investment is necessary to offset the failure of private investment.

It is hard to argue against any theory based on so many conjectures, such as a lack of future inventions. Concerning the interest rate and the sensitivity of investment to small changes in it, let us consider the effect upon the price of bonds. Suppose that the interest rate is at 2 percent and that a bond which pays $2.00 per annum sells for $100.00. Now suppose that the rate of interest were to fall to 1.8 percent. A bond of long term paying $2.00 would then have a capitalized value of $111.11. This would represent a rate of gain in capital value of 11 percent for those who bought the bonds at $100.00, in addition to which they would have the $2.00 interest payment, making a total gain of 13 percent during the year in which the market rate of interest fell from 2 percent to 1.8 percent. The very expectation of such a fall in the rate of interest (if the rate is expected to remain low for some time, as is indicated by the secular stagnation claim) should send intelligent investors stampeding to buy bonds. This would provide a good market not only for old bond issues but also for any new issues which paid anything over 1.8 percent at the time of issue.[11]

Concerning the marginal efficiency of capital, the whole return depends on the cost of capital equipment and on variable costs in relation to selling prices. An adjustment in cost-price relationships may work miracles in the marginal effi-

---

[11] See Professor Haberler's report on Capital Formation published by the National Industrial Conference Board, 1939.

ciency of capital. Wages constitute the principal element in
most variable costs. If we are committed to a policy of unchanged (or rising) money wages, it may be that some form
of inflation will be necessary to reduce the real wages to the
point where labor can be fully employed.

In connection with the liquidity preference argument, it
is difficult to determine whether secular or cyclical causes
are more responsible for the present semi-stagnation of the
investment market. It may even be that our old friend "lack
of confidence" is the prime cause for any present desire for
liquidity.

Professor Hansen has made a very strong case for the influence of the rate of population growth upon the demand for
capital in the last fifty years or more. His analysis stands as
a warning to anyone who attempts to predict the future upon
the pattern of the past. We may, however, raise one question in connection with the population problem. Will not
the changed age grouping of the population (caused by decreasing birth and death rates) result in a somewhat dimin-
ished "propensity to save"? We may expect an increased
proportion of those who are "living on their savings" and a
decreased proportion of those who are "saving for their retirement." At best, however, this might be only a partial corrective and could hardly offset any tremendous decrease in the
demand for capital.

A Possible Cyclical Policy for Government Borrowing

We have already raised the presumption that government
borrowing in the recession phase of the business cycle is more
apt to prevent funds becoming idle rather than simply to
displace private investment or to scare it off, as might be the
result of such government action during the recovery period.
It has also long been proposed by many economists that pub-

lic works projects be undertaken as soon as private investment starts to fall off. Experience has shown that it is difficult, if not impossible, to plan public works projects and to
put them into operation rapidly enough for them to be of
much effect in cushioning the decline.

It might be possible, however, for governments to defray
all expenses by taxation during normal or prosperous times
and then to reduce taxation and replace it by borrowing when
business conditions start to decline. This policy would be
most helpful if those taxes which were reduced or eliminated
were those which are part of business costs. It would then
be desirable to have a budgetary surplus in times of prosperity
to retire the outstanding debt, the heavier taxation at this
time working as a contributing factor in preventing excessive
inflation. This program is not suggested as a cure-all, by any
means, but it does seem to offer a measure for better timing
of the inflationary and deflationary effects of government
financing.

Spending Our Way to Prosperity

No part of this chapter should be considered as an argument against government relief for the unemployed. We
have, however, raised some doubts as to the possible extent of
secondary employment through government spending *unless
there is additional induced private investment*. Regardless
of the numerical value of the multiplier, additional secondary
income will be created on *that part only* of government deficit
spending which represents a net addition to total money flow.
The amount of secondary employment that may be created
through secondary income might be seriously curtailed by
(1) rising wage rates and (2) rising prices of commodities
(still assuming no induced private investment). Meanwhile,
the government will be incurring additional interest charges

both on that part of the deficit which represents creation of
new income and on that part which represents mere replacement of private investment.

Most advocates of the government spending policy do not
contemplate repayment of the government debt.[12] They do
hope that sufficient secondary income will be created out of
which taxes may be raised to balance the budget. Note, however, that if the propensity to consume is the sole source of
secondary income, once the multiplier has approximated its
final value government expenditures must remain unchanged
if total income is to be sustained at the new high level. If
the budget is to be balanced, taxes will have to be equal to
interest payments on the past debt plus the amount of current expenditures. It follows, if any attained income level is
to be sustained, that either: (1) The additional taxes must be
drawn from what would otherwise be idle money, or (2)
recipients of interest payments on government bonds must
have the same propensity to consume this part of their income
as was implied in the original multiplier, or (3) recipients
of government interest payments must immediately invest
them in new private investment. On any huge volume of
new taxes it seems somewhat overoptimistic to assume that
condition (1) will be entirely fulfilled. To the extent that
a large proportion of the bonds are held by banks and insurance companies, we cannot rely on condition (2). This
leaves us dependent to a considerable extent on condition (3).
In other words, private investment must be prepared to take
over whenever the deficit starts to be reduced, or government
deficits must continue in an increasing spiral merely to maintain any income level attained by government spending. Professor Hansen seems to be far more aware of this danger than

---

[12] It can be proved mathematically that debt repayment must result in a lower
total income than existed before the spending started if sole reliance is placed
upon the propensity to consume.

Mr. Keynes: "Public spending is the easiest of all recovery methods and therein lies its danger. If it is carried too far, we neglect to attack those specific maladjustments without the removal of which we cannot attain a workable cost-price structure, and therefore we fail to achieve the otherwise attainable flow of private investment."[13]

Since ultimate reliance must be placed in some measure upon private investment, the opponents of the spending program may be permitted a few pertinent questions: How is such private investment to be stimulated in the future? What is the nature of the stimulants that they cannot be applied in the present rather than to invoke such a huge volume of government expenditure? If we are to depart from the strict Keynesian theory of the multiplier and to rely on private investment that may be induced by government spending, then it would seem that the government program should be designed to induce the greatest amount of capital investment rather than to "increase consumer purchasing power."

---

[13] *American Economic Review*, Vol. XXIX, No. 1, March 1939, p. 14.

CHAPTER V

Problems of Transportation

THE ECONOMIC importance of transportation can hardly be exaggerated, because, as Adam Smith pointed out long ago, the division of labor is dependent upon the extent of the market; and it is the nature and costs of transportation which determine the extent of the market. Low-cost transportation facilities also increase the mobility of labor, allowing workers to move from regions where they are poorly paid to those where better wages prevail. All of the advantages of inter-regional and international trade arise only because transportation of goods and people makes such trade possible.

It is, perhaps, idle to attempt to calculate the immeasurable value of transportation as a whole. We are repeatedly forced to consider whether a specific means of transportation between two given points is worth what it costs. In the case of an existing means of transportation, all that is necessary is that the value of the service rendered be equal to the costs of operation and maintenance in order to justify its continued existence. In the case of proposed transport routes or facilities it becomes desirable to calculate whether the benefits expected from it will cover costs of construction as well as costs of operation and maintenance. This problem will likewise involve the selection of the most economical means of transportation. For example, through certain parts of African and South American jungles no means of transport more elaborate than bearers carrying packs and walking a trail is economically justified, even the small cost of the crudest unsurfaced road being too high for the possible volume of traffic to be carried. On the other hand, between two populous manufacturing centers nothing short of a four-track standard-gauge railroad, a four-lane concrete highway, and airplane service may be adequate to handle the volume and diversity of traffic which can most profitably be carried. Before considering more specific problems, a brief discussion of the field and function of the various forms of transport may be a help in acquainting us with the general picture.

Roads

Roads are one of the oldest means of transportation. Their economic importance has varied from time to time, as has their place in the transportation system. Although the ancient Roman roads were built primarily for military purposes, they soon became important arteries of commercial transportation.

During the Middle Ages the art of road building declined and with it the importance of wagon roads as a means of transportation. The soft surface of Medieval roads set very low limits upon the weight of the loads which might be carried and consequently made roads an extremely expensive means of conveyance as well as a slow and uncertain one. The lack of strong governments during the Middle Ages also exposed road-borne freight to the danger of confiscation by highwaymen. Even where the highwaymen were suppressed, the feudal barons over whose domain the goods passed often levied heavy tolls on merchandise crossing their territory.

The intolerable condition of early English roads is attested in the diaries of numerous travelers of the period. The repeated introduction into Parliament of various measures intended to improve the condition of the roads is evidence of the seriousness of the problem. One of the most amusing was a regulation that all freight-carrying vehicles must have tires eighteen inches wide—a vain hope to prevent the rutting of the soft roads by heavy vehicles.

Modern road construction dates from the road engineering of Metcalf, Telford, and MacAdam, the latter of whom discovered the process of mixing crushed stone with the topsoil of the road to give it a hard surface. The Macadam road still bears his name. Although the Roman roads were built by the state, many American Colonial and some English roads were built and operated by private companies. Toll gates and toll bridges which were maintained to charge people for the use of such roads may still be found standing in some parts of the country. A high-speed toll road is even now being proposed to cross the State of Pennsylvania from Philadelphia to Pittsburgh and a privately owned toll road up Mt. Washington is still in operation.

Although there were some important arterial highways in the early history of the United States, such as the Cumberland Road, the Boston Post Road, and the Cherry Valley Turnpike, the roads were much less important carriers of heavy freight than the rivers and canals and the railroads that were later developed. Until comparatively recently our road systems have been developed largely as "feeders" for the other forms of transportation and for serving small communities where the volume of freight traffic did not justify the building of branch railroad lines. The development first of passenger automobiles and more recently of trucks and busses has again made the roads an important form of conveyance of long-haul traffic.

Motor truck transportation of large consignments of heavy freight for long hauls is not, even today, as economical as railroad transportation of the same type of loads. On many types of loads the trucks have one distinct advantage: There need be only one loading and one unloading to carry the goods from the point of shipment to the place where they are actually to be delivered. Not only is this a saving in handling costs but also, particularly on short hauls, it may result in a considerable saving in time of delivery.

The friends of the railroads also tell us that truck transportation is being unfairly subsidized in that the trucks travel over publicly built highways and do not pay their fair share of the cost of construction and upkeep of the roads upon which they travel. There is undoubtedly some truth in this claim. Just what amount the "fair share" of such costs would be has yet to be determined. We should not forget that many railroads were subsidized during their construction periods by large gifts of public lands.

The comparative infancy of the airplane and the recent improvements in freight and passenger locomotives on the railroads makes it impossible for us to prophesy what the final position of roads will be in our transportation system either for freight or passenger traffic. For some classes of traffic it is likely that the roads will again return to the status of "feeders," for example, in carrying passengers to and from airports. For other classes of traffic the roads may prove to be the most economical or convenient even on long hauls.

In the case of public roads, their free use makes it difficult to measure their productivity. However, when a decision is being made as to whether a new road is to be built, a reasonable test that the authorities may apply has been suggested by Professor Machlup. An estimate could be made of the amount of revenue that could be earned by the road if it were operated as a toll road. If this is in excess of the estimated cost of constructing and maintaining the road, then the gain in real income to the people from building the road and allowing free use of it will be in excess of the costs. In cases where relief labor is used on the roads, it may be justifiable to deduct the cost of this labor from the total cost of the road in making the estimate, if this relief labor would otherwise have been supported in idleness or employed on nonuseful projects.

Waterways

Where both shipping and receiving points are conveniently located as regards navigable water, water-borne transport has always been, and is likely to continue to be, the cheapest means of conveying heavy freight. Except where the waterways are artificial or must be kept navigable by artificial aid, there is absolutely no cost for roadbed. Ships can also carry a greater weight and bulk per horsepower of engine than any other form of conveyance.

There are, however, many serious disadvantages under which water transportation labors. It has always been a comparatively slow means of transport and is likely to continue to be so. It is also relatively inflexible, as in the case of direct shipments, when both shipping and receiving points must be on navigable water. To obtain business from beyond these points there must be a combination with other means of transportation, for canals cannot ordinarily be run to warehouse doors as can the spur tracks of railroads. For many kinds of package freight, the cost of unloading from freight cars into boats and then loading again into freight cars at the other end of the water haul makes it advisable to ship the entire distance by rail rather than by a combined rail and water route. For bulk cargoes which can be handled mechanically, the advantage is the other way around. Iron ore, for instance, is handled so efficiently by the mechanical loaders and unloaders in the Great Lakes ports that the ore is regularly shipped by train to Duluth, loaded on boats, and reloaded into freight cars at Ashtabula, Conneaut, and Fairport, Ohio, for shipment to the steel mills in Pittsburgh and Youngstown. So great is the saving in costs of this combined rail and water route that the steel companies, rather than to ship directly by rail from the mines, maintain huge storage piles of ore both at the plants and at the lower lake ports to carry them through the winter season when navigation is closed. A similar advantage is found in the shipment of grain by water, since the grain is likewise handled mechanically in bulk cargo lots. The difference between the prices of grain in Buffalo and Chicago in summer and winter regularly reflect the increased cost of all-rail shipment in the winter.

Canals were once an extremely important form of water transport but they have suffered a decline since the advent of the railroads. They are quite expensive to build and maintain and their courses are sharply limited by the topography of the land. Most modern canals (such as the Suez and the Panama) have been built not to compete with existing land transportation but rather to shorten sea routes or to connect two important water transportation systems. The development of Diesel-engined barges is, however, bringing about an increase of traffic on many old canal systems and may lead to a slight extension of some of them. The comparative unseaworthiness of the old canal boats on lakes or oceans, as well as their extreme slowness on the canals themselves, was a serious handicap to them in competing with other forms of shipping.

Railroads

Since the 1850's the railroads have become the backbone of our transportation system and in spite of present difficulties (financial and others) give every promise of remaining as such, at least for the near future. The ability to haul long trains of heavily laden cars with a single source of motive power, the possibilities of rapid transport over unobstructed roadbeds, continuous operation night and day, the wide number of places that can be reached by rail, and the comparative safety of railroad transportation are advantages which are not easily superseded. That the major railroads are able to survive one financial reorganization after another and one legal handicap after another is ample evidence of their important place in our transportation system.

Perhaps even now the word "system" should not be used in connection with our railroads if we are thinking of railroads in general rather than of certain particular lines. Certainly nothing less systematic can be imagined than the early construction and organization of our railroads. The first railroads were usually built to connect two cities that were fairly close together with little, if any, thought as to where the line was finally to extend. In the early days the different railroads used differently gauged tracks, so that even where two roads happened to intersect, the cars from one could not run on the other. The first long trunk line was organized by Commodore Vanderbilt, who bought up a number of short lines extending up the Hudson and across the State of New York and connected them to form the New York Central lines between New York and Buffalo.

Much of the haphazard nature of our railroad lines is traceable to the era of railroad-building fever which followed Vanderbilt's initial success. The stock market literally went crazy in the buying of railroad securities; funds could easily be secured for the construction of almost any railroad to almost any place. (Some of the roads were actually constructed and some were not.) Most of the railroads which were started at this time were intended by their sponsors to reach the Pacific Coast eventually. The evidence of this fond hope still persists in the phrase "and Western" which embellishes the names of many roads that were started at this time—for example, Delaware, Lackawanna & Western; New York, Ontario, & Western; Norfolk & Western. Many others tried to imitate Vanderbilt's successful scheme of attempting to buy existing lines to unite into a railroad system. During this competitive period many small lines and branches were purchased, not so much for their value to the system which acquired them, but often merely for the purpose of attempting to thwart the plans of rival builders of railroad systems. Many of the new roads that were constructed, instead of following the route indicated by efficient transportation or volume of traffic, simply turned their courses to go through the towns or villages which would grant them the greatest amount of subsidy or which would purchase the greatest quantity of their stocks and bonds. Although there were no Rotary Clubs or Chambers of Commerce in those days, the local boosters organized themselves and bent every effort to ensure the running of the railroad through their town rather than through the near and hated rival town.

Many railroads were built far in advance of the need for their existence, many traversed territory that even today has not produced a profitable volume of traffic, and three transcontinental lines were built when there was hardly enough business to justify one. Since the bulk of the profitable freight and passenger traffic still lay east of Chicago, the competitive effort to tap this source of revenue possibly resulted in even more overbuilding of railroads in the East than in the West. There followed an era of cutthroat competition which resulted in extremely curious rate structures; the roads cut their rates to absurdly low figures between points where there was competition and then tried to make up the difference by charging extortionate rates between points on their own lines where there was no competitor. It was not at all uncommon for through freight from Chicago to New York to be charged a lower rate than was charged on the same class of freight between two cities only one hundred miles apart. More will be said about rate structures later. Notice, however, that during this period of cutthroat competition it was not sufficient for a town to have one railroad entering it in order to have low freight rates and hence adequate transportation for business purposes. There would have to be two competing roads. That the railroads themselves were not averse to cutting into a rival's protected territory explains the construction of many branch lines that are practically useless today.

After a period of supremacy in most classes of freight and passenger traffic, and then a period of relative decline, the railroads today are attempting to regain lost traffic. Through the experimentation with streamlined trains and new types of motive power, they are attempting to compete with the airplanes for the fast passenger and express business. By lower fares and better accommodations than formerly, they are attempting to regain passenger business from the bus lines and to attract people from private automobile driving. With store-door delivery on many types of merchandise, they are striving to meet the competition from the motor trucks for freight traffic. It is too early to determine what the effects of these various measures will be, either on the railroads themselves or on the competing means of transportation.

Airlines

The fact that airplanes and airlines are still in a state of relative infancy leaves us in doubt both as to the future of airlines themselves and as to the competitive inroads they will make upon other forms of transportation. It seems almost safe to prophesy that the use of the airplane will be confined mainly to relatively light loads and to classes of traffic which place a premium on speed. The amount of motive power required merely to lift the plane, its crew, and its gasoline supply tends to place severe engineering limits upon the amount of useful load which even the largest and best designed modern planes can carry. Since a failure of either motive power or structure of the plane usually means a serious accident, the planes must be serviced better and be replaced more often than would be the case with trucks or busses. In consequence, the airlines are forced to charge considerably higher rates for the same weight or bulk of load than do other forms of transportation, and their business is thus confined to those classes of traffic in which the superior speed of the plane is a sufficient justification for the payment of the higher rates. (Aside from its speed, the plane also has an advantage in being able to carry freight into otherwise inaccessible spots, such as the transport of mining machinery to the new Canadian gold fields and to points in the Andes.) In spite of its limitations, the airplane is destined to become a much more important factor in our transportation system than it is at present. The rate of its progress will be governed largely by the adoption of proper safety measures for air transport.

Transportation Rate Making

One of the most difficult problems in transportation is that of determining proper rate schedules for the various classes of freight and passenger traffic. Many of the problems of rate making are quite similar, regardless of whether the rates are set by an unregulated carrier or whether they are to be determined by some regulatory body such as the Interstate Commerce Commission. The unregulated carrier would, of course, be seeking the point of maximum net returns, while the regulatory body is charged with the duty of limiting earnings to a certain fixed percentage on the valuation of the property. Nevertheless, both are confronted with the problem of setting the different rates for various classes of freight and passenger traffic. We shall use the railroads for an example of rate making policies, but it will be found that the principles developed are applicable, with some slight modifications, to other transportation agencies.

Unregulated Rates

The problems of a railroad that is free to set its own rates will first be discussed; later the qualifications imposed by government regulation will be introduced. Writers on railroad rates are fond of using the terms "cost of service rendered" and "charging what the traffic will bear." When an examination of the use of these terms is made, however, it may be seen that "cost of service rendered" is simply another name for marginal cost and that "charging what the traffic will bear" is the marginal revenue principle.[1] The process of fixing railroad rates is then simply one of attempting to equate marginal cost and marginal revenue in exactly the same manner as that which was discussed in the determination of prices under monopoly and monopolistic competition.[2]

A railroad is in a position to determine with a fair degree of accuracy the marginal costs associated with any particular addition to its freight or passenger business; experience will show the amount of the additional fuel and wage cost involved in running one more train over its lines. Likewise (with somewhat less accuracy), the cost of additional wear and tear on rolling stock and roadbed occasioned by running this one extra train can be estimated. The cost of adding one more car to a train which is already running on schedule may also be determined. This cost will not be constant for each added car but will start to drop sharply with the second car on the train. It will finally reach a low point and then increase very slowly as more cars are added, until the hauling capacity of the locomotive is noticeably overburdened. A train of fifty freight cars may have less than double the variable cost of a train of twenty-five cars. A point will eventually be reached at which it is cheaper to split the load between two trains

---

[1] I am indebted to Professor Machlup for this observation.
[2] See Meyers, Albert L., *Elements of Modern Economics*, pp. 83-143, Prentice-Hall, Inc., New York, 1937.

rather than to add more cars to the same train. Particularly in the case of passenger business it may be found that it is desirable to add another train, running at a different hour, before the point of least cost of adding more cars to the first train is reached. This will occur when a sufficient amount of traffic can be attracted by the convenience of a train at a different time to offset the somewhat higher cost of its operation before the full capacity of the first train is reached.

We hear much about the burden of heavy fixed charges in connection with the operation of a railroad. Interest charges on cost of construction will continue whether any trains are run or not. Expenditures for the signal system, maintenance of rails and roadbed, and similar expenses will remain about the same whether ten or a hundred trains a day run over its lines. While the number of clerical help and station employees can be varied somewhat in response to changes in the volume of traffic, this will usually be found advisable only in response to long-continued changes in volume of traffic and not with daily or weekly changes. Except for train crews and engine and car repair shops, most of the labor force of a railroad must be organized to handle its peak loads and cannot be materially reduced in temporarily slack times.

Although fixed costs bulk large in the total cost of a railroad, and although their amount may be the factor which determines whether the road operates at a profit or a loss, fixed costs have nothing to do with the determination of rates by an unregulated carrier. If marginal costs and marginal revenue are equated, this procedure will yield the greatest possible surplus of revenue over variable costs, which may happen to be enough to pay part or all of the fixed costs or to yield a profit, as the case may be. (Sometimes the attempt is made to allocate a part of the fixed costs to some particular class of traffic, but this procedure has no economic sense nor significance. It may be of some practical use only in attempting to defend lawsuits involving railroad rates before an economically ignorant judge or jury.)

It has been stated before that "charging what the traffic will bear" is nothing more nor less than taking proper account of decreasing marginal revenue in setting railroad rates. The fact that the railroads are in a much better position than most sellers to practice price discrimination in fixing their charges gives rise to many interesting problems.

In the case of freight traffic the demand for transportation is a derived demand, the direct demand being for goods at the point of destination. The demand for transportation services is thus derived from the demand for the goods themselves. In examining the conditions under which a railroad may maximize total revenue by charging a high or low freight rate on a particular commodity between two certain points, we can do no better than to apply Marshall's[3] four principles governing the elasticity of derived demand. The four conditions for high freight rates are as follows:

(1) The services of the railroad should be essential, or nearly essential, to the delivery of the commodity at the point of destination, no good substitute means of transportation being available at a moderate price. The closest possible substitute, of course, would be another railroad running between the same points of origin and destination of the commodity. The degree to which other means of transportation approach being close substitutes for railroad services will depend both upon their nature and the nature of the product. For example, the railroads enjoyed almost a perfect monopoly in the transportation of perishable fruits and vegetables until high-speed refrigerated trucks were developed.

(2) The commodity itself should be one for which the demand is highly inelastic, so that a check to its supply will

---

[3] Marshall, Alfred, *Principles of Economics,* Eighth Edition, Book V, Ch. 6, p. 385, Macmillan & Co., Ltd., London, 1927.

cause consumers to offer a much increased price rather than go without it. This condition implies that there are no products in the community of destination that the people will purchase readily if the price of the commodity in question rises materially. It also implies that local production of the given commodity is impossible except at extremely high costs; otherwise, although high freight rates might yield large revenue for a short time, if they stimulated local production of the article they might result in a total loss of all traffic on this commodity to this community.

(3) Only a small part of the delivered cost of the commodity should consist in the cost of transportation. Thus, a freight rate of $20.00 a ton would double or more than double the delivered cost of coal in most communities and would thus result in a serious decline in the amount of coal purchased, whereas a freight rate of even $100.00 a ton on silk neckties would constitute so negligible a part of the delivered price that it would hardly be noticed by the buyer and would cause almost no decline in purchases; consequently freight traffic would not fall off because of the high rate.

(4) Even a small decrease in the amount of the commodity purchased should cause a considerable fall in its price at the point of origin. In this case, even though the demand for the product at the point of destination may be somewhat elastic, producers of the product will pay the high freight rates and accept lower prices for the product in order to avoid discouraging its sale by a high delivered cost.

It is not necessary, of course, for all four of these principles to be fulfilled in order for freight rates to be high on a certain commodity between certain points, but the greater the extent to which each one is fulfilled in practice, the higher the freight rate which will yield maximum total revenue, or in other words, the steeper will be the slope of the demand curve for that transportation service.

Discrimination in Freight Rates[4]

Price discrimination consists of the selling of the same service (or good) by one seller to different buyers at different prices. Discrimination is possible only when buyers can be divided into groups which are really different markets. This implies two conditions: (1) that buyers who are charged a higher price cannot or will not enter the lower-priced market; and (2) that the service cannot be resold by those who are charged the lower price to those who would have to pay the higher price if they bought from the original seller. In the case of freight rates, this grouping or classification is comparatively easy, since it is impossible to change one commodity into another[5] for the purpose of securing a different freight rate, nor will a freight rate which is applicable only between two designated towns be available for shippers between other points.

When the different classes of customers have different elasticities of demand for the service, discrimination yields a greater total revenue than that obtained by charging the simple monopoly price. A group with a very inelastic demand for transportation may then be charged a high freight rate without much diminution in the volume of traffic received from them. At the same time another group with a more elastic demand may be offered a low freight rate in order to induce them to ship in large volume. In this case a simple monopoly price (the same for both groups of customers, nondiscriminatory) would not be high enough to take full advantage of the

---

[4] This section is based largely on the work of Joan Robinson. Those who desire a more detailed and thorough discussion of price discrimination than is possible in a text of this sort should read Chapters 15 and 16 in her *Economics of Imperfect Competition*, Macmillan & Co., Ltd., London, 1934.

[5] Except, of course, that raw materials or finished products, or parts or assembled machines, may be shipped, depending on which has the cheaper freight rate. In the case of lower rates on automobile parts than on assembled cars, this really represents a difference in cost to the railroad (the unassembled parts are less bulky) rather than an example of true price discrimination.

inelastic demand of the first group, nor would it be low enough to take full advantage of the large volume of traffic to be obtained at low rates from the second group.

For purposes of simplicity, discrimination was described above as though it were practiced between two groups only. If, after this first division of customers has been made, there still remain within either group shippers whose elasticities of demand for transportation are different, it will then pay to subdivide that group still further and charge different rates to each subdivision. It will pay to continue to subdivide and discriminate so long as any group still contains customers with different elasticities of demand. The important practical difficulties are the finding of means of classifying customers which correspond with their respective elasticities of demand, and the fear that too much discrimination may bring about calls for legislative action by the government. *Perfect discrimination* would consist in charging a different rate to each shipper whose elasticity of demand for transportation differs from that of any other shipper.

While the railroads have by no means achieved perfect discrimination, they must be credited with a fairly thorough attempt in this direction. The reader who is interested may ask his nearest freight agent to show him the rate classification book. He will be given a book the size of a city telephone directory listing the different ways in which freight rates are classified. It may be interesting to note the different bases that are used by a railroad to classify traffic for the purpose of charging discriminating rates:

Commodity discrimination consists in the charging of different rates per ton mile on different commodities of approximately equal bulk. (Bulkier commodities, since they use more space, cost more per ton to carry; hence a higher rate that represents only this difference in cost is not discriminatory.)

For example, fluid milk and fuel oil are of nearly the same specific gravity and both can be handled in bulk[6] in tank cars. Milk, however, fulfills fairly well our four conditions for a high freight rate (see p. 92), while fuel oil conforms to scarcely any of them. (1) The substitute means of transportation for milk are few, and with the single exception of trucks on short hauls, distinctly inferior. Fuel oil can be carried any distance by water or truck without risk of spoilage. (2) The demand for milk itself is much less elastic than the demand for fuel oil at most points of destination; many other sources of heat are reasonably good substitutes for fuel oil, but there are no really close substitutes for milk. (Canned milk is the closest substitute for fluid milk but most people prefer the fluid.) (3) Fluid milk sells at 12 cents to 17 cents per quart (equal to 48 cents to 68 cents per gallon) retail in most large cities, while fuel oil retails at about 7 cents or 8 cents per gallon. Thus a freight cost of 12 cents per gallon would constitute only one-fourth of the delivered price of milk, while a freight cost of even 10 cents per gallon on fuel oil would more than double its delivered price in most cities. (4) Dairy herds are decreased very slowly in response to declining farm prices of milk. Milk will spoil if not sold within a day or two, and if not sold as fluid, must be sold to the creamery or evaporating plant at much lower prices. Fuel oil, however, may be shipped abroad easily if domestic freight rates are too high. Thus, the elasticity of the domestic supply of fluid milk being much less than that of fuel oil, the farmer may be much

---

[6] It is true that milk must be shipped in glass-lined tanks, but both oil and milk shippers often furnish their own tank cars, thus making this cost to the railroad the same for both. While milk must be carried as fast freight and oil may be carried as slow freight, nevertheless, the fact that about the same amount of milk is shipped every day allows the railroad to adjust its working force very closely to the volume of traffic in milk. The shipments of oil, being intermittent, may happen to come just at the time when the road is busy with a large volume of other traffic. Thus, the actual carrying costs to the railroad may not be materially different as between milk and oil.

more easily forced to bear a large share of the freight cost than the oil refinery.

The railroad man would say that "the traffic in milk will bear a higher freight rate than will that in fuel oil." We say that the elasticity of demand for milk transportation is less than the elasticity of demand for oil transportation; therefore, freight rates which result in a volume of traffic that makes marginal revenue and marginal cost equal will be higher in the case of milk than in the case of fuel oil. The reader who is familiar with other commodities may find it interesting to analyze in a similar way the possibilities of freight rate discrimination between them.

Local discrimination in freight rates consists in charging, on different hauls, freight rates on the same commodities which are not proportional to the difference in cost in carrying the goods. We should note immediately that a rate which is lower per ton mile on a long haul than on a short haul is not necessarily discriminatory.[7] We may regard it as clear evidence of discrimination, however, when we see a higher *total* freight charge for the same commodity for a short haul than for a long haul, or when two different hauls of different length

---

[7] A train crew can only be hired for a certain minimum length of working day. Costs of loading and unloading will be the same regardless of the length of the haul. On steam locomotives, the amount of coal lost in building up steam pressure and allowing it to die down will be about the same for one mile as for one hundred miles. None of these are fixed costs, since they would not be incurred at all if the train were not run. It may be seen, however, that these elements of average variable cost will be very high for the first mile and then will decline rapidly per ton mile, as the length of the haul is increased, until a certain minimum cost point is reached. In terms of marginal cost, all the cost elements mentioned above will be in the marginal cost of the first mile. The marginal cost of the second, and immediately subsequent, miles will consist only of the coal necessary to haul the train one more mile and the infinitesimal additional wear and tear. At intervals of every 200 miles or so the railroad ususally finds it advisable to change engines and train crews. If followed rigidly, this practice would introduce a considerable amount of "lumpiness" into the cost schedule. However, where a particular haûl is only slightly in excess of the standard distance, the same engine will be kept on the train and the crew paid overtime wages. Thus, while marginal cost will rise somewhat for the added mileage, it will not rise as much as if engine and crew were changed for an additional distance of only ten or twenty miles.

are carried for the same freight charge. The principal and perhaps the only occasion for local discrimination in freight rates consists in the existence of the other possible means of transportation and in the rates charged by other carriers for service between the same local points.

Competition between a railroad and some other form of transport (a waterway, for example) is in the nature of monopolistic competition. The two services are not perfect substitutes for each other. A waterway may be slower and may offer more difficulties in loading and discharging cargo. Between any two points where water competition exists, rail freight rates will not be equal to water freight rates for all classes of traffic but rather will be based on the value of the difference in service which it is estimated exists in the minds of the shippers. On many classes of traffic, the railroad may not find it advisable to put rates low enough to attract shipments from those who are completely indifferent to the difference in service. On the other classes of traffic, the volume to be gained by a low rate may be such that the most profitable rail rate is as low as, or perhaps even lower than, the water rate.

The unregulated competition of two railroads operating between the same two cities approaches the nature of pure duopoly, since the services of both are nearly perfect substitutes for each other. It is seldom, however, that competition exists between two railroads for business from all the towns along the lines of either road. More usually the roads are so constructed that competition exists between them as to important terminal cities but so that at intervening points each road traverses a different route through different towns. In such a case, the rates will discriminate against the towns where no competition exists. Two roads may be competitive between New York and Buffalo, or between New York and Chicago, with little competition at many intervening points. Under these circumstances, in the period before railroad regulation it was not at all uncommon to find lower total freight charges (not merely lower ton mile rates) between New York and Chicago than were charged for less than half the distance on each line between points where no competition existed.

Since a railroad can gain by carrying any load for any rate above variable costs rather than to lose that particular bit of traffic, competition between railroads tends very readily to become "cutthroat" in character. Before rates were regulated, competition among the several roads on through freight between Chicago and New York was often of this character. A classic example is recorded in which the rate on live cattle from Chicago to New York was driven down to $1.00 per carload. Thereupon Jay Gould, of the Erie Railroad, proceeded to make money by going into the cattle business and buying cattle and shipping them over his rivals' lines at the low freight rate. (The profit in this would last only until the New York price of cattle dropped, or the Chicago price rose, to the level indicated by the low freight rate.)

Rate "wars" of this sort will not endure for long. Either the roads come to an agreement to divide the traffic between them at some rate which is more profitable to both, or else the road with the stronger financial backing may force the weaker road to sell out. In any event the result is a return to higher monopolistic rates. There are some temporary advantages to be reaped by certain localities during these rate wars but there are also long-run ill effects to offset them at least in part. Exceptionally low freight rates may cause heavy concentration of industry in the favored locality. After the rate war is over and rates are raised again, many firms may find that they can no longer compete with firms in other cities more advantageously situated under the new rate schedules. Either a costly moving process results or many of the firms are forced out of business. The community also may then suffer a heavy

burden in caring for the unemployed workers who had previously been attracted to it.

Another peculiarity may be noted in connection with local
discrimination: The actual cost of high freight rates will tend
to be borne more by either the shipping or the receiving community, depending upon the competitive means of transportation in each place. Thus, if an isolated farm community is
served by only one railroad (and no good highways or other
means of transport), the farmers who ship into a large city
which is entered by other railroads will have to bear the full
burden of highly discriminating freight rates. People in the
city will pay no more for the farm produce from this community than they have to pay for similar goods from other
regions enjoying lower freight rates. Contrariwise, on in-
bound freight the community served by only one means of
transportation will have to bear most of the cost of high freight
rates. Unless the difference in freight rates is paid by the
buyer, sellers will not ship into this community when they can
send their goods to other markets for less. Under discriminating rates, the community which has no competition in transportation is thus penalized in two ways. It must accept low
prices (after freight is deducted) for the goods it sells and it
must pay high prices for the goods it buys.

Personal discrimination consists in charging different rates
to different shippers for the same commodities between the
same local points. So long as personal discrimination is practiced with the sole motive of obtaining the greatest profit for
the railroad, it is no more and no less reprehensible than commodity or local discrimination. Personal discrimination, however, is often practiced for other motives. The officers of a
railroad may be large stockholders in a particular corporation
(often a coal company in the past) and so may grant lower
rates to this company so it may improve its competitive position. Bribery may be practiced by a particular shipper to se-

cure rates favorable to himself. Many motives, other than profit to the railroad, might be listed as the occasion for personal discrimination. Where this kind of personal discrimination is practiced it will not appear openly in the published rate schedule. In the past the favorite method was the granting of secret rebates to favored shippers. A more subtle method is to base the discrimination upon what is apparently a commodity or local basis. Thus if the favored shipper's commodity differs in any way from that of his competitors, a lower freight rate may be placed on his particular type of commodity. If he happens to be the only manufacturer in a particular town, then freight rates may be set lower on that commodity from that town than it is from the competitive towns.

Passenger Fare Discrimination

The principles involved in passenger fare discrimination are quite similar to those involved in freight rate discrimination. Considerably greater difficulty is found, however, in dividing passengers into groups which will correspond to the different elasticities of demand for transportation.

Passenger fare discrimination is achieved by offering types of service which are somewhat different and then depending on the customers to group themselves. On European railroads the fear which many people have that they will be considered *declassé* if they are seen traveling second class, enables the railroads to charge a great deal more for first-class accommodations than the difference in cost between rendering first- and second-class service. The premium which another group places upon cushioned seats and somewhat more comfortable surroundings likewise enables the roads to charge a difference greater than the difference in cost for second-class coaches over third class.

In the United States the discrimination occurs between coach and Pullman fares and between regular and excess-fare trains.

Another form of it is found in the low rates charged on so-called excursion specials. It will be noticed that these trains are usually run at rather inconvenient hours and quite often require the passengers to sit up overnight on a day coach. This is done to discourage commercial travelers, and others who would normally be making the trip without special induce-ment, from taking advantage of the low fares on the excur-sion. Another form of discrimination is the difference charged for upper and lower berths on Pullmans. We may note that this difference does not take advantage of the full possibilities of the situation, since trains regularly leave the stations with all lowers filled but with perhaps only half of the upper berths occupied. Whether it would be advisable to drop the price of upper berths (to divert passengers from the coaches) or to raise the price of the lowers (to obtain more revenue from those who would pay the higher price and to induce the others to use upper berths) is a matter that could be determined only by experiment.

A very important form of passenger fare discrimination exists in the sale of low-priced weekly or monthly "commuta-tion tickets" between suburban points and large cities. The elasticity of demand for this class of service is probably greater than for any other kind of passenger business. Low commu-ters' rates are an important element in inducing people to live in the suburbs and to ride the trains rather than to drive their own cars.

Public Policy on Rate Discrimination

In popular speech the term *discrimination* is practically synonomous with *unfairness,* and the charging of different rates to different customers is often condemned without fur-ther reflection. We cannot dismiss the question so easily in the case of the railroads, however. We must raise questions both as to what really does constitute a standard of "fairness" and as to what alternative methods of railroad rate making are practically expedient.

Perfect competition would result in the entire absence of discrimination, and freight rates would differ only by the actual difference in costs. Under perfect competition a ton of diamonds (if no armed guards were required) would pay the same freight rate as a ton of coal. Even under perfect competition, if the volume of traffic is greater in one direction than in the opposite direction, the "return loads" will bear a lower freight rate. The variable costs in this particular case would be only the difference in cost between hauling loaded and empty freight cars. Perfect competition, however, is an impossibility in the field of transportation. In the case of the railroads themselves we are confronted with monopoly, duopoly, or at most oligopoly; there are very few points in the country between which even four or five railroads compete. Between a railroad and other forms of transportation the situation is one of monopolistic competition. In unregulated rate making, therefore, the practical comparison is not between perfect competition and discrimination, but rather between a simple monopoly price and a discriminating monopoly price.

As a matter of pure theory, it may interest the reader to know that Professor A. C. Pigou,[8] one of the most socially minded economists, believes that under certain circumstances perfect discrimination may be a fairer method of pricing than perfect competition. He points out that perfect discrimination charges each buyer exactly the full amount that the product is worth to him individually. Thus prices are charged in accord with the "ability to pay" rather than imposing a single price on all, regardless of difference in income or in desire for the product.

In the case of the railroads, however, we return to the com-

---

[8] Pigou, A. C., *Economics of Welfare*, p. 286 ff., The Macmillan Co., New York, 1933.

parison of simple monopoly price with discriminating charges.[9] There are some cases in which a railroad might not be built at all if it were not for the possibility of charging discriminating rates. Consider, for example, an isolated point in northern Canada which is capable of producing both gold and lumber. By charging a high rate on gold ore and mining machinery and a low rate on lumber there may be sufficient revenue to warrant building a railroad, but if the road were forced to charge the same rate on all freight, the revenue might not be large enough to induce its construction. In cases like this, discrimination must be credited with a net gain for the community. In view of the fact that goods continue to be shipped by rail, the services of the railroad presumably are worth at least the amount of the rates charged both to those who pay the high rates and to those who pay the low rates. The building of the railroad thus represents a gain for them.

In circumstances where some transportation service would be provided even if discrimination were not allowed, the comparison becomes more difficult. If discriminating prices are higher than simple monopoly price for one group and lower than simple monopoly price for another, we must balance the losses to those who are charged the higher price against the gains to those who are charged the lower price. On this point Joan Robinson says:[10] "For instance, members of the more elastic market (for whom price is reduced) may be poorer than members of the less elastic markets, and we may consider a gain to poorer buyers more important than a loss to richer buyers." She says this, however, because she is thinking of discrimination as practiced directly in pricing consumers' goods. In the field of transportation, the least elastic demand may happen to come from a poor farming community which is served by no other means of transport,

[9] Cf. Robinson, Joan, *Economics of Imperfect Competition,* Ch. 16.
[10] *Ibid.,* p. 204.

and the most elastic demand may be that of a wealthy industrial city which is served by many railroads and other transport agencies.

If marginal costs are falling and if volume of traffic would be increased by discrimination, then there are some situations in which discriminating monopoly price would be lower than simple monopoly price in the less elastic as well as in the more elastic classes of traffic. If these circumstances prevail, then all shippers will benefit under discriminating freight rates as against simple monopoly rates.

Wasteful Use of Resources and the Need for Regulation

So far our discussion would indicate that unregulated rate discrimination is preferable to unregulated monopoly price in railroad rate making. There are certain aspects of unregulated discrimination, however, which are distinctly harmful to the public interest. Most important is the waste of the resources of production which is involved. This waste occurs in two ways: (1) through needless duplication of transportation facilities; (2) through poor economic organization of other productive activities that depend on transportation. Where there is a large volume of traffic that is being charged high rates under discrimination, there will be an attractive opportunity for competition to enter the field. The existing railroad may be physically capable of handling even the full volume of traffic that would be available at lower rates, and might very likely be able to do this at much lower cost than if the traffic were divided with another road. In such a case, the duplication of facilities by a second railroad would be a sheer economic waste. To prevent this type of waste, it is now provided by state and Federal laws that a new transportation line must secure a "certificate of convenience and necessity" from an appropriate commission before it may start to operate.

Perhaps even more important than needless duplication is

our second class of waste: the improper organization of national resources that results from distorted rate structures. This is caused both by commodity and by local discrimination, but the latter factor is probably the more important. Regions which are "favored" by low freight rates will tend to carry production far beyond the point of increasing costs. Other regions which may be equally, or even better, equipped by nature for the production of the same commodities may find that lower production costs are not sufficient to offset high discriminatory freight rates, with the result that they either do not produce at all or produce only for a local market. In domestic trade, discriminating freight rates may prove as effective a barrier to realizing the advantages of specialization and division of labor as are high tariffs in international trade.

Personal discrimination is generally condemned as leading to the development of a monopoly by the favored shipper. The question then turns to whether monopoly or competition is more to be desired in the shipper's industry. But even in an industry where monopoly is best suited to public policy, we shall perhaps be better served if the firm that achieves monopoly by forcing others out of business does so by the means of lower production costs rather than by freight rate favoritism.

Rate Regulation

The unfairness, both real and imagined, of railroad rates charged during the era of cutthroat competition and monopolistic discrimination soon led to demands for rate regulation. The period from 1869 to 1887 was marked by the introduction of laws attempting to deal with this problem in many of the state legislatures. An attack on the high and discriminatory rates on grains, livestock, and other farm produce constituted one of the chief elements in the Granger Movement in the Midwestern states.

State legislation and the establishment of railroad commissions by the state to regulate rates could apply to rates within the state only. At best the scope of this regulation was sharply limited and at its worst it complicated the problem. Many state commissions were not above setting discriminating rates themselves which would operate to favor industries within the state as against those outside the state.

The Interstate Commerce Commission was established by an Act of Congress in 1887 in an attempt to secure better practices in the setting of interstate rates. At first there was considerable conflict between the Interstate Commerce Commission and the various state regulatory bodies and a series of adverse court decisions virtually emasculated its power. Later court decisions and new legislation have clarified and extended the powers of the Commission until it now has jurisdiction over all interstate rates and may also order the changing of rates within a state where it can be shown that these rates have an effect upon interstate commerce. At its inception the power of the Commission was confined to detecting and prosecuting cases of rate discrimination as defined in the original act, and even in this duty it was hampered by defects in the way in which the law was drawn. Gradually the power of the commission has been extended until it now has power to determine both maximum and minimum rates in all cases affecting interstate commerce.

In setting rates, the Commission is required by law to allow the railroads a rate of return of 5 3/4 percent upon the "value" of their property. The problem of determining the fair value of this property, as in the case of other utilities whose rates are regulated, has proved extremely difficult of solution.[11]

After a long period spent in the correction of the more ob-

---

[11] See Meyers, Albert L., *Elements of Modern Economics,* Ch. XVI, Prentice-Hall, Inc., New York, 1937.

vious abuses in railroad rate structures, the Commission is at present faced with the problem, not of preventing the railroads from earning too much, but of enabling them to earn enough income to survive. In doing this the Commission is itself forced to adopt, at least in part, the policy of "charging what the traffic will bear" (marginal revenue principle) and we find discrimination between different classes of traffic on that basis. Considerable attempt has been made to avoid discrimination between localities, although rates are by no means uniform throughout the country, particularly where waterways are competitive with railroad lines. The Commission can and does prevent the competitive undercutting of rates by different railroads. Probably no rate structure can ever be devised that will be entirely satisfactory either to the railroads or to all shippers and passengers. The best that can be hoped for is the attainment of the most effective compromise among the conflicting interests.

In allowing the railroads to earn "a fair rate of return," the Commission, in setting rates, is really taking over one of the functions of management. However, we must not regard all of the disputes about rates between the Commission and the railroads as differences of opinion as to what constitutes good management. The recent passenger fare controversy is a good case in point. It is well known that the elasticity of demand for transportation may be different in different phases of the business cycle, thus causing higher or lower rates to yield the greater revenue according to circumstances. When the Commission proposed to drop the basic passenger fare from 3.6 cents to 2 cents per mile, the opposition of the Eastern railroads was probably motivated more by the fear that rates would not be revised upward when occasion warranted than by the immediate prospects of revenue at the 2-cent rate. After a trial of the 2-cent rate the Commsision raised the rate to 2 1/2 cents.

Shortly after this, some of the roads voluntarily petitioned for a reduction to 2 1/4 cents, probably feeling that experience showed rates could be revised upward and that the immediate promise of revenue was better at the lower rate.

Present Problems of the Railroads

Aside from rate structures, there are many difficulties which account for the unhappy situation in which most railroads find themselves today. These may be reviewed briefly:

Many railroads are much overcapitalized. They are burdened with bond issues so great that it is impossible for them to earn interest upon them even with considerable increases in their present volume of traffic, and a great number of these roads are so situated that an increase in rates would reduce rather than increase their total revenue. The only permanent solution to this problem is bankruptcy, which will wipe out these bond issues based on fictitious valuations. There has been a reluctance to face the fact and accept this solution in the past because of the large amount of the securities of these roads which were held by banks and insurance companies; the evil day has been postponed by one breathing spell after another in the hope that some bit of luck would change the situation.

By means of laws and trade union rules the railroads have been largely prevented from effecting economies in the use of labor. Many of these restrictions were originally promulgated in the name of safety but they have not been sufficiently flexible to allow the roads to take full advantage of changes in motive power and methods of operation.

There is much needless duplication of rail facilities between different points. If this traffic were confined to a fewer number of roads running at or near capacity, many operating economies could be achieved. For this reason the railroads have been requested to submit plans to the Interstate Commerce Commission for approval whereby the existing roads will be merged to form "systems." At least one serious obstacle to this plan presents itself: If the stronger roads, in absorbing the weaker ones, are compelled to assume the present burden of fixed charges borne by these roads, this would in many cases more than overbalance the economies to be achieved by consolidation. To date the Commission and the railroads have failed to agree on the plans for any important systems. It would seem plausible that the ultimate goal should be the consolidation of all railroads into perhaps four or five systems, one for each region, since we have seen that competition here does not achieve the benefits that it brings in some other industries. The problem of regulation would be no more difficult than it is at present, and probably would be simpler.

Many roads are in possession of some branch and spur trackage which is being operated at a definite loss and should be abandoned. Whenever such a move is proposed by the roads, the community affected usually protests loudly to the Commission. It would seem that no community is entitled to demand railroad service which it is unable to support by a reasonable volume of traffic.

Competition by trucks, busses, and airplanes has cut seriously into railroad traffic volume in recent years. Insofar as these means of transportation are being subsidized through not being compelled to pay their fair share of the costs of roads, airports and air beacons, the railroads may have a legitimate ground for complaint. It would seem to be an advisable policy for the long run to confine new subsidies for these other forms of transportation to fields where they can continue to give better and cheaper service, after subsidies are withdrawn, than the railroads now provide.

Public Ownership of the Railroads

Many people have argued for and against government ownership and operation of the railroads. The debate usually centers around the question of government *versus* private efficiency in operation. Well-managed government projects and poorly managed private enterprises are offered as evidence by one side and well-managed private business and poorly managed government activities are offered as evidence by the other. An objective answer to this question is almost impossible.

It might be more to the point to assume, for the purposes of the argument, that governmental and private efficiency are equal, and then to ask to what extent government ownership and operation of the railroads would solve the problems outlined above. In the first place, government ownership, in and of itself, would not solve the problem of overcapitalization. If the government were to take over the roads and assume all existing financial obligations at face value, it would be in exactly the same position as the present owners, and losses would have to be paid out of taxes and the bonds redeemed from the same source. Under no circumstances should the government pay more than the current market value of the outstanding securities. Purchase at such a price would be equivalent to bankruptcy proceedings, which could achieve the same results and leave the roads in private hands. It might be argued that the government would not overcapitalize in the future, whereas after reorganization private owners might be tempted to do so; however, the Securities and Exchange Commission now provides a means of preventing this.

If we are to judge from the present trends of labor legislation, the government would probably be in no better position to economize in the use of labor than are the private owners at present. In fact it is likely that the government would be even more hampered in such economies.

The government could eliminate duplicating rail facilities but this would be perhaps no more effective than a single all-inclusive railroad system in private hands. If it is stipulated that no employees are to be laid off, either the government or a private owner would be equally restricted in the economies to be achieved from such a reorganization. As far as the elimination of non-paying branch lines is concerned, there might be even more political pressure to prevent this than there is at present, when the decision lies with the Interstate Commerce Commission.

Competition with trucks, busses, and airplanes would be the same under government ownership of railroads as under private ownership. Any restrictions which might be placed on this competition could be enacted as well under one system as the other. A plan might be advanced under which the government would own these other means of transportation as well and would then apportion service and traffic on the basis of general transportation efficiency. Under such a plan government ownership of a transportation system of such magnitude might be better than private ownership because motor car manufacturers, airplane manufacturers, and the makers of railroad equipment would each be tremendously interested in having the system use as great an amount of his type of equipment as possible, to the exclusion of the others. If the owners of such a private system were financially involved in any of these manufacturing companies, such companies might be unfairly favored. How much political favoritism of the same type there would be is, of course, problematical.

In the determination of rate structures (except for rates within the states which do not affect interstate commerce), the government has nearly as much authority at present under the Commerce Commission as it would have if it owned the roads. If the rates are to be prevented from becoming purely political in character under government ownership, they must be under the jurisdiction of some body which is at least as free from politics as the Interstate Commerce Commission.

After an examination of all these questions, the relative efficiency of government and private business is still to be determined. The issue, after all, will probably be decided on the basis of political philosophy rather than by economic theory.

CHAPTER VI

Problems of Agricultural Policy

THE MUTUALLY interrelated problems that may be grouped under the general heading of "the farm problem" have much with which to challenge the interest of the serious student of economics, since they involve the application of almost every principle of economic theory. As with many other questions of national economic policy, the problem is political as well: The pure economic theorist may propose a solution for the farm problem which is based on sound economic logic; the administrator, however, who attempts to put such a plan into effect must face the realities of both domestic and international politics. His question is not so much "What is the best plan?" as it is "What is the best plan which can be adopted in the existing political situation?" As regards any particular measure, it is not simply a question of "Is this measure desirable?", but rather "After all the political concessions that will be necessary to secure its adoption have been made, will this measure still be desirable?"

At the very outset the question, "Is there any justification for special aid to the farmer?" must be proposed. In opposition to such aid it is urged that the farmer as a business owner stands a chance to make a profit and assumes a risk of loss; therefore, there is no more and no less reason to aid him in bad times than to rush to the aid of a manufacturing capitalist who suffers reverses. The farmer who, when wheat is selling at

$2.00 a bushel, mortgages his own farm in order to buy an additional farm is a land speculator and deserves no better fate than an urban real estate speculator who makes a similarly unwise investment. In many cases changes in taste and dietary habits have decreased the demand for certain farm products, but the danger of these changes occurs constantly to manufacturing producers, and nobody takes up collections for the destitute ex-manufacturers of hoop-skirts. The mere fact that the farmer is in bad straits seemingly would entitle him to exactly as much, and no more, consideration than we give to the unemployed industrial worker.

In spite of these arguments, there are certain grounds on which the farmer may legitimately, and with self-respect, claim the consideration of his problems by the Federal government and the American people. The farmer is injured by the special privileges which are granted to other groups: The American tariff policy forces the farmer to buy in a domestic market while he must sell in a world market. Clothing, building materials, and household goods are all protected by tariffs which raise the price that the farmer has to pay for them. Corn, wheat, cotton, tobacco, and the other major crops are produced in such quantities that an exportable surplus results, and it is the price which prevails in world markets which determines the domestic price for such products.

There are other inequities besides the tariff: Labor unions are allowed to organize quasi-monopolies of their craft to raise wages, which practice increases the prices of many of the products that the farmer must buy. Most of the products which the farmer must buy are either produced by monopoly or by firms operating under conditions of monopolistic competition. One of the chief reasons for the plight of the farmer is that agriculture in general is one of the few branches of industry in which conditions approaching those of pure competition still survive. It is not an exaggeration to say that the farmer must sell in a highly competitive market, while most if not all of the nonagricultural products which he has to buy are produced and sold under conditions of varying degrees of monopolistic price control.

A very brief review of the historical changes which have taken place in American agriculture may put us in a position to understand better the present agricultural problems. Even in Colonial times, American agriculture was on an export basis. Wheat, corn, tobacco, and later cotton were and have continued to be the principal crops upon which the farmers of this country depend for cash income. Even in these early days, the demand situation prevailing in European markets was one of the very important factors influencing the price which American farmers received for these crops. However, when we probe more deeply into the matter, we discover many contrasts between the situations prevailing under early farming and those that prevail at present. The early development of American agriculture paralleled in time the industrial progress of England, and presently of the United States. Both in Europe and to a lesser degree in America, people were concentrating in industrial manufacturing cities and population was increasing rapidly. Consequently, the demand for agricultural products, both foodstuffs and agricultural raw materials, was an ever-expanding one. The chief problems which confronted the United States then were simply those of expanding agricultural production and providing adequate means of transportation to bring the agricultural products to hungry cities. Farmers suffered occasionally from drought and other adverse weather conditions, as they always have and probably always will, but where transport facilities were adequate, for farmers to suffer from a surplus of agricultural production was a condition that was almost entirely unknown. Particularly heavy crops did depress prices and cause farmers to grumble, but such a thing as a general surplus of practically all agricultural products was unheard of.

Agricultural problems before the twentieth century were chiefly and almost solely problems of production. Practically all agricultural leaders devoted their efforts to increasing the yield and improving the quality of agricultural products. The workers of the natural sciences became the chief helpers of agriculture. New varieties of plants better able to withstand the climatic conditions of various localities were developed; means of controlling insect pests were studied and perfected; scientific breeding improved farm animals; new systems of crop rotation tended to retain the fertility of the soil. This process is still going on and improvement is still being made in the means of agricultural production. However, the primary problem of the American farmer at the present time is not so much how to produce a crop as how to dispose of it at a profitable price once he has produced it.

Perhaps one single fact may make us realize vividly the change which has taken place in agricultural production: In 1787, the year the Constitution was framed, it required 19 people living on farms to feed and clothe one person in the city, in addition to feeding and clothing themselves; today 19 people on farms can provide for the agricultural requirements of 66 people living in cities.[1]

Production Responses to Price Changes

Since agriculture is characterized by conditions closely approximating those of pure competition, we should expect to find marginal farms dropping out of the production of various crops as prices fall and new farms beginning production as prices rise. The theory states, however, that these changes may be expected to take place "in the long run." These

---

[1] Secretary of Agriculture Henry A. Wallace, in a speech at Des Moines, Iowa, August, 1938.

changes do take place in practice but the increases in units of production in response to rising prices are much more rapid than the decreases in production units following falling prices. Several factors account for this difference.

Some crops require either special machinery or special methods of production. Rice, for example, requires extensive irrigation. When, in response to a higher price, irrigation facilities have been provided, the tendency is for the farmers to try to hold on for a few years in an attempt to realize something on the investment. It usually requires about three successive years of low prices to cause any substantial reduction in rice acreage; many other crops require more than one year of low prices to cause acreage reduction. In the case of tree-grown crops such as fruits and nuts, responses in actual production to changes in price are much slower both in increases and declines. A few years of relatively attractive prices may cause expansion of orchards but these trees do not begin to bear fruit for several years. Once they are bearing, even several years of low prices may still find the grower reluctant to cut them down. Aside from vagaries of nature, the only force operating to decrease production will be the failure to replace old orchards and old trees as they die or cease to bear. If he can avoid it, the grower will not ordinarily pick the fruit unless the price promises to cover the cost of picking and marketing. Unless weather damage or insect pests decrease the crop, prices may remain at or near this low (variable cost) level for several years without causing a substantial decrease in production.

Many types of soil and climate are technologically suited to the growth of a wide range of crops. When we take freight rates and marketing facilities into account, however, we find that the number of commercially feasible crops is considerably below the number of botanically adapted crops in most localities. Even crops which are closely related in methods of production may exhibit considerable marketing differences. For example, many parts of the Western cattle range country are equally well suited to the grazing and care of milk cows. They are too far away from large cities, however, to allow shipment of fresh fluid milk or even the production of evaporated milk and butter and cheese, and the higher freight rates prevent them from competing with the present milk-producing areas which are closer to the centers of consumption. The development of refrigerator cars and fast freight service in recent years, however, has had a tendency to widen the number of commercially feasible crops for many localities. The South has benefited particularly by this development, since Southern truck crops mature earlier than those in the North and they are able to command an early season premium in price which helps to overcome the cost of the long haul.

When the number of commercial crops is sharply limited, either by natural or economic factors, even shifts from one crop to another may avail little in relieving the farmer from the effect of disastrously low prices. For example, in some parts of the Southeast the two chief crops competing for the use of the land are cotton and peanuts. Any large shift from cotton to peanuts in response to low cotton prices may find the farmer receiving as low or lower cash return per acre of peanuts as he would have had if he had continued to raise cotton. While the elasticity of demand for peanuts may be somewhat greater than the elasticity of demand for cotton, it is not great enough to prevent serious declines in price if there is a great addition to the supply.

Even before the World War, when agriculture was more prosperous, many farmers had the bitter experience of shifting their entire acreage from one crop to another, only to find themselves one year behind the price changes in the market. This kind of experience has led many of the more conservative farmers to give up attempting to forecast prices and instead to divide their land among a few of its best uses in the hope that price fluctuations in the various crops will cancel out to yield them a more stable income. Other farmers may be led by experience to hold steadily to a single crop in the hope of "making a killing" when years of high prices occur. Some potato growers in Idaho figure that they can afford to stay in business on one good price year out of five, and that with two or more good years out of five they will show a profit. Either of these practices, if followed by any considerable number of farmers, has a strong tendency to delay acreage changes in response to price. Supply is thus inelastic for short periods.

So far we have been discussing simply the influences affecting acreage changes as the determinant of agricultural production. The number of acres planted to a given crop is the one factor affecting production which is most subject to control in accordance with the judgment of the farmer as to anticipated prices. If, for the moment, the question of government control (or influence) is ignored, the only important element other than price that will be apt to deter the farmer from planting his intended acreage to a particular crop is the presence of unfavorable weather at planting time, which makes it difficult or impossible for him to work his fields. Production, of course, is a function of yield per acre as well as of total acreage.[2]

The yield per acre is a factor which is far less subject to the farmers' control than the acreage planted. Weather is an important factor in determining the yield of all crops, and in many instances weather alone can spell the difference between a total crop failure and a record yield. Nevertheless, assuming "normal" weather conditions, or similar weather conditions, in two or more successive years, there are many prac-

---

[2] Planted acreage is also the best single statistical measurement of the farmers' desires to expand or contract production of a given crop. Fertilizer sales may give a rough indication of the desire to increase yields, but there is generally no way of knowing to what crops the fertilizer is to be applied.

tices which the farmer may adopt which will tend strongly to influence the yield per acre and hence the total production: He may use fertilizer or (within limits) he may increase the amount of fertilizer used; he may buy a variety of seed which is known to give greater yields; he may increase the number of times the field is cultivated; he may make a more active effort to control insect pests for which known remedies are available.

In general, the relation between changes in the price anticipated by the farmer and changes in the above practices to influence yields is somewhat more complicated than in the case of acreage variations. If the amount which can be added to the yield by any one of these practices is known, we multiply it by the anticipated price to obtain the anticipated increase in total revenue. If, then, the cost of the practice falls anywhere short of this sum, it will appear profitable for the farmer to act along these lines. This is simply a rough approximation of our principle of equating marginal revenue and marginal cost.

However, certain secondary influences present themselves, which may tend toward prolonging the increased yields even at much lower anticipated prices than the one which influenced the first decision. When soil has been fertilized for a few years, a sufficient amount of fertilizer may remain in the soil to yield fairly large crops even though no more fertilizer is added for a year or two. This, in fact, is a normal expectation. When superior seed has passed the developmental stage and is produced in commercial quantities, its difference in price over poor seed is generally so slight that it pays to use good seed if the crop is to be planted at all. After the crop has been planted, spraying or dusting for insect pests may be the only means of saving all, or any considerable part, of the yield. It will then pay to spray or dust if the anticipated receipts from the crop (after harvesting and marketing charges are deducted) are anything above the cost of spraying or dusting itself, disregarding all previously incurred costs.

In the case of farm machinery, farmers should figure depreciation and interest charges in addition to the operating costs, and make sure that all these costs will be covered by an increased value product before they purchase the machine. (At this moment the cost is not yet incurred, hence variable.) Yet farmers who do this may find that the price of the product falls and that the increased yield from greater cultivation does not return all these costs for the use of the machine. Other farmers may not figure costs carefully at all—indeed many of them have bought tractors simply from the motive of having something to ride on rather than having to walk behind the plow or cultivator. In any event, once the machinery has been purchased it will continue to be operated so long as the costs of fuel, oil, and repairs are less than the expected returns. (Depreciation and interest will now be fixed costs.)

Decreases in yields are due far more to weather conditions than to voluntary contraction by the farmer. Methods of increasing yield, which are adopted in response to high prices, will be continued in years of low prices as long as the anticipated price of the product promises to cover the variable costs of their use. The most important way in which lower prices may tend to reduce yields is by leaving the farmer short of cash or credit with which to buy fertilizer and equipment. (Judging by the credit policies of fertilizer and equipment companies in many regions, this is not a serious factor at present.) In most major crops produced in the United States the long-time trend of yields has been steadily upward. Even in cotton, several years of low prices failed to discourage farmers' efforts to increase yields and the 1937-1938 season found fertilization, plus very favorable weather, producing an all-time record yield. The tables which follow show the ten-year average yields in each of several major crops for the United

States and for certain states which may be considered typical. The 1937-1938 season yields are also shown separately.

TABLE III

TEN-YEAR AVERAGE YIELDS, UNITED STATES

	Wheat (bu.)	Rye (bu.)	Oats (bu.)	Corn (bu.)	Cotton (lb.)	Tobacco (lb.)	Potatoes (bu.)
1870–79	12.5	10.8	26.1	26.5	195.3	754.7	83.9
1880–89	13.2	12.1	28.0	26.0	184.5	712.5	83.0
1890–99	13.7	12.7	27.2	26.0	201.8	754.2	82.6
1900–09	14.4	13.3	28.8	27.3	193.4	824.4	94.9
1910–19	14.2	12.5	31.0	26.0	193.1	808.4	97.2
1920–29	14.0	12.7	29.7	26.9	171.6	772.8	110.6
1930–38[1]	13.3	11.7	27.4	22.8	206.2	820.4	111.4
Crop Year 1937–38	13.6	12.9	32.7	28.2	264.6	897.1	123.1

[1] Nine-year average.

TABLE IV

TEN-YEAR AVERAGE YIELDS, IMPORTANT STATES

	Wheat Kansas	Rye N. Dak.	Oats Iowa	Corn Iowa	Cotton Miss.	Tobacco N. C.	Potatoes Maine
1870–79	13.6		33.9	37.4	208.6	470.7	108.0
1880–89	13.9	10.1[2]	33.7	34.7	196.9	398.7	114.1
1890–99	13.4	10.8	31.8	34.3	209.5	536.7	129.4
1900–09	13.8	13.3	30.6	38.1	203.5	622.8	175.8
1910–19	13.5	10.3	37.3	38.9	185.5	647.2	206.4
1920–29	13.2	12.0	35.4	40.1	197.7	675.8	246.5
1930–38[1]	12.3	10.1	31.4	35.6	245.8	794.8	269.9
Crop Year 1937–38	15.1	10.8	45.0	45.0	368.0	884.0	287.0

[1] Nine-year average.
[2] Eight-year average.

These tables do not give an entirely true picture of the increase in productive efficiency of farming for this period. During the last two or three decades covered by the tables, production of grains and potatoes has been widely extended in the "dry land regions" of the West. The relatively poor showing of wheat, rye, and oats is due partly to the spread of "extensive" farming methods and partly to dust storms occasioned by the type of farming. The fact that the average yields for the country as a whole have continued to increase despite the inclusion of these poorer lands in cultivation is evidence of a still greater increase in efficiency than that shown by the yields. On the other hand, the fact that acreage control programs, particularly in cotton and tobacco, have been in effect during the 1930-1937 period may tend to distort the picture in the other direction. Farmers who are given an acreage allotment will naturally take their least productive acres out of cultivation.

Farming of New Land and Farm Abandonment

The above discussion of production responses to price changes dealt with adjustments made by a farm which continues in operation, that is, one which continues with shifts and variations from one crop to another and in attempts to secure high yields. There is one other way in which production may vary in response to price, that is, in the organization of new farms on previously unused land in response to high prices and the abandonment of old farms as prices fall. Both of these responses are apt to be slower than shifts from one crop to another, but even here increases in production in response to price tend to take place much more rapidly than decreases in production due to farm abandonment. The prospect of a few years of high prices may make it appear worth while to work lands of comparatively low fertility which it would not pay to cultivate at lower prices. High prices may also make it appear profitable to clear "waste land" of underbrush and stones and bring it into cultivation.

It may take several successive years of low prices in most of the possible alternative crops to cause much reduction in production through farm abandonment. Mere foreclosure of a mortgage does not mean that a farm is taken out of production. When a mortgage is foreclosed, the holder of the mortgage has a choice among three courses of action: He may allow the farm to be sold for what it will bring at public auction, in which case the buyer will continue to operate the farm; or he may bid the farm in himself and then either operate it or rent it to someone else (perhaps to the previous owner). Even if no other buyer makes an offer, we may be sure that the mortgageholder will attempt to operate the farm as long as there is any prospect at all of recouping some part of his losses. Generally this means that for some few years the farm will continue to be operated as long as the anticipated returns promise to cover the additional costs of a year's operation. If taxes have been paid up to date, these variable costs need not even include taxes. The operator can gamble on one year's return and if this does not include enough to pay taxes, he may allow the county or state to seize the land at a tax sale and keep in his pocket whatever income there is above other costs. Lack of alternative occupations, particularly in business depressions, is another factor operating to delay farm abandonment.

Taking a farm out of production is thus seen to be a very slow response to price. More rapid abandonment is usually occasioned by dust storms or other natural calamities which make the prospects appear poor for raising any crop at all, regardless of price. Farm abandonment in response to several successive years of low farm income is usually preceded by a period of several years of cutting costs, those most commonly dispensed with being fertilizing, terracing, and other soil-building practices. The farm is not usually abandoned until it is "worked out." If there is any danger that we will be threatened with a shortage of arable land in the future, there is thus some justification for the payments made by the Agricultural Adjustment Administration for "soil-building practices."

After all the above influences have been allowed for, there is one still more important reason why agricultural production is not voluntarily controlled in an effort to govern price. Since each individual farmer is responsible for so small a part of the total production of any crop, each one realizes that he cannot affect the price to himself by the infinitesimal amount which he individually may withhold from, or throw on to, the market. It requires the reduction of output by all, or a very large number of, farmers to raise the price from the supply side of the market. The only consideration which will cause substantial voluntary reduction of acreage (without agreement, benefit payments, or compulsion) is the firm belief of a great proportion of farmers, prior to planting time, that the price of the crop will be very low. Cultivators of particular crops have assembled in meetings from time to time and counseled each other to reduce acreage. Usually the more they believed one another's promises, the more they believed that the price was going to be high. Consequently, it frequently happened that each farmer went home and planted, not less, but more acreage than the year before.

The question may be argued as to whether control of agricultural production is desirable. If it is conceded that such control is advisable, it must be obvious that the initiative of the individual farmer cannot be relied upon to achieve it. Planted acreage depends mostly on the price forecast in the mind of each individual farmer. If all farmers believe the price will be high, it is likely to be low. If all farmers believe the price will be low, it will probably be high. When "balanced agricultural production" has been achieved, it has usually been the result of a happy and fortuitous combination of right and wrong guesses on the part of the farmers.

Problems of Farm Valuation and Farm Debt

The value of a farm is its capitalized net income. That is, if the annual average net income of a farm is divided by a given rate of interest, the result is the capital sum which would have to be invested at that rate of interest to yield a similar net income. This formula, however, does not begin to solve our problem. The true value of the farm must be based, not on the past net income, but on the anticipated future net income. If the farm has been properly cared for and not "worked out," the past yields may give us a fair indication of the average production to be expected in the future; but former prices are most unreliable as a guide in determining the prices at which those future yields may be sold.

There is always a danger that farms will be overvalued after a few years of high prices. Wars, crop failures in other parts of the world, and violent upswings of the business cycle may each result in short periods of high farm product prices. In these periods prospective buyers of farms are always apt to pay too much attention to the net income of the past year or two and fail to realize that the high prices and consequent high net income cannot be expected to continue. As a result they rush to buy farms at excessively high prices and commit themselves to mortgages in order to buy them. Bankers and other lenders in farm communities have usually been equally short-sighted in extending excessive mortgages on overvalued farms during periods of high prices.

When a few years of low prices follow a period of high prices, farmers who have bought farms at inflated values find that they are unable to meet even interest payments on the mortgages, to say nothing of making repayments on the principal sum. Such times usually find some farm groups demanding "more liberal" farm credit while others are asking some form of price inflation or farm aid.

Liberal credit in the form of government or government-guaranteed loans at interest rates lower than market rates of interest can save the farmer only if his farm has not been too greatly overvalued and too greatly mortgaged. To see how this works, let us assume that, when wheat is selling at $1.50 per bushel, a farmer with $3,000 cash buys a farm for $10,000, giving a $5,000 first mortgage at 6 percent and a $2,000 second mortgage at 8 percent for the unpaid balance. (To keep the problem simple, we will assume that wheat is the only crop for which the land is fitted.) Various possible circumstances are shown in the following table:

TABLE V

Price of Wheat	Farm[1] Net Income	Farm[2] Value	Interest on $5,000 1st Mortgage	Interest on $2,000 2nd Mortgage	Debt Repaid	Unpaid Interest
$1.50	$600	$10,000	@ 6% $300	@ 8% $160	$140	. . .
1.00	360	6,000	@ 6% 300	@ 8% 160	. . .	$100
1.00	360	6,000	@ 3% 150	@ 4% 84[3]	126	. . .
.80	200	3,333	@ 3% 150	@ 4% 84	. . .	34

[1] These figures are assumptions perhaps in rough accord with facts.
[2] In calculating farm value, we assume a rate of interest of 6 percent in each case, which is, of course, an oversimplification.
[3] Second mortgage is increased by $100 to cover previous unpaid interest.

The first line of the table shows us the farmer's expectations when he buys the farm. After meeting all other expenses he would have $140 to apply on paying back the principal on his mortgages. (We assume that his living costs, which we deduct in computing net income, are met out of his own wage as a farmer. Properly speaking the interest charges are also costs, but in our table we wish to show the relationship between these charges and the cash available to meet them.) Under these circumstances, if the farmer continues to pay the $140 each year plus the interest charges saved by its repayment, he will be able to pay off the second mortgage in about ten years and the first mortgage twelve years after that. In twenty-two years he would own a $10,000 farm free of debt if the price of wheat stays at $1.50 and if average yields and other costs remain unchanged.

The second line of the table shows the situation in which the farmer would find himself if, in the first year after he bought the farm, the price of wheat should fall to $1.00. The farmer's original investment of $3,000 has been wiped out; the value of the farm is $1,000 less than the combined amount of the first and second mortgages, and $100 of the interest charges remains unpaid. The farmer may be threatened with foreclosure if this situation continues.

The third line of the table represents the situation as it would be if some government farm credit agency offered to take over the existing debt of 3 percent on the first mortgage and 4 percent on the second mortgage. If the price of wheat remains steadily at $1.00, even with these liberal interest rates it will now take the farmer thirteen years to pay off the second mortgage and additional eighteen years to pay off the first mortgage. If, however, the farmer does not expect the price of wheat to rise above $1.00, he would be unwise to accept these terms at all. By accepting these terms, if the price of wheat does not average higher than $1.00, he would be paying $7,100 for a farm worth $6,000 in addition to the $3,000 already lost. He would do better to allow the farm to go at a foreclosure sale and then either rent a farm or try to buy one at a value more in line with the price of wheat. Nor should the credit agency take over the mortgages on these terms if there is any expectation that the price of wheat will average $1.00 for a number of years. It should insist that the mortgages be scaled down before it assumes them. The only consideration that would justifiy the terms shown in line 3 of the table is the firm belief on the part of all concerned that the price of wheat will rise shortly and will average higher than $1.00 for long years to come.

Let us suppose, for a moment, that such a price rise is anticipated and the terms are agreed upon. Line 4 of the table shows what would then happen if, instead of rising, the price of wheat should decline to 80 cents and promise to remain there. The value of the farm would drop to one-third of its original purchase price, and the farmer would lack $34 of even meeting the low interest charges, without paying a cent on the principal.

We find, then, that more liberal credit is of real help to the farmer in times of low prices only if the farm has not been too greatly overvalued when originally purchased and only if prices may be expected to rise again soon. The table also illustrates the fallacy of the old rule which regarded 50 percent of the value as a "conservative" loan. Fifty percent of value is conservative only on conservative values and not on valuations based on prices that are temporarily extremely high.

There is, however, a sociological reason for special consideration of the problem of farm mortgages. Urban businessmen who go bankrupt are usually found to have their homes in their wives' names so that they do not lose them, but the foreclosure of a farm mortgage usually means the loss of a farm family home. Also, a farm mortgage usually covers the farmhouse as well as the land and other farm buildings. Even if the farmer were able to keep his home after a foreclosure, it might be of very little use to him if he is forced to seek work in some distant locality. Farm owners are always known to be a conservative group, but a group of dispossessed farmers, or of those threatened with the loss of their farms, will be ready to follow any crack-pot who promises them relief.

Inflation as a Remedy for the Farm Debt

Inflation offers a dubious solution of the farm mortgage problem from the point of view of the individual farmer, and no solution of the problem at all for the country as a whole. In order for the farmer to free himself from mortgage debt through inflation, the prices of farm products must rise more than the prices of the goods and services the farmer buys and *must remain higher* for a sufficient length of time for him to be able either to pay off the mortgage or to sell the farm at its higher valuation. Unfortunately, no formula has yet been devised by which prices can first be inflated and then stabilized. Both experience and plausible economic theories indicate that every period of inflation is followed by one of deflation; nor has any monetary scheme yet been propounded for inflating the prices of one category of goods (for example, farm products) without also raising other categories.

If a farmer sells his farm during a period of inflation and another farmer buys the farm at the inflated value, giving a mortgage as part payment, the identity of the debtor is changed but the farm mortgage problem still remains for the country as a whole. Farm prices rose steadily and rapidly from 1921 to 1925 and remained at a high level until 1929 (the index of farm prices rose from 128 to 154 from 1921 to 1925 while the index of prices paid by farmers rose only from 152 to 157), yet the number of farmer bankruptcies in 1925 was over five times as great as it was in 1921, and even in 1929 it was three times as great as in 1921. In 1933 the United States devalued the dollar in an avowed attempt to improve farm prices (among other reasons). Table VI (page 132) shows what has been accomplished towards debt reduction.

It is unfortunate that for many of the items in the table data are available only for the census years 1930 and 1935. While the table shows a considerable improvement in the farm mortgage debt situation, little, if any, of this improvement can be credited to the devaluation of the dollar. All of the following influences were at work to reduce mortgage debt: (1) A considerable amount of the debt was reduced by mortgage foreclosures (if the mortgageholder resold after foreclosure, the new mortgage was undoubtedly smaller in recognition of the lower value of the land). (2) From 1933 through 1937 the Agricultural Adjustment Administration paid out over two billion dollars, much of which went to the owners of mortgaged farms. (3) Agricultural prices were improved during this period by: (a) crop curtailment under the A. A. A.,

(b) the drought, (c) purchases of farm products by the Federal Surplus Commodities Corporation, (d) the failure of the Canadian wheat crop, (e) accumulation of foodstuffs by European countries as a result of war scares, (f) cotton loans above market values. When all these influences are taken into consideration, it is difficult to credit dollar devaluation with much

TABLE VI

FARM PRICES, FARM MORTGAGE DEBT AND
RELATED STATISTICS

	1930	1931	1932	1933	1934	1935	1936	1937
Index of Farm Prices..	126	87	65	70	90	108	114	121
Prices Farmers Pay....	145	124	107	109	123	125	124	130
Farm Mortgage Debt (Billions of $).........	9.21	...	...	...	...	7.64	7.50	7.25
Number of Mortgaged Farms (Millions)......	2.53	...	...	...	...	2.35	...	...
Average Debt per Mortgaged Farm..........	$3,652	...	...	...	...	$3,253	...	...
Value of Agricultural Capital[a] (Billions of $).	57.7	51.9	43.7	36.2	37.2	38.6	...	...
Farm Mortgage Debt as Percent of Value of Agricultural Capital[a].....	16.0	...	...	...	...	19.8	...	...
Farm Foreclosures[b]....	20.8	26.1	41.7	54.1	39.1	28.3	26.2	22.4

Source: *Agricultural Statistics 1938* and *Agricultural Finance Review*, Vol. 1, No. 1, U. S. Department of Agriculture.
[a] Value of all agricultural capital. No figures available for value of mortgaged farms alone.
[b] Number per 1,000 of all farms changing hands by forced sales and related defaults.

effect in raising farm prices, to say nothing of mortgage reduction, in which causes (1) and (2) must likewise be taken into account.

If present farmers are to be freed from debt by means of inflation alone, there will have to be an inflation equal to that which occurred in the period ending in 1929 and, as a consequence, the country will perhaps have to suffer a depression like that of 1932, or worse. Even such a course would not solve the farm mortgage problem for the country. Undoubtedly there would be farms sold and mortgaged at the high valuations of the inflationary boom and a new crop of farm debtors would be asking for aid in the inevitable depression.

Farm Mortgage Debt and the Nature of Competition

Since agriculture is characterized by conditions closely approximating those of pure competition, economic theory teaches that there is a persistent tendency for prices to be equal to the cost of production. Therefore, there is no ordinary surplus income to be expected out of which a farm mortgage can be repaid. There are only a few conditions under which a farmer can hope to repay a mortgage out of the receipts from the sale of farm produce: (1) If the farm is purchased at a price sufficiently below its eventual value, the surplus income is available for mortgage payment. (2) If the farmer is able to pay a sufficient portion of the original purchase price in cash by not spending the interest of his own investment, he may have funds available for mortgage repayment. (3) If the farmer uses a large family as farm hands without paying them, he may use what would have been their wages for mortgage repayment. (4) If the farmer is a more competent farmer and farm manager than the average, his superior ability may increase yields or lower costs so that some surplus will be available for mortgage payments. (In a perfectly competitive economy he could secure the same return as a wage by being a hired farm manager, but from lack of opportunity for such employment people may not recognize his ability so that he may have to run his own farm to secure the equivalent of a fair wage.) (5) Better than normal weather conditions in a particular locality may produce a surplus income through higher yields, provided that yields are not high enough in other parts of the country, or the world, to depress prices unduly.

Most of these conditions involve a considerable amount of

self-denial on the part of the farmer in order to repay the mortgage. Whenever a farm is sold at a price which represents the full capitalized value of its economic rent, mortgage repayment is apt to prove extremely difficult if the mortgage represents a major proportion of the original purchase price. When we consider that in many parts of the country farmers have also been obliged to obtain short-term credit for seed, fertilizer, and payrolls on distinctly disadvantageous terms, the wonder is not that so many farmers fail, but rather that so many of them finally manage to own their farms. The answer is to be found partially in the very low standard of living of many farm families. A great many of those who manage to own their farms free and clear of debt will be found to have purchased their farms at depressed values. Comparatively few of those who purchase farms in years of inflated values will be able to hold on to them. Again we are confronted with the problem of forecasting; not only must the farmer be a forecaster to determine what crops to plant, he must forecast the general course of farm prices before he even buys a farm, if he is to be successful.

Methods of Raising Farm Income

No one who is at all familiar with agricultural conditions will contest the statement that farmers in many large sections of the country have been suffering, and in many cases are still suffering, from a prolonged and serious period of greatly reduced incomes. The merits and defects of the farmer's claim to special consideration by the government have already been discussed. Regardless of whether one approves of farm aid or not, political realism will indicate that the strength of the farm vote will insure some form of attempt to improve farm income regardless of which party is in power. It is, therefore, very much to the point to examine the various measures, proposed or in operation, which are designed to increase farm income.

Export Subsidies

Although they differ as to the mechanics involved, many farm aid programs include as one of their main features some form of subsidy to encourage export of "surplus commodities." All export subsidies are open to two very serious objections: (1) Importing countries are very likely to impose higher duties to offset the subsidy. (2) Exporting competitor countries are also likely to give subsidies if the United States starts the practice. (Our present export subsidies on wheat and flour were introduced to meet the competition of various forms of export aid given by Canada and, since our program started, Australia and the Argentine have followed suit.) To the extent that either of these methods cancels the effect of the original subsidy, the subsidizing governments will be losing money without aiding the farmers at all. Offset (1) enriches foreign treasuries at the expense of our own. Offset (2) means giving the foreign consumer the benefit of low prices if importing countries do not raise tariffs. If the subsidies given by all competing exporting countries are equal, no one country is likely to gain in exports at the expense of the others. If the demand of the importing countries is very elastic, total exports of all subsidizing export countries may be increased. If the domestic demand is then less elastic than the foreign demand, total increase in income to the farmers as a result of this form of price discrimination against domestic consumers might possibly exceed the cost of the subsidy to the government. In many crops there is grave danger that the cost to the government might exceed the benefit to the farmer, even if foreign tariffs were not raised. Under such circumstances, it would be much better to pay the cash directly to the farmer rather

than to make part or all of the cash a gift to the foreign consumer or to the foreign government.

A variant of the subsidy scheme is the proposal to set a fixed
and profitable price on the part of the crop that is sold in the
domestic market and "to sell the rest for what it will bring" in
the world market. It is now being pushed politically under
the slogan of "guaranteeing to the farmer the cost of production
on crops sold domestically." This may sound fair and appeal-
ing to the man on the street, but the student of economics need
not be considered cynical if he starts asking some embarrassing
questions. What do they mean by cost of production and
how will it be calculated? Is a separate cost to be calculated
for each individual farmer on each crop? A force of one million men could hardly do the job in a year's time, even if all
farmers kept an accurate set of books, which most of them
probably do not. (Perhaps this is a way of solving the farm
problem—there might be so many men working for the Department of Agriculture that there would be nobody left on the
farms.) Or is the marginal or average cost of the highest cost
farmer to be taken as a base? If this is the case, overproduction
will make present surpluses seem small by comparison. Or
is someone to make an inspired statistical guess as to what constitutes the "typical" or "average" or "bulkline" cost of production for each crop? Such a program would arouse howls
of protest from producers whose cost was higher than the
estimate and would probably still constitute an incentive for
lower cost producers to expand output. We have said nothing
about the problem of setting different prices for different
grades of each crop. (In some crops, tobacco for example,
the number of grade and type combinations runs well up
into the hundreds.) May we be pardoned for asking what is
meant when we are promised a "guaranteed price equal to
cost of production"?

Leaving aside the cost problem, the higher the arbitrary

price is set, the lower will be the amount of domestic consumption and the greater the proportion of the crop that will have to seek foreign markets. Our exports have been disappointing in volume even at the fairly low prices of recent years. It is difficult to compute what prices would be necessary to move all of the large surpluses abroad. Still, a low export price will not act as a deterrent to the individual farmer. Again we are confronted with the fact that no individual farmer acting alone could depress the world price by expanding his own production, but this would certainly be accomplished if all farmers acted in concert to expand production. The plan offers an additional motive to each farmer to expand. He is guaranteed a "fair return" on part of his crop and so is in a better position to take a gamble on the rest. The bitter experience of many other countries demonstrates that prices cannot be controlled for long without controlling production.

Relief Purchases of Surplus Farm Products

The purchase of surplus farm products for relief purposes offers many attractions. Certainly we are all horrified by the spectacle of "people starving in the midst of plenty," and the distribution of surplus agricultural products would be a means of attacking the problem. As far as the relief measure for the unemployed is concerned, the only question which can be raised is whether the method of government purchase and distribution is cheaper than that which would prevail if relief clients were paid cash and allowed to make their own purchases. Even if this question is decided in the negative, the claim might still be made that a wisely paternalistic government may provide the people with a more nutritious and better-balanced diet than they would buy for themselves.

When, however, the avowed aim of these purchases is to improve distressed farm prices, and the relief objective is made somewhat secondary, some other questions of theory must be considered.　In the first place, if the government agency purchases at prices much above those prevailing in the market, it is faced with three somewhat unpalatable alternatives: (1) It must be prepared to buy any amount up to all of the crop which is offered for sale at the price; or (2) it must be prepared to face charges of favoritism in buying at the high price from some farmers and not from others; or (3) it must devise a cumbersome and probably extremely expensive system of prorating purchases among all growers of the crop.　(Even this last method will probably be criticized by individuals who feel that more of their own or less of their neighbor's crop should have been purchased.)

By far the better method of purchase is the "offer and acceptance" basis.　Under this method the government agency asks sellers to submit bids at which they are willing to offer their crop for sale and the agency then accepts the bids up to the maximum quantity it wishes to buy or the maximum price it wishes to pay, beginning with the lowest bid and working upward.　This system has the advantage of removing "distress" lots from the market and leaving the rest of the crop in firmer hands.　It would also seem reasonable to infer that those who offer to sell at the lowest prices are most in need of a government outlet for their crop.　Farmers have been known to criticize this method, however, claiming that dealers say, "This is the price the government is paying," and then attempt to beat down the price on the rest of the crop to that level.　In some scattered instances this claim may be true.　Such dealers, however, are always looking for an excuse to pay low prices and if this one were not available, they would find another. When the government is actually removing some of the surplus crop from his local market, the farmer should be able to see through this excuse.

The effect of relief purchases upon prices may be expected to vary considerably from one crop to another.　In the case of citrus fruits, celery, and other articles not ordinarily found in the diets of the lowest income groups, consumption is probably increased by relief purchase and distribution.[3]   In the case of dried prunes, potatoes, and other low-priced staple foods, the amount of increased consumption may be questioned.   Even in these crops, some results may be obtained in price by strategic timing and geographic location of purchases to relieve particularly glutted markets of distress merchandise.   One qualification must be introduced here, however: In years of large crops and extremely low prices, some portion of the crop is usually left unharvested.   In general this burden falls heaviest upon the farms most distant from market as they must bear heavier freight rates as well as the harvesting charges. Under such circumstances, *if we can assume that the relief clients would have bought some of the product had it not been given to them,* then purchases from these more distant areas distributed for relief in the cities will tend to depress the price received by nearby growers.

Even though they may be very effective in raising prices of particular crops in individual years, the long-run effect of relief purchases may still be open to question.   The average farmer expects some bad-price years as well as good-price years in any crop.   The effect of a few low-price years in succession is to drive out marginal producers or to cause some acreage reduction so that the price of the crop tends to improve.   However, if farmers in general get the idea that the government stands ready to "bail them out" by relief purchases whenever a low-price year occurs, acreage may be steadily overexpanded.   Under these circumstances the government could not be blamed if it confined relief purchases to those crops, those regions, and those farmers who were willing to make some sacrifice to help

---

[3] Except possibly where the demand for the product by those not on relief is highly elastic so that they are discouraged from buying a similar amount by the price rise which is achieved.

themselves in the form of acreage reduction or marketing agreements.

Marketing Agreements

Marketing agreements are a somewhat less-known feature of the work of the Agricultural Adjustment Administration and offer some interesting possibilities. The original A. A. A. Act, and the parts of it reenacted in the Marketing Agreements Act of 1938, relieve farmers and handlers from the provisions of the Sherman Anti-Trust Act in making agreements conforming to the provisions of the Marketing Agreements Act and approved by the Secretary of Agriculture.

One provision which marketing agreements may contain is limitation of shipments by grade and size regulations. When there is an oversupply of a perishable crop, a considerable part of the crop will be left to spoil in the field, on track, and in terminal markets. It is highly desirable, both from the point of view of the producer and the consumer, that this wastage be confined as far as possible to the lower grades of the product. In years of large crops, for example, cull potatoes and even No. 2s may not bring much more than freight charges in terminal markets, yet their presence in the market often tends to depress the prices of No. 1 potatoes by much more than the simple effect of their addition to the total supply. Unscrupulous dealers buy these low-grade potatoes at distress prices and then advertise a "sale" of potatoes at extremely low prices. Consumers, unable or unwilling to go to the trouble of making grade comparisons, then expect other dealers selling first-grade potatoes to meet these prices. Grade and size regulations, together with compulsory government inspection, offer a means of combating this evil.

Another provision allowed under the Marketing Agreements

Act is the pro-ration of shipments: that is, handlers are limited to the shipment of an agreed percentage of each farmer's crop. Since it is somewhat difficult to enforce and expensive to administer, pro-ration is generally resorted to only when grade and size regulations appear insufficient to meet the surplus problem (for example, when all or nearly all of a crop is able to meet the highest grade requirements). Under grade and size regulations, an inspector's certificate is sufficient evidence that a car may be shipped. Under pro-ration, it is necessary for someone to check each man's quota against past shipments to see whether the quota is being exceeded by the shipment in question.

Whenever the demand for any crop is sufficiently inelastic, the withholding of part of the crop from market will increase total revenue. When it is remembered that no shipping charges (and in some cases no harvesting charges) are incurred on the part of the crop that is not sent to market, we can see how the farmers' income can be augmented considerably by such restriction. Grade and size regulations and pro-ration offer a means of equalizing both the burden and the profit of such withholding.

Marketing agreements have one serious legal handicap: They can apply to shipments in interstate commerce only. Thus they tend to become only partially effective in the case of a crop of which a large percentage is marketed within the state where it is grown. In such cases they would have to be implemented by individual state laws to the same effect in order to become 100 percent effective. Some states do have laws requiring the grade of the product to be stamped on all consumer packages. In such states, consumer preference may be as effective in preventing the marketing of culls from within the state as grade and size regulations are in preventing culls from entering the state.

Reduction of Acreage

In a pamphlet entitled "America Must Choose," [4] Secretary of Agriculture Wallace gives us the essence of the American farm problem.   In it he points out that if we are to follow the course of extreme nationalism as indicated by our previous tariff policy, we must be prepared to take from 40 to 100 million acres of farm land out of production—40 million if we take out good land, 100 million if we take out poor land.   This course would place all the sacrifice on the farmers.   On the other hand, Secretary Wallace points out that if we are to sell all our surplus farm produce abroad, we must be prepared to reduce our tariffs sufficiently to import one billion dollars worth more of goods than we did in 1929.   This course would impose the entire burden of sacrifice on the manufacturers.   He proposes a "planned middle course" to retire approximately 25 million acres and to import 500 million dollars worth of goods more than in 1929.

Many people may raise the question as to why farmers should be "paid for taking land out of production" when low prices will force them to do it anyway.   The answer to this is twofold: (1) As we have seen above, voluntary acreage contraction in response to price is an extremely slow process; (2) such land will probably not be taken out of production until its fertility is destroyed.   If there is any hope that foreign trade in agricultural products will be restored, or if there is any prospect that expanding American population, or one with an expanding income, will be able to buy the products of our soil in the future, we should not risk this loss of the soil.   A difference should be noted here between the original Agricultural Adjustment Act of 1933 which provided payments for mere reduction of acreage, and the Soil Conservation and Domestic Allotment Act of 1936 which bases payments upon the re-

---

[4] *World Affairs Pamphlets,* No. 3, 1934, published by Foreign Policy Association, New York, and World Peace Foundation, Boston.

placement of soil-depleting crops by soil-conserving crops and
upon other soil-building practices. There is, of course, little
excuse to pay the farmer simply for "not raising crops," but if
such payments are made for reforesting, planting green manure
crops, or other soil-building or fertility-conserving practices, it
may be found in the end that we have adopted the cheapest
means of retaining our national heritage.

The Ever-Normal Granary

The basic idea underlying the ever-normal granary program
is the carryover of surpluses from periods of excessive production in various crops to periods when production falls short
of normal requirements. The plan is applicable to grains and
other crops which are capable of storage for at least a full year.
(If there is again a surplus in the second year, the first year's
carryover may be sold and replaced from the second year's
crop to continue storage along with the second year surplus.)
The success of the plan hinges upon the occurrence of a short
crop before too many successive years of large crops intervene.
If it had been applied in the past two or three decades, it apparently would have worked, provided that annual production
would not have been changed by the plan itself.

If the loan and storage features were the only elements in
the plan, there is a serious danger that the plan would defeat
its own purpose. Short crops have occurred in the past from
a combination of reduced acreage and bad weather or other
natural causes. If loan and storage keep the price above that
which would prevail in years of large crops, then there is little
incentive to acreage reduction, and sole reliance must be placed
on natural causes for the occurrence of a year or years in which
the surplus carried over can be disposed of. To guard against
this, the present experiment provides that loans are available
to those farmers only who are "co-operators" in the acreage
reduction program. It also provides for the imposition of

marketing quotas, upon a vote of two-thirds of the producers, whenever the Secretary of Agriculture deems them to be necessary.

One vital factor in the success or failure of the plan is the prices at which the loan rates are set. The setting of too high a loan rate will result in a market price which prevents the absorption by the market of even a normal year's consumption requirements, and an excessive amount of the crop will go "into the loan." A loan rate which is even equal to the market price may well be too high, since the farmer is thus guaranteed at least the present market price and a chance to wait without risk for higher prices. (The terms of the loan prevent the government from recovering from the farmer if the stored crop is eventually sold for less than the amount of the loan.) The present cotton loan situation should not be blamed upon the Department of Agriculture. Both the making of these loans and their amount (either as a direct amount or by a rigid formula) was made mandatory by Congress. Also, present acreage provisions were not in effect in time to cover the 1937 cotton crop.

In the case of wheat there is also a special crop-insurance program. "Under this program the insurance is against losses in yield through unavoidable causes and provides either 50 percent or 75 percent coverage. Both insurance premiums and insurance indemnities are computed in wheat rather than money, so that the insurance reserves provide in effect an additional storage granary to be filled in years of fair or high yields and drawn upon in years when yields are low." [5] To the extent that this insurance feature operates successfully, like all insurance it will tend both to eliminate risk and to eliminate profits. Recent experience may have made the farmer more receptive to

[5] *Agricultural Adjustment, 1937-38,* U. S. Dept. of Agriculture, Agricultural Adjustment Administration.

the idea of a small and steady income rather than a chance of large profits or large losses. Whether he will continue in this frame of mind remains to be seen.

At best, however, many of the above methods of improving farm income are temporary expedients. In the end our solution to the farm problem may be found to come by indirection. As Professor Sprague has pointed out,[6] if we can make our economic system work as it should to provide full employment to people in the cities and to draw some of the population from the farms to the cities, the farm problem will disappear by itself.

The "Back to the Farm" Movement

Some incurable romantics are advocating a complete decentralization of industry with plants located in rural small towns and the workers engaged in part-time farming. If such a plan involved the synchronization of slack times in the factory with harvest times on the farms and the use of the workers as harvest hands instead of floating labor, there might be some sense to it. The proposal, however, is for each worker to have his own small farm. Such a plan, if followed extensively, would insure the impoverishment of thousands of specialized fruit and vegetable and chicken farmers if many more people raise these products for their own use, and so would still further decrease the demand for the products of the factories. It is a negation of all of the advantages we have found in specialization.

It would, of course, be nice for the employer to feel that his workers had something to "fall back on" when the plant shut down. Such a plan would also tend to increase the immobility of labor and so tend to decrease labor's bargaining power. Rather than make the farmer the victim of this kind of "depres-

---

[6] *American Economic Review*, Vol. XXVIII, No. 1, March 1938.

sion insurance," let us find a way of avoiding extreme business fluctuations and turn the clock forward instead of turning it back. We have spent much money and effort in educating professional farmers to be good farmers. There is no need to turn around and try to make jacks-of-all-trades out of good factory hands.

CHAPTER VII

Forms of Business Ownership Organization

THE VARIOUS forms that business ownership may take are prescribed by law, and a large body of legal doctrine has grown up around each of these forms. At first sight it might appear that we are dealing with a purely legal question. However, the legal advantages and disadvantages, the privileges and immunities which are associated with each form of the business unit carry with them certain economic consequences which make the form of business ownership organization a question of economic importance. Since the very definition of each form of business ownership organization is a legal question, we shall have to pay some attention to their legal aspects, although our main attention will be directed to the economic problems involved in each form of the business unit.

The Single Proprietorship

The single proprietorship may best be explained as a one-man business organization. This does not mean that the proprietor will have no employees, but it does mean that he is the sole owner of the business. All of the business property belongs to him, and he alone is responsible for all its debts; he will receive all the profits which are made from this business and will suffer all of its losses.

When an individual is operating a business under the single

proprietorship form, the law does not distinguish between the individual and his business. Any careful individual will keep two sets of accounts, one for his personal income and expenditures and another for the income and expenditures of his business. In this way he will be better able to judge whether he is operating his business properly or not. The law, however, makes no such distinction; in its eyes the business firm and its owner are one and the same person. All of his personal fortune may be levied upon to satisfy the debts of the business, and any of his business assets may be seized to cover unpaid personal debts.

The single proprietorship has many distinct advantages. Whatever profits there are go entirely to the owner and need not be shared with others. Since there is only one individual to make decisions, these can be made quickly and can follow a consistent individual policy. Since the owner is free to discharge any employee, he can rid himself of dishonest and incompetent individuals much more readily than would be the case if these individuals happened to be partners in a partnership or stockholders in a corporation. Since the owner's entire personal fortune is at stake, he has the strongest motives to watch the business carefully and to run it as efficiently as possible. In many retail trades, people seem to derive a certain satisfaction in dealing directly with the owner of the business so that this form of ownership organization is peculiarly well-adapted to small retail establishments. An individual proprietorship can be started with a minimum of legal expenditures; there is no corporation charter to be procured, no incorporation fees to be paid, and the firm is free from taxes levied against corporations.

There are, however, certain limitations and disadvantages attached to the individual proprietorship. The capital of the firm will be limited to the individual's personal fortune plus the amount he is able to borrow on his personal credit. There will be no one except hired employees to whom the owner can entrust the running of his business during his absence. The success of the individual proprietorship depends largely on the ability of the owner to master all branches of business management. He must be both a shrewd buyer and a capable salesman; he must be somewhat of an accountant; and he must be familiar with the technical details of whatever business the firm is engaged in. He must be a competent executive to direct the employees. It is true that individuals may be hired to take over some of these functions; the ability of hired managerial employees, however, will depend to a considerable extent on the amount of salary the firm is capable of offering to attract them. The amount of such salaries will depend upon the size of the firm which, in turn, depends upon the amount of capital the individual is capable of raising. One great disadvantage of the individual proprietorship is that a business failure will involve the owner's entire personal fortune. He can, of course, place his home and certain other personal property in his wife's name, but if his wife should then happen to desert him, he would have no means at all of recovering this property. The individually owned firm also lacks continuity; in case the owner dies or decides to retire, it may be impossible to sell the firm for anything near the amount it has previously been worth as a going concern.

Partnership[1]

The simple business partnership consists of two or more individuals who are joint owners and joint proprietors of the business. There is a partnership agreement which specifies the amount each partner will contribute to the business, and fixes his share of the ownership and his share in the profits. This agreement may be verbal, but it usually is and should be

---

[1] In discussing this and other forms of business ownership, the legal aspects given are those common to most states. The reader should consult his own state laws for features that may be peculiar to his state.

written. The different partners may contribute both cash and services to the business, or some may contribute merely cash and others their services, or cash and services may be contributed in varying proportions by the different partners. The partnership agreement usually recognizes differences in value of the contributions of the various partners by providing for corresponding proportions in the share of the profits and the assets of the business. The partnership agreement will usually stipulate also the proportion in which each partner is to bear the losses in the event of failure. In the event of bankruptcy, the courts will endeavor to carry out such terms as far as possible. However, should any partner be unable to meet his share of the losses, the courts will hold each and every other partner liable up to the full amount of his personal fortune.

Legally, each partner is responsible for, and will be bound by, any act committed by any other partner in the firm's name, regardless of any private understanding among the partners themselves. For example, two partners may have an agreement that one is to do the buying and the other the selling for the firm, nevertheless, should the buying partner decide to go out and sell goods much below cost, the other partner would be held responsible for delivery of the goods. Likewise, should the salesman partner have a notion to buy a particular lot of goods at absurdly high prices, the other partner would be held equally liable for accepting and paying for the goods. Debts contracted by any partner in the firm's name are a debt against all the partners. Should one of the partners borrow money in the firm's name and then keep it himself, the other partners might bring suit against him for fraud, but *regardless of whether they collected anything from him or not,* they would still have to pay the debt.

At first sight these provisions may seem somewhat harsh, but they are based on a sound principle. It would be almost im-

possible to do business with a partnership if all partners had
to be consulted every time anything was to be sold to the firm or
bought from it. In most minor matters it would likewise be a
needless waste of the partners' time. Consequently, it is a
practical necessity that each partner be free to negotiate for the
firm. To protect the public, it is then necessary to make each
responsible for the other's actions. It is then up to the partners to watch each other to see that they do not commit acts
which are undesirable for the business. In some respects, one
should exercise more care in choosing a business partner than
in choosing a wife.

The Limited Partnership

In some states, limited partnerships are allowed. Such a
partnership must have one or more general partners and may
have one or more limited partners. The status of the general
partners is the same as that outlined above under the simple
partnership. The limited partner is allowed to have the
amount of his possible loss limited to his share in the business,
but he is subject to certain restrictions: (1) He may contribute
cash only and not services to the business; (2) his name must
not appear in the firm's name; (3) he must not attempt to do
business in the firm's name. If he violates any of these provisions, he loses his status as a limited partner and automatically
becomes a general partner. The reason for these provisions
is to avoid having people deceived into thinking that a limited
partner is a general partner. For instance, without these provisions, if I could persuade John D. Rockefeller, Jr. to invest
$5,000 as a limited partner with me and we then adopted the
firm name "Rockefeller & Meyers," I could probably obtain unlimited loans from any bank; or if Rockefeller went out to buy
goods for the firm, we could obtain practically unlimited credit.
On the other hand, if these people knew that he was only a

limited partner, the firm's credit would be limited to $5,000 plus their best estimate of my own meager ability to repay possible losses.

Advantages of the Partnership

The partnership can ordinarily obtain more capital than the individual firm, both through taking in more partners who will contribute capital and through the increased willingness of the banks to lend more to a group of individuals than to a single individual. It can take in partners possessed of different skills to manage the various special aspects of the business, and since these partners will share in profits or losses, they may possibly devote more conscientious effort to their tasks than they would as hired employees, either of a single proprietorship or of a corporation. If there is any truth in the adage that "two heads are better than one," it will be applicable here. In the temporary absence of any of the partners, the business may still be left in responsible hands. In dealing with the public, the partnership will still possess much of the character of a "personal business" which is characteristic of the single proprietorship. The partnership is likewise free from legal requirements and taxes imposed on corporations as such.

Disadvantages of the Partnership

Although superior to the individual proprietorship in raising capital, the partnership is still somewhat sharply limited in this respect. In spite of conspicuous exceptions (such as J. P. Morgan & Co.), the capital of the average partnership will be found to be small. In general, it is necessary to take in more partners in order to raise more capital. As the business expands, it may be increasingly difficult to find people willing to invest money in the firm who will also be desirable partners in other respects.   Another possible serious disadvantage is disagreements among the partners on matters of business policy. Unless these can be settled amicably, the partnership will have to dissolve.   No partner can sell or transfer his holdings in the firm without the consent of the other partners.   Unless he can find a new partner satisfactory to them, he will either have to buy out the other partners, sell out to them at whatever price they will give, or force a dissolution of the partnership.   If any partner dies, his heirs will be under the same disadvantage. The surviving partners will likewise be under a handicap; if the share of the deceased is not willed to someone whom they consider a satisfactory partner, they must either be willing to buy out the heir or face dissolution of the partnership.   The liability of the partners for each other's acts and the unlimited liability of all general partners is also a disadvantage.

The Joint-Stock Company

The joint-stock company is a kind of transition type of business ownership organization halfway between the partnership and the corporation, possessing many of the features of both types.   The owners are under the same degree of full liability as in the general partnership.   Instead of the partnership agreement, ownership is represented by transferable shares of stock similar to those of a corporation, and management is centered in a board of directors elected by the stockholders.   The joint-stock company possesses practically all of the advantages of the corporation except limited liability.   It is free from the disadvantage of acquiring and conforming to a corporation charter, and it is not subject to corporation taxes levied as such.   However, the unlimited liability of stockholders has appeared to be such a disadvantage in selling stock that the joint stock company has not met with much favor in this country.   It is far more common in England.

The Corporation

A corporation is an artificial person, created by law, for the purpose of accomplishing some object. The first corporations were not business organizations but were religious, fraternal, benevolent, or educational institutions founded by a royal charter which conferred certain privileges and immunities upon them. The older English Universities and the Medieval Guilds were among the first corporations.

The business corporation is an adaptation of this form for business purposes. A group of persons will apply to the state to grant it a charter for the purpose of doing business as a corporation. If the charter is granted, a corporation is created which may do business in the firm's name; it may sue and be sued in the firm's name, exactly as an individual person; it may own property and may borrow and owe money. Although the stockholders own the corporation, they are not held liable individually for the actions of the corporation as it is considered to be a separate person. Ordinarily, the possible loss of the stockholder is limited to the amount which he paid for his shares. In the case of banking corporations, in some states the stockholder may be held liable for double the amount of the face value of the shares which he holds.

Some states have had the idea that the corporation charter might be used as a means of exercising some sort of control over the corporation. The charter would state rather rigid limits as to the kind of acts the firm might perform, and general laws were passed regulating their acts. In practice, the diversity of state laws and the laxness or cupidity of some states have largely defeated this purpose. Under the interstate commerce clause of the Constitution, a corporation created by one state is able to do business in any other state; consequently, new corporations have taken out their charters in those states which are most lenient. After the United States

Steel Corporation was granted a charter by the State of Delaware which allowed it to "engage in any kind of business in any part of the world," there was a rush to incorporate under the laws of that state and the state has since become notorious as a "corporation mill." The state has received so much revenue from a small corporation tax on numbers of business firms whose real centers of business are all over the country, that its own residents are practically tax-free. Technically, the corporation is supposed to have its main office in Delaware, but this is evaded by setting up a "dummy" office. The doors of Wilmington office buildings are plastered with the names of hundreds of large business firms whose principal place of actual business is New York, Chicago, or other large cities in other states. Some other states have attempted to set themselves up in the business of "selling corporation charters," and as a result, the remaining states practically have had to abandon their efforts to regulate corporations through their charters. It has been proposed from time to time that corporations, particularly those doing interstate business, be required to incorporate under Federal rather than state laws, but as yet no action has been taken on this matter.

The Simple Business Trust

The word "trust" in popular speech usually means combination or monopoly. This arose from the fact that some of the first large business combinations to be prosecuted in the courts had adopted the trust form of organization. More accurately, the word "trust" refers to a form of business ownership organization which need not have any large-scale or monopoly aspects. The simple business trust, sometimes called the Massachusetts trust because it received its greatest development under the laws of that state, is a form of organization under which the title to business property is placed in the hands of a board of trustees who manage the business in the interests of the former owners, who are then called the beneficiaries of the trust. (This is in contrast to trusts for the purpose of safeguarding inheritances in which the beneficiaries are usually third parties.) The deed of trust which transfers the property will specify the powers and duties of the trustees. Usually equity in the trust is evidenced by trust certificates which may be transferred like shares in a corporation, to which they are quite similar in all respects except that of voting. The deed of trust often specifies that no liability shall attach to shareholders or trustees.

For most purposes the trust would appear to be at least equal to, and in some respects superior to, the corporation. Trustees are ordinarily possessed of greater freedom to act for the business than are directors of a corporation. To the extent that trustees are held more responsible for their actions than are directors, this may be a greater protection for the minority shareholder than his vote in a corporate organization. The main reason why the trust form is not more widely used is probably due to the stigma attached to the name in the various "Anti-Trust" agitations.

Co-Operative Organizations

Co-operative organizations are often formed by consumers for the purpose of buying and by farmers for the purpose of marketing their products. Some few manufacturing co-operatives have been formed by workmen, but these have had little success. The co-operative is usually organized as a corporation to do business under a corporate name, but it has certain features distinct from the ordinary business corporation: (1) In the true co-operative, each member has one vote regardless of the number of shares that he holds. (2) After a low fixed dividend (really an interest payment) is made on each share, further profits are shared on a "patronage" basis; that is, each member receives dividends in the proportion which his purchases or sales through the co-operative bear to the total purchases or sales.   The question of the field and function of the co-operative is a separate subject which we will not discuss here.

Business Ownership and Business Government

The various forms of business ownership organization are really forms of business self-government and may be compared with various forms of political government:[2] The single proprietorship is an absolute monarchy; the partnership is an oligarchy; the corporation is a republic (with voting based upon a property qualification); the trust may be compared to the mandate; the co-operative is a democratic republic.

Within the corporation, the analogy to political government may be carried even further.   The corporation charter is its constitution; its by-laws correspond to legislative enactments; the board of directors is an administrative body empowered to carry out the provisions of the charter and by-laws and allowed to pass some administrative rulings of its own.   The active control of the corporation by a small group of stockholders is somewhat similar to that exercised by the political bosses of a dominant party when the opposition is negligible.

Types of Corporate Securities

Corporate securities are of two general classes each of which has many subclassifications: *stocks,* which represent ownership in the corporation, and *bonds,* which represent claims of funded debt against the corporation.   We shall be able to discuss here only the most important aspects of the principal types of stocks and bonds.   The reader who wishes further information on this subject should consult a good text on corporation finance.

Common stock represents the ownership and, unless the interest on bonds or the dividends on preferred stock are in default, usually represents the voting control of the corporation.

---

[2] This analogy is a teaching device used by Professor J. M. Shortliffe of Colgate University in his classes.   I have not seen it developed so extensively elsewhere.

Common stock is issued in shares. The percentage of the total number of shares held by any individual indicates his proportionate share in the total of dividends and assets accruing to the common stockholders in general. Evidence of this ownership is given in the form of a stock certificate which states the number of shares that the holder owns, dividends on which may be paid only after all interest on bonds and all preferred dividends have been paid. In the event of dissolution of the company, the common stockholders receive whatever is left after all debts, bonds and other prior claims have been paid. Unless otherwise stated, after interest and preferred dividends have been paid there is no limit to the dividends which may be paid on common stock except the earnings of the company and the discretion of the board of directors. The owners of common stock thus stand the greatest chances of both profit and loss. Since all other claims must be paid first, common stock is often called the most risky form of investment. This statement holds true, however, only as among different classes of securities *in the same company*. The common stock of a prosperous company may easily be a safer investment than the bonds of a corporation which is suffering reverses.

Classified common stock is sometimes issued. In such cases there will be two or more classes, usually called Class "A" and Class "B," only one of which has voting power. (There is no uniformity as to which class, "A" or "B," receives the voting power.) There is no excuse for the issue of this type of stock. It is purely and simply a trick device to allow a few individuals to gain control of a corporation without being required to invest as great an amount of money as would be required to purchase majority control of unclassified common stock. The holders of the non-voting stock are deprived of the power to protect themselves through voting and are not guaranteed any fixed dividends.

Preferred stock carries the provision that a certain fixed dividend (a specified number of dollars on stock with no par value, or a specified percent of par for stocks with par value) will be paid on the stock before any dividends are paid to common stockholders. It may be either *cumulative* or *noncumulative* preferred stock. On cumulative preferred stock, this year's specified dividend, *plus unpaid dividends for all past years,* must be paid before any dividends are paid on the common stock. On noncumulative preferred, only the specified dividend for *any one year* need be paid before the dividends are paid on the common stock. Noncumulative stock is hardly worthy of the name "preferred" since it is so easy for the stockholders to be cheated out of dividends. For example, suppose that a corporation has $1,000,000 in common stock and $1,000,000 in 6 percent noncumulative preferred stock. The first year it earns, let us say, $120,000, a sum which is enough to pay a 6 percent dividend on both preferred and common stock. The directors, however, say that it is advisable to set up a reserve, invest the earnings in government bonds or other earning assets, and vote to pay no dividends on either preferred or common stock. The following year, if the company again earns $120,000, the directors may say that it is now well-established and needs no reserve, so they sell the government bonds, or other assets, and this, plus the current year's earnings, makes a fund out of which they pay *only this year's* dividend of 6 percent on the noncumulative preferred stock and pay the remaining sum as an 18 percent dividend on the common stock. Since the directors usually hold the majority of the common stock and usually own very little preferred stock (usually none if it is noncumulative), it will be to their interest to juggle the earnings from one year to another in this way. There is practically no legal remedy for the preferred stockholders in the situation we have outlined above, crude as it is, and there are still more subtle ways of concealing earnings from one year to the next. The only sure safeguard against this particular form of cheating is *not to buy preferred stock unless it is cumulative.*

The preferred stock of different companies may carry many different provisions, either to safeguard further the preferred stockholders, or to provide for their further participation in large earnings when they occur. To be certain of exactly what these provisions are in the case of a particular stock, the corporation's charter should be consulted.[3] One rather common provision is that, in the event of dissolution of the company, a certain fixed sum be paid to the preferred stockholders before the common stockholders receive anything. When this provision is made a stock is said to be *preferred as to assets.*

A provision is sometimes found that, after the preferred stockholders have been paid their guaranteed dividend, and after the common stockholders have been paid an equal percentage, further earnings will be divided equally between the two groups. Where this provision is in effect it removes some of the disadvantages from noncumulative preferred stock.

Another provision occasionally made is that, whenever preferred dividends are unpaid, preferred stockholders may vote their stock along with common stockholders at meetings of the corporation. This affords some measure of protection to the preferred stockholders but it is dependent upon the ability and willingness of this group to organize for their own protection. In the case of a stock which is widely scattered in small holdings, this may be difficult. It is not unknown for stockholders (either preferred or common) to surrender their proxies to a "stockholder's protective committee" which really represents the existing management of the company.

---

[3] Or in many cases, the information may be obtained from *Moody's Manual* or *Poor's Manual.*

Bonds represent the long-term funded debt of a corporation. Since no one individual, or even one bank or insurance company, may be willing or able to loan millions of dollars to a single corporation, bonds constitute a way of "cutting the debt into small pieces" that may be disposed of more readily. This is an advantage even to the large bank or insurance company that might be willing to buy a whole bond issue. In the event that it needs money later on, a claim divided in the form of bonds will be more readily salable than the claim of a large debt in a single lump sum. Bonds are usually issued in denominations of $100 or $1,000 although, in order to attract the small investor, bonds of $50, $20, and even as low as $10 are sometimes found. Bonds may be classified according to the nature of the claim of debt of which they are small pieces.

Mortgage bonds are bonds that are secured by a mortgage upon all or some part of the physical property of a corporation. They may be either claims against the real property of the corporation, in which case they are *real estate mortgage bonds,* or they may be secured by a mortgage on movable property, in which case they are called *chattel mortgage bonds* (for example, bonds secured by a mortgage on railroad freight cars). There are first, second, and even third and fourth mortgage bonds in some corporations. In such cases, when foreclosure or bankruptcy takes place, the first mortgage bonds must be paid in full before the second, the second before the third mortgage bonds, and so on. Note well that the mere presence of the word "first" in the title of a bond issue does not necessarily mean that it is an absolutely first claim on the assets of the corporation. We often find "first refunding," "first convertible," and "first debenture" bonds issued by a company which already has two or three prior mortgage bond issues outstanding.

Debenture bonds are simply a claim against the general assets of a company *that are not otherwise specifically pledged.* In case there are no other bond issues of the company outstanding, debenture bonds are just as good as mortgage bonds. If we call mortgage bonds "pieces of a mortgage," we may call debenture bonds "pieces of a long-term promissory note." If there are large issues of mortgage bonds outstanding, debenture bonds in the same company may constitute an extremely risky junior security. Even where no other issues are outstanding, *unless it is specifically provided against,* the company may issue mortgage bonds on property against which debenture bonds have previously been the sole claim, thus impairing the value and the possibility of redemption of the debenture bonds.

Value of Bonds

In the event that interest payments are not made when they fall due, or that the principal is not repaid when the bond matures, bondholders may foreclose or bring an action in bankruptcy against the corporation. The value of a bond will then depend upon the proportion of the company's assets which it represents *when such assets are sold at a forced sale.* (Such value will not exceed the face value of the bond, since any surplus over this amount goes to the stockholders.) Since the "secondhand" value of capital equipment at a forced sale is ordinarily much less than its original value, it follows that no bond issue is "secured as to principal" unless it is made in a considerably smaller amount than the original purchase price of the assets against which it is a claim. The more specialized the capital assets against which bonds are issued, the more will their value be dependent upon the corporation as a "going concern." Consequently, unless bondholders are willing and able to take over a business and operate it for themselves, their right of foreclosure is useful only as a threat to the management and is by no means a guarantee of the return of the invested principal.

Unless adequate allowance is made for maintenance, the

depreciation of plant and equipment may impair the value upon which a bond issue rests. It is also to the interest of the bondholder to see that there is provision for a sinking fund which will repay the bonds at maturity. Otherwise, particularly in the case of long-term bonds, the company's excess earnings may be paid out in high dividends, leaving nothing but the possibility of borrowing again as a means of repaying the bond issue.

In addition to the circumstances peculiar to the individual company, there are many general market factors which will affect the value of bonds. When the market rate of interest on new capital investment declines, old bond issues will tend to rise in value.[4] In extreme inflation, bonds, because their principal and interest is payable as a fixed number of dollars, will lose their attractiveness as an investment. Mild inflation, after a period of depression, may raise the prices of low-grade bonds to the extent that it increases the earnings of the various companies which have issued them. Railroads and public utilities will be apt to profit less from this source than will industrial corporations since their rates, being fixed by regulation, are not apt to rise rapidly, and increases in traffic volume, due to inflation, may be offset by higher operating expenses.

Abuses of the Corporate Form of Organization

We have already mentioned some abuses of corporations. Before going further into specific abuses, we must raise the question: "Who controls the corporation?" Whoever controls a corporation is responsible for its abuses (seldom legally responsible, unfortunately); even if he does not perpetrate them nor profit from them, he is in a position to prevent them. The corporation was compared to a little business republic, with the stockholders as electors and the directors

---

[4] See Meyers, Albert L., *Elements of Modern Economics*, p. 252, Prentice-Hall, Inc., New York, 1938.

as representatives. In such a business government, as well as in political government, there are political parties by which the majority may exploit the minority. Political bosses exercise control through controlling the active minority in the majority party, and there are "blocs." Finally we have what corresponds to lobbyists representing outside interests that may bring pressure to bear on the corporation. In actual practice most stockholders seldom take an active and intelligent interest in the affairs of the corporation. If they vote at all, it is usually simply to approve matters (including the proposal of new directors) submitted to them by the board of directors.

The board of directors may be the controlling element, but it is seldom, particularly where the board is large, that the board *as a whole* exercises active control. Many directors may be "dummies" elected to the board to do someone's bidding. Many may be "honorary" directors used as "window dressing" in order to have imposing financial names on the board. The failure of many directors even to attend meetings long ago gave rise to the custom of giving each a twenty-dollar gold piece in order to get a quorum. In practice it will be found that most often the board simply gives "rubber stamp" approval to measures originating with one of the following interests: (1) a single director, or a small group, who may or may not be large stockholders; (2) a large stockholder who may or may not be a director; (3) the active business management of the corporation (President or General Manager); (4) a bank or banking group which is lending to the corporation; (5) the principal buyer of the corporation's product; (6) the principal supplier of raw materials; (7) the corporation's lawyer. This list might be extended considerably further.[5] Any of these "pressure interests" may

---

[5] Dr. Robert Gordon has made an extensive study of this question and the results will soon be published.

be represented on the board of directors but this is not necessary so long as they have one, or a small group, of the directors who will actively present their measures and a complacent majority of the board who will follow the leader.

Excessive salaries voted to officers and executives of a corporation are one of the most common abuses and one that is least subject to legal control. It may appear that it would make little difference to a corporate officer whether he received his earning as salary or dividends; nevertheless, if that part of his salary which is excessive were allowed to go into the general earnings of the company where it belongs, it would be shared *by the minority stockholders.* As a salary, it goes to him alone. In spite of the fact that tremendous salaries are continually reported for executives of large corporations, this evil of excessive salaries is apt to work more hardship upon the stockholders of small corporations. A salary of $50,000 for the president of a small corporation might absorb nearly all the earnings of the business, whereas a salary of $100,000 for the president of a corporation which has two million shares outstanding would amount to but 5 cents per share if the entire amount were distributed and the executive paid nothing. Since it is extremely difficult, if not impossible, to determine what an executive actually is worth to a business, it is hard to say whether any given salary is excessive and, if so, by how much. Quite likely the salary should be in some sort of rough ratio to the net earnings of the company. Rather than draft a general law to this effect, however, the author would prefer to be left free to criticize the man who would draft it.

Juggling of earnings from one corporation to another is a favorite device by which stockholders may be swindled. Where an individual or group has a major interest in one corporation and a minor but actively controlling interest in another, opportunity for unwarranted profit is offered.

For example, if the corporation in which they have large stock holdings is selling products to the other corporation, prices will be fixed very high. If their major interest is in the buying corporation, prices will be set low. Even though this practice is illegal, it is often extremely difficult to prove that it has taken place, particularly where the product is one that is not sold every day on the open market. For example, what is the market price for automobile bodies in lots of 100,000, or what is the fair value of 250,000 horsepower generators? Unless definite proof of overpricing or underpricing can be established, the courts will naturally assume that those doing the buying or selling were acting in good faith.

Misuse of "inside information" for stock market purposes by officers of a corporation is another common abuse. Some officers of a company may be in a position to know the way its affairs are going before this information becomes available to the general public and they may then profit by buying or selling the company's stock. This abuse is far more serious when officers are selling in advance of bad news than when they are buying on the basis of advance information of good news. When officers and directors unload their large holdings, they tend to depress the price of the stock seriously before the small stockholder has even a chance to sell. If it starts to become known in the market that officers are unloading, a panic decline may drive the price of the stock temporarily far below even the price which is justified by the bad news. It requires rather a high type of ethics on the part of officers not to unload and avoid losses when they know that the price of a stock will go down, but there is certainly no excuse for their selling short and making a profit under such circumstances.

Falsification of earnings for stock market purposes is also fairly easy to engineer. Overly generous markdowns of the company's assets for depreciation and obsolescence and the writing off of perfectly collectible items as "bad debts" can make a very large share of the earnings apparently disappear. When the price of the company's stock drops after the publication of this poor earnings report, the "insiders" can buy it at a bargain. In a subsequent earnings period the process can be reversed and the stock sold out at a profit.

Purchase of assets from an officer of the corporation, either openly or through a "dummy" intermediary is fraught with many possibilities of abuse. For example, an officer knows that the company is going to need a certain piece of real estate, so he buys it for himself and then resells it to the corporation at a quick profit. There are many other variants of the scheme.

Watered stock is the issuance of stock the original price of which exceeds the value of the assets of the corporation. This may be the result of giving a large block of stock to the owner of a patent right (not necessarily the inventor) or of giving large blocks of stock to the organizer of the corporation, or to the underwriters who sell the securities, for their "services," the value of the stock being more than the services or the patent are worth. It is not even necessary that stock be given. An excessive cash payment for services would have the same effect.

One way in which the small investor can protect himself against this particular practice is *never to buy the stock of a new company or a new issue of stock by an old company until it has been on the market for at least a year or more.* In spite of what the glib salesman tells you, this practice will not prevent you from "getting in on the ground floor." A study of the price history of the stocks of today's best and soundest companies will show that almost invariably the stock sold for much lower than its original issue price within two years after the original issue. This practice will also save you from buying the stock of many companies which are either ill-conceived or outright fraudulent and which "fold up" within a year or two. While he is marketing a new issue of stock, an underwriter, who has guaranteed to the corporation that he will sell the stock at a certain price, will buy back every share that the public offers for sale in order to protect the price of the stock which he still holds unsold. As soon as the issue is completely sold out, this support will be withdrawn and the stock must seek its own level on the market. If then the company is slow in getting established (as it is very naturally apt to be) and the first year's earnings are disappointing, those who bought in the hope of a quick profit will become tired of waiting and will unload their holdings. Then, and not before then, if the long-time prospects still look good, is the real time to "get in on the ground floor."

The list of abuses of the corporate form of business ownership which we have given could be almost indefinitely extended. Should, therefore, the corporate form be abolished? No. It would be impossible to organize large-scale businesses without it and in many lines we must have large-scale business organization if we are to have the product at any kind of reasonable price. The answer lies in attempting to remedy the abuses as far as possible. The Securities and Exchange Commission is a step in the right direction. If we can maintain the present high type of its personnel, its powers should be still further extended. Regardless of how good our laws or how well they are enforced, however, the investor will still find it necessary to exercise self-protection and judgment.

CHAPTER VIII

Large-Scale Organization, Combination Monopoly, and Unfair Competition

SOME authors treat large-scale business organization and combination as if the terms were synonymous, and others even include monopoly as if its meaning were not different from the other two. While there may be some few attributes which are characteristic to all three, we shall keep our thinking much clearer if we take the trouble to distinguish carefully between them and to note the principles which are peculiar to each. Large-scale organization may come as the result of combination or it may be simply the result of the steady expansion of a previously small firm. Large-scale business may be of any degree of competition or monopoly. Nearly perfect monopolies may exist in an enterprise of any size and they may or may not be the result of previous combination of firms.

Economies of Large-Scale Production

Ability to take full advantage of the economies of specialization and division of labor. We assume, of course, that the large firm has a big enough market either to absorb its entire capacity of output or to keep it running at a reasonably high percentage of capacity most of the time. The large firm, then, will be able to keep each man working at a highly specialized task. This allows for the development of greater

169

skill and speed at the particular operation and avoids the loss of time occasioned by changing from one operation to another.[1]

Ability to use specialized machinery. In firms selling a large output of a more or less uniform product, it becomes possible to do nearly every operation on a machine developed to perform that particular operation in the most rapid manner since the machine cost per unit of output will be small when total machine cost is spread over a large output. Even if such machinery is not yet in existence, a very large company can often afford to hire engineers to design it. In some industries which involve very few operations (such as papermaking and sugar refining) the basic machinery may be so costly that a firm must operate on a fairly large scale to use machinery at all.

Ability to pay large salaries for men of special ability. This enables the large firm (if it has the judgment to select them) to hire the best men for the "key positions": engineers, division superintendents, sales managers, and so forth.

Ability to obtain lower prices through quantity buying. Almost all raw materials are lower priced when purchased in large quantities, and freight rates on materials are always lower in carload lots. Another economy which might be classed either with this or with the previous one is the ability to hire a purchasing agent and to hire experts to test materials purchased.

Ability to utilize by-products. Small plants often find it necessary to throw away low-valued by-products, or even to hire someone to carry them away. Large plants, on the other hand, may have a sufficient quantity of the by-product to enable them to set up a separate plant to process it into some readily salable product that will show a profit on the operation.

---

[1] Meyers, Albert L., *Elements of Modern Economics,* p. 114, Prentice-Hall, Inc., New York, 1938.

Ability to conduct experimentation and research. Large firms can afford to set up elaborate and expensive experimental and research departments to develop and test new products and new methods of manufacture. The Westinghouse and General Electric Laboratories are conspicuous examples of this. For a small company a few costly experiments which yielded negative results would mean bankruptcy. Large companies are able to hire some of the foremost scientists and to conduct a tremendously large number of individual experiments. The law of averages is almost bound to give them a few profitable results which will overbalance the cost of the failures. The experimental method, when it is sufficiently well financed, may save many of the costs of the "trial and error" method. The DuPont Company, for example, built a "pilot plant" in order to solve most of the problems of manufacture before building their large plant to manufacture their new "Nylon" textile fibre.

All of the economies we have listed are peculiar to *large-scale* business enterprises. If particular combinations or highly monopolistic firms happen to exhibit some of these economies, it will be because they are also large-scale businesses, and not because they are combinations or monopolies. Combination of a number of previously small business units may result in a large-scale business which is able to achieve the economies of large-scale production, but it is the size of the business and not the mere fact of combination which is responsible for the economies. We shall find later some economies which are peculiar to combinations and monopolies.

Disadvantages of Large-Scale Business Organization

Extremely susceptible to business cycle. The dependence on volume of output renders the large business subject to heavy losses in business depressions when volume of sales declines. Large fixed investments mean mostly large fixed costs which cannot be contracted when output has to be contracted. The high-salaried "key men" will have to be retained if the organization is to be kept intact; their salaries also tend to become part of the fixed cost.

Comparatively inflexible. Large-scale businesses find it necessary to develop routine procedure to handle most of their minor business decisions and business practices. This very routine places them at a disadvantage in handling many business opportunities which are open to smaller and more flexible firms. In manufacturing, the large firm is seldom equipped to handle small orders, particularly if the specifications are even slightly different from their standard products. Consequently, in business declines when large orders are not forthcoming, the large firm may be forced to shut down or curtail output seriously while smaller firms may be able to keep going through their adaptability to meet the needs of particular small customers. In retail selling, opportunities to buy distress lots of merchandise and to resell them at a profit often appear. Large firms may be forced to decline many of these opportunities because the quantity of goods is small and because it may not be wise policy for them to whet their customers' appetites for goods at bargain prices which they cannot supply in sufficient volume to meet the demand.

The extremely large investment in specialized machinery means a tremendously heavy cost even to improve and modernize the product, to say nothing of changing from the manufacture of one product to another. Thus, the large firm tends to develop an "inertia" which may tend to keep it manufacturing the same product in the same way, sometimes for a considerable time after the public taste for the product has changed.

Limitations of large-scale management. This is probably the chief disadvantage of large-scale business. The larger the business, the more the authority that must be delegated to minor officials, which leads to the "dilemma of management."[2] Either great reliance must be placed upon the judgment of minor officials and hence high-salaried men must be hired, or many arbitrary rules must be laid down for their guidance thus tending to increase the inflexibility criticized above.

Economies of Combination

As mentioned before, to the extent that combination results in large-scale business, it will be capable of effecting the economies (and will be subject to the disadvantages) of large-scale business. These are listed above and we shall not discuss them further. There are, however, certain economies and certain disadvantages which result from the combination of existing business firms. There are two major types of combination, horizontal and vertical. *Horizontal combination* is the combination of two or more firms in the same stage of the industry (for example, a combination of a number of blast furnaces making pig iron). *Vertical combination,* sometimes called *integration,* is the combination of two or more firms in successive stages of an industry (for example, the combination of an iron mine, a blast furnace, a steel plant, and a structural steel works).

Horizontal Combination

Elimination of cross-hauling. When two or more firms located in different geographic areas are combined, a considerable saving in freight costs may be achieved by supplying the demands of each region from the factory closest to the customer: For example, if two formerly competing firms, one located in Chicago and the other in New York, are combined, the New York firm will no longer ship goods into Chicago and *vice versa;* instead, the Chicago factory will supply the Middle Western market and the New York factory

---

[2] Meyers, Albert L., *Elements of Modern Economics,* p. 115.

will supply the Eastern states. Any firm which is large enough to set up branch factories at strategically located points can, of course, achieve the same economies. Even a large firm, however, may find it more convenient to buy out, or merge with, an existing firm in a distant territory rather than to set up a new plant in that locality to compete with the old firm.

Elimination of duplicate selling expenses. When two firms are combined, it is no longer necessary to send two salesmen to call on the same customer since one can now do the work. This does not necessarily mean, however, that if two firms each having the same sized sales force are combined, only one-half of the previous number of salesmen will be needed. Each firm may have some customers on which the other has not been calling. The sales force can be curtailed only to the extent that duplication has previously existed. The combined firms might be found to have, say, three-quarters of the previous total sales force, each salesman covering a smaller territory more intensively. Similar economies may be achieved in advertising expenses to the extent that the two firms previously competed for the same market.

Elimination of other duplicated costs. The services of purchasing agents, accounting departments, research departments, and other nonmanufacturing departments may be combined and a considerable reduction in personnel achieved by the combination of two previously competing firms. Usually the greatest proportionate reduction can be achieved among the higher salaried executives in these groups. The total amount of detail work to be done by clerks and other minor employees may be nearly as great for the combined firms as it was when the two were separate.

Economic utilization of capacity. When a fairly large number of plants are brought into a single combination, it may be found that lower costs can be achieved when demand is slack by operating some of the plants at their optimum, or least cost, output and keeping others shut down entirely, rather than to run all the plants at reduced output as would be the case under competition. It will generally be found too that some of the plants have lower unit costs at optimum capacity than others. When this is the case, production can be confined to the lower cost plants in dull times, the highest cost plants being operated only at such times as the price of the product warrants.

All of the above economies of combination are predicated upon the assumption that an actual operating merger is formed. If the combination is a mere financial or ownership arrangement and the identity and operating set-up of the existing firms is retained intact, naturally none of these economies will result. The actual operating merger achieves economies which may be passed on to the public in the form of a lower price of the product if the company so desires, or if circumstances force it to do so. The mere ownership merger, without an operating merger, may simply be a means of avoiding price cutting and maintaining excessive cost structures.

Disadvantages of Horizontal Combination

Product differentiation as a limit to the possible economies of combination. When an intensive effort has been made to create demand for particular brands of a product, the mere fact that the two or more companies combine is not apt to make the customers willing to shift from one brand to the other. If one company has been spending millions of dollars to convince its customers that "dated coffee is the only fresh coffee" while another has been spending similar sums to extol the merits of "vacuum-packed coffee," and the two should happen to combine, it might prove considerably embarrassing to retract the statements of one or the other and package coffee in only one way in order to achieve sales economy. If the separate brands are to be maintained, the selling economies achieved by combination may be negligible or nonexistent. Even where the products are in different price classes, and so somewhat less directly competitive, this limitation persists. It will be noticed, particularly in the larger cities, that General Motors has different sales agencies for every one of its makes of cars. This is probably because they have found that a dealer who does not care whether he sells a customer a LaSalle or a Buick may lose a sale to the dealer who is energetically selling nothing but Packards. In the smaller towns the savings in combining salesrooms and repair departments are proportionately great enough to offset this, and one dealer often handles two or more makes of General Motors cars.

Essential and important differences in the actual nature of the product (as distinct from mere differences in brand names and packaging) may make it difficult to achieve the operating economies of combination as well as the selling economies. It will not be possible to shut down some plants and keep others running at best capacity unless a thoroughly standardized product is made by all plants.

Possible hazards in eliminating duplicate employees. In spite of the statement that "a corporation has no soul," business firms are somewhat like human beings. It is not always possible to cut two of them up and take parts of each and to reassemble an artificial being that is as healthy as either was before. Two business firms may each be moderately successful as the result of the personnel which each has, without the relative merits of the different minor executives being particularly apparent. It is entirely possible that the poorer rather than the better men will be retained for most positions when the two companies combine. Many companies have some inefficient employees who are retained in their positions simply because of their friendship or relationship with the controlling interest. It is these very men for whom the "boss" is apt to say the strongest word when the consolidation takes place. Unless the favorites happen to be in exactly corresponding positions in the two firms, the net result may easily be the retention of the inefficient and the firing of the efficient. Each firm may have been able to carry its own "deadheads," but the combination may sink under the combined weight of the two groups. Some other firm may then take on the good employees who are discharged and put the combination out of business. This is an extreme example; nevertheless, we have seen many a combination of metropolitan newspapers fail which tried "to retain the best features of each."

Economies of Vertical Combination

Continuous supply of raw materials and other essential contributory products. The firm which is integrated as far back as the source of its materials can always be assured of the materials it needs to fill orders. Particularly in the metal trades, when rush business follows a period of slackness in which mines have been shut down, serious shortages of raw materials occur. In such times the firm without its own source of supply may have to pay outrageous prices for raw materials, and even high prices may not be sufficient to insure prompt delivery when other firms have also ordered. Semi-finished products and parts may likewise have occasional periods of scarcity for the firm which buys rather than controls them. "Bottle necks" all along the line may be eliminated by a well-planned chain of plants in the different stages between the raw material and the consumer.

Elimination of selling costs at intermediate stages. In the integrated firm there are no selling costs between the raw material producer and the first processor, between the first processor and the second, and so on, as would have to be the case were these successive stages of production separately owned. The cotton in your shirt was probably bought and resold at least ten or twelve times in some form or other before it reached you. On the other hand, the iron ore, coke, and limestone in structural steel are often sold only twice, once to the building contractor and then to the buyer of the building. Selling and advertising may be dispensed with all along the line by vertical combination.

The claim is often made that the advertising of parts and materials directly to the consumer helps the manufacturer to sell the finished product. At best such advertising probably has only a limited effect and is important only when the finished product, or the parts or raw materials, are a comparative novelty to the public. It is hard to imagine today a customer who is torn between the purchase of two makes of cars because one uses his favorite brand of ball bearings and the other uses a certain brand of piston rings. Of course, the integrated firm can, and sometimes does continue to advertise the parts manufactured by its component firms, but it is remarkable how little of such advertising it seems to find necessary. General Motors runs an occasional advertisement for "Fisher" bodies, few for "Delco" starting, lighting and ignition, and almost none for any other part which is manufactured by its subsidiary companies.

Co-ordination of manufacturing processes. Where a number of plants are united in a vertical combination, each can be so organized as to meet best the requirements of the succeeding stage of production. For example, an independent parts manufacturer will have to design his product to fit as many different makes of cars as possible or will have to be prepared to manufacture various types to suit the different makes of cars. A parts plant in an integrated chain will design its product to fit best one or two makes of cars only (the car may also be designed to use the parts), and concentration on fewer types will allow further adoption of mass production methods.

Reduction in total inventories. When the plants in successive stages of production are independently owned, each may be compelled to maintain fairly large inventories both of raw materials and of products which are finished as far as that stage is concerned, in order to be able to supply customers when the orders come in. An integrated firm, on the other hand, can gauge the flow of the entire productive process by the sales of the end product and may be able to keep the total inventory much lower through avoidance of duplicate stocks in successive plants. The independent firm will naturally try to keep its stocks low when buyers are heavily stocked, but such information on buyer's supplies may not be as available to it as it is to the firms which are integrated. Moreover, the independent firm must be ready to meet the demands of any buyer who may come along or he may decide to buy from someone else. The unit of an integrated firm need not hold stocks unless the succeeding stage will require the product soon.

Disadvantages of Vertical Combination

Dependence of entire organization on the marketing of product by the "end firm" or plant which produces goods in their most finished form. Unless the selling organization at the end of the integrated chain of plants is able to sell all of its products, all of the preceding stages will either have to curtail output or shut down as the case may be. If the primary plants have dispensed with their selling force, they will not be in a position to solicit business from independent manufacturers when their own organization is unable to absorb their produce. Even if they maintain a small selling force, they will not ordinarily be able to obtain much business from independents in slack times. Those independents who do have orders to give for parts or materials will prefer to place them with other firms on whom they can continue to rely for supplies in a period of prosperity, rather than to buy from a link plant in an integrated chain which will decline or cancel orders as soon as its own organization can absorb its product. Moreover, the greater the degree of specialization achieved by the integrated plants, the less suited will they be to supply the needs of a general market.

Inability to take full advantage of low costs in depressions. In times of depression, raw and semi-finished materials often sell at prices much less than their replacement cost. Independent firms in the stages of production closer to the consumer may buy these materials and place their product upon the market cheaply. Even if the integrated firm should buy these materials rather than manufacture its own, it would still be burdened with the fixed costs of its own mines and primary factories.

Dilemma of excess or idle capacity. The various plants of an integrated firm will be designed to meet the requirements of the plant in the next stage; but what is meant by "requirements"? Are they maximum, minimum, or average requirements? If the plant is designed to supply the maximum requirements at least cost, it will be operating at higher than minimum cost at all times when the next plant does not require so great an output. If the plant is designed to meet the minimum requirements of the next plant, then the next plant must be prepared to buy its additional supplies on the open market in times of rising prices and may run the risk of failing to secure them at all. Designing a plant to meet average requirements is at best a somewhat unsatisfactory compromise between these two evils, being alternately subject to both. This problem of selection of the optimum size of plant in the face of fluctuating business conditions is faced, of course, by the independent firm as well as by the units of a vertical combination. However, the independent firm may be in a better position to secure more business by small price cuts than the integrated unit which sells in the open market only occasionally. The greater the degree of specialization of the integrated unit plant, the less will be its opportunity to utilize its excess capacity by selling to outside firms.

Economies of Perfect Monopoly

By a perfect monopoly we mean an organization which controls either the entire output of an industry or one which controls the entire market for a commodity in a given locality.[3] Most of what are commonly cited as economies of monopoly are really the economies either of large-scale production or of horizontal combination. It is true, however, that in many industries monopoly may be able to practice these economies to a greater extent than can either large-scale firms or combinations which do not control the entire output or market. In fields where the potential market for the entire product is small, even two or three firms only may mean that the division of the market among them leaves each with an output which is too small to achieve the economies of large-scale production. In such circumstances, if the demand for the product was fairly elastic, monopoly price would probably be lower than oligopoly[4] price and much lower than the price set by a few firms which operated under a price agreement.

The monopoly is in a position to carry on what we have listed as the economies of horizontal combination to their extreme possible limit. Cross-hauling is entirely eliminated. Duplication of services may be completely avoided. Such advertising as is done will be designed simply to increase total consumption of the product and not to push one brand at the expense of another, and there can be little doubt that advertising expense would be greatly reduced.

---

[3] Or we may say that it is a firm whose product has no close substitutes.

[4] Oligopoly is a situation in which there are few sellers, each of whom takes account of his rivals' price policy.

Monopoly as a stimulus to integration. When a firm has an assured control of the market for a product, this may be an inducement to gain control of the earlier stages of production, perhaps even as far back as the raw materials. On the other hand, if the monopoly is the chief or only customer for the raw materials or semi-finished products (monopsony), it might be more profitable simply to beat down the prices of the supplying firms rather than to acquire ownership of the firms themselves. The threat of potential competition might be a more effective motive to induce attempted control of the source of supply.

It may be questioned whether a firm which has a monopoly of a source of raw materials can gain anything further (assuming it is already charging the full monopoly price) by attempting to enter the field of manufacturing finished products. There is one set of circumstances under which a further gain can be made: If the purchasers of the raw material are themselves making large profits by fabricating it into finished goods, the monopoly owner of the raw material supply, by competing with them, may force them to accept lower prices for the finished goods. If there is then any considerable elasticity in the demand for the finished goods, this may be the means of selling a greater quantity of the raw material at the same high price. In general, it will be found that when the owners of the supply of raw materials begin making finished or semi-finished products, they tend to confine their efforts to those lines in which the raw material comprises as large as possible a part of the value of the finished product. (For example, the Aluminum Company of America manufactures pots and pans and aluminum paint, but does not attempt to make automobiles, airplanes, or typewriters, although all these use a considerable amount of aluminum.)

The field in which the greatest case can be made for the economies of monopoly is in that of public utilities, such as the furnishing of water, gas, electric and telephone services. While these economies are not different in nature from those we have listed for large scale organization and combination, the wastes which occur through the duplication of facilities and the savings which may be achieved through the elimination of these wastes in the field of public utilities are so great that many economists have classified the public utilities as "natural monopolies." The use of the term "natural" may be questioned, but the advantages of service by a single company are so obvious that an exclusive charter to render such service is usually granted to a single company by the government of a community.

Disadvantages of Monopoly

Monopolies lack the stimulus of competition which forces the competitive firm to be alert to discover new ways of lowering costs. Research may be neglected and the industry allowed to become completely moribund. This may be particularly true in cases in which the maximum net earnings of the company are limited by law. Unless the company is allowed to participate at least to a certain extent in the savings which may be achieved, there is no motive at all to seek lower costs. In such circumstances the companies rather tend to conceal earnings by "padding" their operating expenses.

Rigid prices. Once a monopoly has hit upon what appears to be a satisfactory price, there may be a tendency to maintain this price for a considerable period of time regardless of fluctuations in general business conditions. This tendency may result in much greater fluctuations of output and of employment than would be the case if prices were allowed to decline during the recession and depression phases of the business cycle. If the monopoly is one which produces raw materials or semi-finished goods, the maintenance of rigid prices may force a greater decline in output and employment among the firms that buy its products than would occur if these firms were able to obtain the raw materials cheaper during periods of business decline. The more rigidities are introduced into our economic system, the more the pressure that will have to be borne by those elements which still remain flexible, such as the volume of employment.

Combinations in Restraint of Trade

At the beginning of this chapter combinations were discussed mainly from the point of view of their abilities and disadvantages in securing economies in production and selling costs. Those combinations which are organized mainly for the fixing of prices and the restraint of competition must now be considered. Since every operating combination will tend to reduce the number of competitors and so may tend to reduce price competition, it is not always easy to distinguish between the two types. Greater control over prices, rather than the achievement of economies, may be the dominant motive to combination. As an arbitrary line of demarcation we shall assume that, in the combinations now being discussed, the identity of the individual firms is maintained. The combination attempts to fix prices rather than to allow competitive prices to prevail.

The Simple Price Agreement

The simplest form of combination in restraint of trade is a mere agreement among previously competing sellers that they will all sell at the same price. Such agreements have no standing in law and will not be enforced by the courts. If the price agreed on is profitable, each member of the agreement will attempt to sell all that he can at that price and then will be tempted to cut the price slightly in order to secure more business. At first the price may be adhered to in a nominal way, but concessions, which are really price concessions, will be given in the form of more liberal credit terms, extra delivery service, extra quantity discounts and the like. Finally comes the stage of open breaking of the agreement. When price agreements of this sort have lasted any length of time, it has usually been because there were one or two very large firms which dominated the industry. When this is the case, the large firm may threaten to undersell and force out of business any smaller firm that breaks the agreement. If the smaller firm's business is concentrated in a particular locality, the large firm may undersell it in that particular region without cutting its prices elsewhere, and the threat may be effective in enforcing the agreement for a considerable period of time.

The Price and Quota Agreement

If the voluntary price agreement is to be maintained for any length of time, it is imperative that each member receive a "fair" share of the business so that he will not be so strongly tempted to violate the agreement. One method which is sometimes used in an attempt to bolster the agreement is the allocation of sales quotas or production quotas to the various members. Any member who then sells in excess of his quota is fined a certain amount per unit on the excess sales and this sum is divided among the other members of the agreement. There is, of course, no more means of enforcing the collection of fines than there is of enforcing the price agreement itself. However, if the quota system gives each member a satisfactory amount of the business, each may then feel that it is better to adhere to the agreed price and remain within his quota rather than trust to his own chances of survival in an open "price war" which might be precipitated by his violation of the agreement.

The Territory Pool

Another device which is sometimes used to strengthen the price agreement is the territory pool. Under this arrangement the sales area is divided up and each member is given a territory in which he has the exclusive right to sell. This device has the advantage over the quota system in that it may be easier to detect violations of the agreement when a member sells outside his alloted territory than to determine whether he is selling a volume in excess of his quota. Unless the territory is very carefully divided, however, and unless sales in each territory conform to the expectations when the division was made, members may easily become dissatisfied with the share of the business that they are receiving and the agreement will collapse.

Selling Pools and Cartels

A much stronger form of price agreement is provided for in the selling pool. Under this form each member delivers his output to a central selling organization which sells for all the members only at the agreed price. It also provides an accurate means of seeing that the sales of each member conform to his quota. In Germany this type of organization is not against the law and these "cartels" have even been reorganized by a special "Cartel Law." Under the amendments to the Cartel Law passed in 1933, the Minister of Economics may form compulsory cartels in any industry whenever he thinks that this is necessary to the welfare of the Reich. He may also: (1) prohibit for a certain length of time the establishment of new enterprises in a particular industry, (2) prohibit the enlargement of existing plants, or (3) limit their output.[5]

---

[5] See Kessler, W. C., "The New German Cartel Legislation," *American Economic Review*, Vol. XXIV, September 1934, p. 477 ff., for a full discussion of these amendments.

The early experience of the German cartels again demonstrated the old principle that prices cannot be controlled without controlling production. Some of the earlier cartels established quotas for their members on the basis of a fixed percentage of the plant capacity of each member. This device broke down in a rather curious manner. Member firms, which already had excess plant capacity due to the quota restrictions, enlarged the size of their plants in order to obtain a larger quota expressed as a percentage of the larger plant capacity. It was also found that when profitable prices were established new firms sprang up outside the cartel. This meant that the structure of the cartel itself was threatened unless it could either freeze the new firms out of business or force them to enter the cartel and assign them a quota, which would necessarily decrease the size of the quotas of the older members. It was experiences such as these that led to the passage of the new cartel legislation mentioned above.

It is interesting to note that one of the avowed objectives of the German cartel legislation has been to preserve the existence of the smaller firms and to prevent their being absorbed by the larger firms. The prevention of cutthroat competition by the establishment of the cartels was expected to accomplish this end.

Collusive Bidding on Contracts

Most governmental agencies advertise for bids on government contracts with the understanding that the contract is to be awarded to the lowest bidder. This procedure is required by law on contracts awarded by many Federal, state, and local government agencies. In addition to obtaining lowest costs, it is also one of the greatest safeguards against bribery and favoritism in the awarding of contracts. Although it is no absolute guarantee against such practices, it does make them more difficult. Some large industrial concerns, and buyers of building construction in particular, also use the procedure of asking for bids on contracts.

Two systems of collusive bidding are used by conspiring contractors to defeat the purpose of requesting bids. The simpler method is for all the supposed competitors to submit identical bids. Although it is sometimes still used, this method is naïve, since the submission of identical bids is almost *prima facie* evidence of collusion.[6] A more subtle method and a more difficult one to detect is for the various contractors to get together and agree on which one is to have the contract and at what price. He then submits his bid and all the other contractors submit different higher bids. If the various contractors all keep silent and adhere to their agreement, it is extremely difficult to obtain evidence that this practice is being used.

This second method is not apt to be successful for any length of time, however, unless the number of bidders is fairly small and the volume of total business is great enough so that each firm will secure a sufficient amount of business to induce it to keep to the agreement. In cases where a particularly large contract may give a disproportionate share of the business to one firm, this problem is sometimes met by a supplementary agreement that the previously designated "successful" bidder shall award a part of the work to one or more of the other firms on subcontracts.

The most conspicuous example of this type of collusive bidding agreement that has been brought to light was discovered in the investigation of the building trades scandal in New York City which finally sent two of the principals to prison. In this case, the contractors' "ring" was supported by building trades union labor. In return for closed shop con-

---

[6] As this is being written, the United States Attorney General's office is bringing an action under the Sherman Act against tire companies that submitted identical bids on government contracts.

tracts and high wages, the unions agreed not to work for any contractors outside of the agreement. This kept the number of possible bidders small. Unable to stand success, they kept on raising the prices until the cost of building in New York reached such fantastic heights that it was obvious that something was wrong and the investigation was started.

Disadvantages of Price Agreements

It may be said with a fair degree of truth that, from the point of view of the general public, the price agreement has all of the disadvantages and practically none of the advantages of an outright ownership and operating monopoly. There will be none of the economies of large-scale production except as the individual firms happen to be of large size. Furthermore, the restriction of output to conform to quotas by such large firms as do exist will tend to prevent them from operating at minimum cost. Of the economies of combination, the elimination of cross-hauling will exist only in the form of price agreement which we have described as the territory pool. Elimination of duplicate selling organizations may occur in the case of sales pools or cartels, only if they are expected to last for many years, so that the member firms feel like taking the risk of giving up their own sales organization. Otherwise, none of the economies of combination is available to the price agreement which retains the identity of the separate firms.

Since so few of the economies of large-scale production, of combination, or of monopoly are available to the firms under a price agreement, it follows that their costs will be higher than that of an operating monopoly in the same field. Under the simple price agreement, it is also impossible to close down a few of the plants in order to run the others at optimum capacity. It is thus safe to say that it is practically certain that prices will be higher under a price agreement than they would be either under some form of competition or under outright monopoly.

The greater loss to the public, in the form of higher prices, under a price agreement than under an outright monopoly is obvious. It must also be remembered that higher unit costs represent a wastage of our economic resources.

Advantages of Price Agreements

There are some alleged advantages to the public in price agreements over monopoly. Though prices are uniform, competition may exist in the form of services or quality of product. In any event, such competition will not exist either under the territory pool or under the selling pool. Even where sales quotas are allotted, competition on the basis of service or quality is not apt to exceed that necessary to obtain the full amount of the quota for the firm. Since such quotas, in order to obtain higher prices, are usually lower than full competitive output, it is not likely that much service or quality competition will be deemed necessary. Service and quality competition are thus seen to be confined largely to the simple price agreement without sales quotas. Even under the simple price agreement, whenever service and quality competition become really keen it will usually be found that this is a prelude either to the breakdown of the agreement or to the adoption of more stringent forms of price control.

The claim is also made that price agreements tend to keep the smaller firms in business. Even if this is true, of what advantage to society is the retention of the identity of small firms if they no longer compete on the basis of price, and probably do not compete even on the basis of service or quality? Most of the vaunted virtues of small firms cease when the firms cease being competitors. If a few large firms "gobble up" the small ones, the prices that they charge may or may not be higher than the prices which were charged when the small firms were in genuine competition with them; but the prices charged by a few large firms are apt to be less than would be the case where there are many small firms operating under a price agreement. Moreover, it is by no means always certain that it is the smaller firms which are receiving the protection under a price agreement. In some few industries where the larger firms may be found to be too large to operate economically, it may be found that the severest competition is coming from the small and medium-sized firms.

It is also alleged that controlled prices under a price agreement tend to "stabilize business conditions." Investigation will show, however, that such "administered" prices go up by a succession of large jumps in the upward phase of the business cycle and then are lowered only reluctantly and gradually in the recession and depression. Each rumor of a jump in price brings about accumulation of stocks by purchasers, and the peak of prosperity is apt to find them with just as excessive inventories as they would have with competitively priced products.

The Sherman Anti-Trust Act

The first important attempt of the Federal Government to attack the problems of combination and monopoly in fields other than the railroads was made in the Sherman Anti-Trust Act of 1890. This act declared "every contract, combination in the form of a trust or otherwise, or conspiracy, in restraint of trade or commerce" either in interstate or foreign commerce to be illegal, and further made it a misdemeanor to "monopolize or attempt to monopolize, or combine or conspire with any other person or persons, to monopolize any part of the trade or commerce among the several states, or with foreign nations." Individual firms which are injured by combinations in restraint of trade or other practices prohibited by the act are also permitted to sue for damages and, if successful, it is stipulated that they receive three times the amount of the damages proved, plus attorneys' fees.

The cases under the Sherman Act were few and unspectacular until the advent of the "trust-busting" era under the late President Theodore Roosevelt. The Northern Securities case (an attempt to combine the Great Northern and Northern Pacific railroads under a holding company) and the cases involving the dissolution orders against the Standard Oil Company and the Tobacco Trust attracted widespread public attention. For a time people actually believed that the act would be effective in curbing monopolies. The subsequent rapid spread of the "Interlocking Directorate" (various directors being on the boards of two or more companies to secure price or other agreements) and of the various forms of price agreement soon proved this belief to be unfounded. A typical cartoon of the time pictured the "Standard Oil Trust" and the "Tobacco Trust" as fat men riding along luxuriously in a limousine while a number of poor "trusts" on the curbstone are saying, "Please dissolve us too."

The rule of reason is a famous legal doctrine which was announced by the Supreme Court in the Standard Oil case. Under a literal interpretation of the language of the Sherman Act, even so small a combination as that of two corner grocery stores might be deemed to be "in restraint of trade" and therefore unlawful. To avoid the cluttering of the court dockets with cases such as this, the Supreme Court, in effect, "read the minds" of the Congressmen and announced that the act was intended to be directed only against "unreasonable" restraint of trade and not against combinations incidental to an otherwise lawful purpose. The court has never put itself on record with a comprehensive definition of what does or does not constitute "unreasonable" restraint of trade, so that no planned combination can be absolutely sure in advance whether it will be deemed legal or not. From subsequent decisions of the court, we may draw the inference that the court directs its particular attention to the questions: (1) whether the combination controls a substantial majority of the output of an industry, (2) whether an attempt is made to control or raise prices, (3) whether competitors are compelled to join the combination or are forced out of business by unlawful means, and (4) whether prospective new competitors are prevented from entering the industry.

The Clayton Act

It finally became evident that there was not much effect in "busting the trusts" after an industry was in the hands of a combination of a few large firms and after effective competition had been stifled. The Clayton Act, passed in 1914, represents an attempt to prevent the formation of monopolistic combinations by making illegal some of the means by which monopoly power was often attained. Specifically it was directed against holding companies, local price discrimination, interlocking directorates, and tying contracts (contracts which bind the purchaser of a product to use certain of the seller's other products in connection with it: for example, requiring the buyer of a cotton compress to use bale ties provided by the seller). These practices were not necessarily made illegal in themselves but were to be considered illegal when the effect was to lessen competition substantially or to tend towards the creation of monopoly. The Clayton Act also made civil damage suits easier than under the Sherman Act by providing that conviction by the government under the criminal provisions of the anti-trust acts was to be considered as *prima facie* evidence against the defendant in a civil suit.

The Federal Trade Commission

The Federal Trade Commission was also established shortly afterwards. Its principal duties are the conducting of investigations to determine whether the anti-trust acts are being violated and aiding the Department of Justice in prosecution; the investigation of trade practices with a view to proposing remedial legislation to Congress; and the prevention of "unfair methods of competition."

Probably the most interesting phase of the work of the Federal Trade Commission has been in the field of exposing and prosecuting "methods of unfair competition." The mere listing of the different types of unfair trade methods which the Commission has had occasion to bring before the courts would fill several pages. Among them will be found: false advertising, boycotting, inducing breach of contract, bribing employees of customers and competitors, conspiracy to cut off supplies of competitors, discrimination, disparagement of competitors, threatening competitors and their customers with patent infringement suits, rebates, closely imitating competitor's name or trade-mark, tampering with competitor's goods in order to make them demonstrate poorly, and the maintenance of resale price by discrimination against price cutters.

It is rather ironical to note that the vast majority of the Commission's actions have been to the effect of protecting the "good will" of the various firms supposed to be injured. We know that "good will" is one important element of monopoly power. Thus, although attempting to prevent the formation of monopolies, the actions of the Commission have contributed much to the rise of monopolistic competition.

Prior to 1938, whatever protection the consumer received from the Federal Trade Commission was most apt to be entirely incidental. "False advertising" was generally proceeded against not because it injured the consumer but mainly because it tended to injure the business of a competitor. Repeated cases have arisen in which a firm manufactured a product identical with (or perhaps even superior to) that of a competitor. If it then packaged its product in a manner to imitate the competitor's package and sold it at a lower price, it would be enjoined from such a practice on the ground that it was "deceiving to the public." Granted that the people are deceived in such a case, it is difficult to see how they are harmed; if the product is identical and the price is lower and will remain lower, it would seem that the deception is beneficial. The damage to the competitor is obvious. It is only fair to state that in a great many cases the imitation is an inferior product. In such cases the public is also protected by the prohibition of package imitation.

This discussion does not suggest any criticism of the Federal Trade Commission itself. That body has simply been administering the law as it has been written and as it was interpreted by the courts. Under the 1938 amendment to the Trade Commission Act, the Commission is now empowered to act in cases of deception which tend to damage the consumer, even though no damage to a competitor can be shown. Congress is now engaged in an investigation (Temporary National Economic Committee) which it is hoped will shape the course of new legislation.

Public Policy on Competition and Monopoly

In spite of the "bust the trust" and "anti-monopoly" slogans which have appeared in various political platforms from time to time, we have by no means arrived at any definite public policy in this respect. Indeed, we have not even considered fully either the means necessary to carry out a policy nor its full implications if carried to its logical conclusion. At present, our system is a curious hodge-podge of enforced and regulated monopolies (public utilities); government-fostered and largely unregulated monopoly, oligopoly, and monopolistic competition (fostered by patents, trade-marks, protective tariffs, and the suppression of "unfair competition"); and finally, a few surviving elements of pure competition in the markets for some agricultural products.

If experience has taught us anything, it is that no particular degree of competition or monopoly is "good" or "bad" *per se,* but rather that the nature of each particular industry will be the most important element in determining what state of competition or monopoly will be the most economical for the community. By "most economical" we mean that which results in: (1) greatest output at lowest prices, (2) most efficient use of resources, (3) most convenient service for the consumer consistent with (1) and (2). These three aims will sometimes be found to conflict with each other and it then becomes a question of which end we desire most or of possible compromises. (For example, do we want the widest possible choice in articles of clothing or do we want the lowest possible prices?) With these aims in mind, let us consider the field and function of the various forms of monopoly and competition in a supposed "ideal" economic system, which still attempts to take advantage of the motivating forces of profits and differential wages.

The Field of Monopoly

Monopoly is indicated as the appropriate form for any industry: (1) in which a single firm can achieve much lower unit costs than would result from any division of the market among two or more firms, and (2) in which duplication of facilities will not result in a sufficiently greater value of service to the consumer to justify the higher cost. The "public utilities" have already been cited as examples of this situation. In the future we shall probably witness some expansion in the number of industries which are called public utilities. (Perhaps retail milk distribution might be the first addition.) When the word monopoly is used in this connection, it of course refers to ownership and operation of an industry by a single firm and not to some form of price agreement or combination in which the identity of individual firms is retained.

In some industries it may be found that demand is sufficiently elastic and that marginal costs are falling over a sufficient range of output so that unregulated monopoly price would be lower than competitive price. In most cases some positive action must be taken if the benefits of low monopoly costs of production are to be passed on to the public in the form of lower prices. The alternatives are then government regulation or public ownership.

The Field of Duopoly and Oligopoly

In industries where large-scale organization is necessary to achieve lowest costs and at the same time the market is too large to be served by one firm of optimum size (and possibly where product differentiation can measurably increase consumer satisfaction), duopoly or oligopoly would seem to be indicated. The manufacture of low and medium-priced automobiles in the United States appears to be the best example of such an industry.

Whether we may rely upon competition to keep prices low depends upon: (1) the willingness of the various firms to engage in price competition and (2) the readiness with which buyers will shift from one seller to another in response to small differences in price. When this is not the case, there may be either recourse to the Sherman and Clayton Acts in an attempt to prevent price agreements (not too successful to date), or the government may take a hand in setting maximum prices. The Department of Justice has recently announced an interesting technique which may be applicable in this situation: anti-trust proceedings are first started as a threat, and then the case is dropped under a "consent decree," which contains provisions covering trade practices and presumably an agreement to reduce prices. The results of this procedure should be interesting. Even its announcement is an indication that we are beginning to be more realistic than we were in the "trust-busting" decades.

The Field of Monopolistic Competition

Where there is a wide variety of tastes to be served, where the manner of service may be an important element in the satisfaction that the customer derives from the product, and where the nature of the industry is such that small firms are numerous and are the most efficient, monopolistic competition would seem to be indicated for the industry. The legal bulwarks of the monopoly element in monopolistic competition are patents, trade-marks and the general protection of "good will" for the owner of a business by the laws and the courts. We have already had occasion to state some of the arguments for and against these special privileges accorded to business firms by the government. (See p. 9.)

Since "good will" could hardly exist without these important elements of government protection, it would seem reasonable that the government should insist that they be used as far as possible in conformity with public interest and not as a means of preventing price comparisons and of confusing or deceiving the buyer. A few simple measures suggest themselves which, if generally required (some are already in partial use), might greatly facilitate price comparisons and so increase the element of price competition. (1) Wherever services are separable, require that they be separately priced and purchased only at the buyer's option. Require, for example, that delivery charges be stated separately from the price of the product and be charged to those who insist on delivery and not to those who carry the goods home themselves. Also make credit a separate and clearly stated charge only against those who use it. (2) Limit packages and containers to a few standard sizes, the gradations in size being such as to be readily apparent to the eye. (3) Establish Federal grades for all products, wherever possible, and require that these grades be printed in large type upon consumer packages. (4) Revise Federal grades so that grades 1, 2 and 3 indicate, at least roughly, the same relative grades for all commodities. (This need not preclude the retention of a "fancy" grade for qualities which are pleasing to the eye only.) (5) Provide that false claims, either in the advertising or on the label of a product, be made sufficient grounds for revocation of patent or trade-mark together with widespread public notice of such revocation and the reason therefor. (For a first offense it might be sufficient to require the publication of a retraction, publication being at the offender's expense and to be given the same publicity as had been given to original false claim.) If this measure were ever proposed in Congress, there would certainly be a howl about "government interference with business," but if a firm's "good name" is to be protected in the courts, it would seem that there should be a requirement that it be a *good* name and not a vehicle for dishonest advertising.

The Field of Pure Competition

After defining the other fields, the field of pure competition is thus narrowed down to those industries in which the most efficient firms are of small size and in which product differentiation can confer no benefit upon the buyer. It may be said, however, that if the regulations suggested in the above paragraph were adopted, many industries now characterized by monopolistic competition would closely approximate the conditions of pure competition. At least competition would be much more on a price basis.

Conclusions

Monopoly is not necessarily an evil; it may be the only form of organization under which low costs can be achieved, but usually it requires some form of government effort to see that the benefits of monopoly accrue to the public. Neither large nor small business has any claim to virtue or deserves to be designated as vice. Each has fields to which it is most economically suited. Where small business is actually most efficient it will probably continue to survive without help. In many industries where there are small "special orders" as well as large markets for standard goods, small firms may survive in the same industry with large firms. If there exist any sentimental worries about what will happen to the small businessman in those fields destined for large-scale organization, he may be pictured in the place where he probably will arrive, as the minor executive in a large corporation. On the average his salary might be expected to be greater than his earnings as an independent businessman. A comparison of the executive employment records of large corporations with Dun and Bradstreet's records of the percentage of small business failures would likely show that he would be more secure with the corporation than working for himself.

For the present our best course would be to allow each industry to adopt the form that is best suited to it (possibly preventing cutthroat competition and piracy during the process), and then to attempt to secure the maximum benefits for the public from that best form. For large noncompetitive business, some degree of price regulation may prove necessary. For small businesses (and to some extent for larger ones), active efforts to force competition on to a price basis may prove to be the solution.

CHAPTER IX

International Economic Policy[1]

BEFORE we can discuss international economic policy we must have in mind some standard of what constitutes national well-being. In these times of depression-warped thinking, it is necessary to reiterate so simple and obvious a truth that the wealth of any country increases only as the quantity of goods which it possesses. The debts which are owed to us by foreigners can be added to this total only to the extent that they can be converted into foreign goods which may be consumed by our people.

We tend to confuse ourselves by thinking of national wealth and national income in the same terms we use for the short-cut calculation of the wealth or income of an individual, that is, in terms of money. When we speak of a man with $1,000,000 in the bank or invested in bonds, we consider him as very well-to-do. In reality this consideration rests upon the knowledge we have of the goods that one million dollars will buy at present prices. If, however, goods were so scarce (or dollars so plentiful) that a cup of coffee sold for $10,000 and a piece of pie for $20,000, we would regard our millionaire as a poor man. The same short-cut thinking exists with respect to changes in wealth. If a grocer buys a stock of goods for

---

[1] This chapter is based primarily on Haberler, Gottfried, *Principles of International Trade,* The Macmillan Co., New York, 1936; Williams, John H., "The Adequacy of Existing Currency Mechanisms," *American Economic Review,* March 1937, pp. 151 ff.; and the teachings of Professor Machlup.

$500 and then sells them for $1,000, we consider that he has done very well for himself. If immediately after he received payment, however, the government should happen to repudiate its currency, his $1,000 will be worthless and he will be regretting that he did not keep his groceries for himself to eat or to barter for shoes and clothes.

We can keep our thinking clearer on the subject of foreign trade if we will occasionally have reference to what Professor Taussig has called "the barter terms of trade." We may then see readily that if, in exchange for an export of 10,000 automobiles, we receive 1,000,000 pounds of coffee or 1,000,000 pounds of rubber, we are much better off than if we received only 500,000 pounds of these articles. The lower the price of foreign goods (in comparison with our own cost of production for the same product), the greater will be our gain from foreign trade. If as a nation we had the economic intelligence of a six-year-old child (who always likes to get more candy for his penny), we would welcome an influx of "low-priced foreign goods" instead of holding up our hands in horror and slapping on tariffs whenever this occurs.

"Buy American"

In these days of economic maladjustment, certain people who are honestly ignorant and others who are attempting to bolster markets for their own overpriced goods are attempting, in every country, to make capital of the slogans, "Buy American," "Buy British," "Buy Italian," and so on. The appeal is to "Keep your money at home" and to "Employ your own workmen." The spread of this idea may eventually lead people to see the absurdity of its own logical conclusion: "Buy in your own State," "Buy in your home town," "Buy in your local neighborhood." The logical end would be, "Don't buy from anybody but yourself." Those who insist that keeping out foreign goods is the way to employ American workmen must explain to us why the depression ever occurred when tariffs, which were already high, were increased steadily from 1920 to 1932.

Economic Nationalism

As threats of war make their chronic appearance, nation after nation begins to toy with the idea of making itself self-sufficient in time of war. The United States is probably better equipped to do this than any other country, unless it be Russia. Let us make some wild guesses as to what it might cost us to achieve self-sufficiency. We now import about six billion pounds of sugar annually (not counting receipts from Hawaii and Puerto Rico). To produce this additional quantity of sugar on the American mainland might easily cost us 10 cents per pound more than we now pay for the imported sugar, or let us say, a total $600,000,000. We now import about 1.2 billion pounds of rubber. To produce this quantity of synthetic rubber (even if it were as good as the natural) might cost us about 15 cents per pound more than the imported product or, roughly $180,000,000. In 1936 our wool imports were about 370 million pounds, and in the war years of 1918 and 1919 they were 420 million pounds. If it cost us only 10 cents per pound additional to produce this ourselves, another $42,000,000 would be added to our bill for self-sufficiency. We have already run the bill up close to one billion dollars per year without mentioning coffee, tea, tin, manganese, and nitrate of soda. Even if we were assured of a war, it would be cheaper to build a naval and air force capable of defending our commerce against any nation or combination of nations, rather than to attempt to produce these products for ourselves. To the extent that vast amounts of most of these imports come from British territory, England would be nearly as interested in protecting these shipments as we would ourselves.

Even though perfect self-sufficiency is an impossibility, intensive efforts towards even partial self-sufficiency may be contributing causes to world economic depression and possibly to war itself. As a result of the World War and of the postwar tariffs we have made ourselves independent of the German chemical and optical instrument industries. Our curtailment or cessation of these and other imports from Germany helped to deprive the Germans of the purchasing power with which they formerly bought from us 300 million pounds of pork products, 200 million pounds of tobacco, 2 million bales of cotton, 80 million pounds of dried fruits, 40 million pounds of rice, and large quantities of other products. Thus, we have contributed, at least in a small way, to the distressed conditions in Germany, which in their eruption spewed Hitler into power.

The Balance of Trade

In the long run, the value of a country's exports to the rest of the world must be equal to its imports from the rest of the world. It must be remembered that exports and imports include not only physical goods but also the so-called "invisible items" in the balance of trade: that is, shipping and insurance services performed by foreigners (or by us for foreigners), tourist expenditures, immigrant remittances to relatives in the home country, and similar items. For gold-producing countries, gold itself may be considered simply as one commodity exported.

Note that the only balance which has any significance is the balance between one country and *all other countries;* to compare the balance of trade between any two countries is an idle statistical trick, utterly without meaning. We may regularly import a greater value of goods from England than we export to her; at the same time, however, our exports to Canada exceed our Canadian imports, while simultaneously,

Canadian exports to England exceed Canadian imports from England. To look simply at the "balance" with England and to say that because it is "unfavorable" we must take measures to import less from England, is to ignore the fact that this would be the simplest and surest way to destroy Canadian purchasing power and so to reduce our exports to Canada. A retail coal dealer always has an "unfavorable" balance of trade with the mineowner from whom he buys his coal, whereas he always has a "favorable" balance of trade with his retail customers. He would be properly contemptuous if told that it was wrong for him to buy more coal from the mineowner than he sold to him. It would not be necessary for us to belabor this obvious truth were it not for the fact that the spread of "bilateralism" is evidence that those entrusted with the foreign trade policy of various nations are apparently still ignorant of it.

Purchasing Power Parity

We are all familiar with the fact that the price of a transportable commodity in New York cannot for any great length of time exceed the price of the same commodity in Chicago by more than the cost of transportation. Exactly the same situation exists between two different countries. Where a tariff is in existence we may consider it simply as a part of the transportation cost. Only one more factor need be introduced: In order to compare a foreign price with a domestic price we must *translate* the foreign price into terms of our own money. To do this we multiply the foreign price by the rate of exchange.

Whenever the foreign price of a commodity, plus transportation costs, is lower than the domestic price, the commodity will tend to be imported. Whenever the domestic price of a commodity, plus transportation costs, is lower than the foreign price, the commodity will tend to be exported. Transportation costs may be higher in one direction than in the other, particularly if one country has a duty on the commodity and the other has not, or if one country's duty is higher than the other. Also, if the general volume of traffic happens to be greater in one direction than it is in the other, transportation companies may offer lower freight rates on "return loads." We may readily see that each commodity has an "export point" and an "import point."

In its simplest form the above reasoning applies only to those commodities that may be transported easily. Some writers on international trade have laid great stress on the difference between what they call "international commodities" and "domestic commodities." According to them, international commodities are those which may be shipped easily from one country to another. They would classify as domestic commodities houses, hotels, personal services, and any goods or services whose nature requires that they be used in the place where they are located. To this group some authors would add those goods whose shipping costs are so high that they are not ordinarily transported for any great distance (obviously this is a mere difference of degree and the distinction loses most of its force between two markets in different countries which happen to be just across the border from each other).

Further reflection will show that this distinction between so-called domestic and international commodities does not introduce as much qualification to our doctrine as would appear offhand, even in the case of goods which are physically incapable of transport. The distinction has force only when one, or a very few, of the so-called domestic goods are differently priced in different countries. Houses may be incapable of movement, but let any considerable number of the prices which make up the "cost of living" be much lower in one country than in another and *people can and do move* temporarily or semi-permanently to take advantage of the difference.

One of the best examples of this occurred when the Canadian rate of exchange was such that an American dollar was worth $1.20 in Canadian money. Since Canadian prices had not risen, this was roughly equivalent to a 20 percent lower cost of living in Canada. Large numbers of workmen from Buffalo, New York, rented homes in Fort Erie, Ontario, just across the river and drove back and forth across the bridge to their work in Buffalo.

In cases such as this, the significant factor which must be over-balanced by the price difference is not the cost of transportation of goods but the cost of transportation of people. In the above example the cost was extremely low, being merely the toll on the Peace Bridge (in many cases the distance traveled to work was actually less than before). Even where the two countries are separated by a long ocean voyage, the principle is still applicable. Low living costs in a foreign country will tend to induce more tourist travel and, perhaps even more important, will tend to induce those who intended to travel anyway to prolong their trip and thus to consume more of the low-priced goods and services. Meanwhile, apartment and hotel owners in the tourists' home country, confronted with vacancies, will tend to lower their high rents and the difference in living costs narrows or disappears.

We can readily see then that, if we are concerned with differences in prices of any large number of commodities, such as might be occasioned by exchange rates or the currency policy of one country or another, the distinction between domestic and international commodities is without much meaning. We can, perhaps, raise the presumption that the so-called international commodities will respond more rapidly to price differences (greater than the cost of transportation) than will the so-called domestic commodities.

There are a few ways in which a country can divorce or partially isolate its own price system from that of the rest of the world: (1) by an absolute prohibition of imports plus a law forbidding its citizens to leave the country (this would soon result in zero exports); (2) by duties which are prohibitive, not merely "protective." This will be effective only so long as prices do not diverge from foreign prices by more than the amount of the duty and other transport costs. To be thoroughly effective this method would also require prohibition of foreign travel; (3) by a system of import quotas. This is a partial method. The closer the quota approaches the amount which would be imported in a free market, the less will be the amount of divergence between domestic and foreign price; (4) by "rationing" foreign exchange. This has much the same effect as import quotas. We shall have occasion to discuss some of these schemes later. At present it is sufficient for us to note that, even if complete purchasing power parity is not always actually in effect, it requires very drastic measures to prevent the prices in one country from influencing those in another.

Price Stability versus Exchange Stability

In the field of domestic and international currency either the government or the banking system must adopt a policy. The government either regulates the quantity of money itself, or allows the banks to do so, or lays down regulations which will govern the quantity of currency that the banks may issue under various circumstances. Changes in the quantity of money are extremely important in causing changes in domestic prices, in exchange rates, and in the volume of imports and exports.

There is considerable difference of opinion among economists as to whether a "stable price level" is a desirable or even a possible means of increasing the stability of the economic system in general (assuming stability to be a desired end).

For the moment, let us sidestep this argument and assume that we are committed to a policy of trying to attain "price stability." We are immediately confronted with a dilemma: "price stability," "exchange rate stability," and "stability of industrial output" are mutually contradictory in a country which maintains any commercial connections with the rest of the world.

Let us see how this works. Assume that two countries which are trading with each other make no attempt to regulate their domestic prices and that the only material banking regulation is that the banks in each country are required to maintain a specified minimum reserve ratio against their deposits. What follows is equally applicable whether both countries are on a gold standard, both on a paper standard, or one on a gold and the other on a paper standard. Assume now that country A has a balance of payments[2] flowing to it from country B (perhaps because A's exports to B exceed its imports, or because the people in B are buying securities on the stock exchange in A, or for any other reason).

In this situation there will be an amount of bills of exchange[3] drawn on people in country B and offered for sale in A which exceeds the amount of the requirements of people in A who have payments to make to B. The banks in A will buy this surplus foreign exchange, thus putting more money (usually created deposit credit) into circulation in A. In consequence, prices in A will start to rise. Since the supply of foreign exchange is a temporary surplus which the banks will have to hold as a balance in a foreign bank until they can resell it, they will not be willing to pay as high a price for bills of exchange as they would at a time when foreign payments and receipts were equal. In other words, the rate of exchange falls somewhat.

[2] See Meyers, Albert L., *Elements of Modern Economics,* Ch. XX, Prentice-Hall, Inc., New York, 1938.
[3] *Ibid.*

What is happening in country B at the same time? The bills of exchange are sent over to the banks in B for collection and deposit to the credit of the A banks, that is, individual deposits belonging to people in B are reduced and deposits to the credit of the A banks are increased. But since the banks in A have bought more bills of exchange than they have sold, this excess will not be drawn upon and will become an idle deposit. Thus idle bank deposits have replaced some active bank deposits in B, and we may say that the velocity of circulation of money has decreased, or that money previously in circulation has been absorbed into idle cash balances. The decreased effective quantity of money in B will tend to cause prices to fall.

Thus we have three factors at work: (1) higher prices in A, (2) lower prices in B, and (3) a lower price of B's money in terms of A's money (that is, a lower exchange rate). All three of these operate to cause people in A to buy more goods from B (or to spend their vacations in B). At the same time, since money in B will buy much more at home than it will abroad, people in B will tend to buy more home-produced and less foreign goods, thus decreasing imports.

If no other conditions are changed, increased demand for B's goods will cause prices in B to rise, decreased demand for A's goods will cause prices in A to fall, and increased demand for bills of exchange in A (to pay for increased imports from B) will cause the rate of exchange to rise again. These forces will continue to operate until the balance of payments is equal and purchasing power parity is regained.

We see that the "impact" of the fluctuation has been "split three ways": Prices in A have fluctuated a little; prices in B have fluctuated a little; the exchange rate has fluctuated somewhat. Notice that the word "gold" has not been mentioned in our explanation. The process that was outlined could have taken place without an ounce of gold in existence. This is what may happen when two countries on the paper standard follow "the rules of the game."

Now let us suppose that, instead of the above situation, the authorities in country A decide that it is desirable to have a "stable price level." They would regard the influx of payments from B with alarm and attempt to prevent its influence in causing prices to rise. This might be done by: (1) raising the discount rate (this tends to make it less attractive for businessmen to borrow from the banks and so results in less creation of deposits); (2) raising the reserve ratio required for banks (if the actual ratio is about equal to the new legal ratio, this prevents any further expansion of deposits); (3) selling government bonds in the open market in an amount equal to the payments from B and holding the money received from the sale as an idle balance (these practices are sometimes called "sterilization" of capital imports although the term is used more often in connection with gold imports).

The failure of prices to rise in A means that this source of increased demand for imports (and restraint on exports) is not present as it was in the first situation discussed. This means that the rate of exchange will have to fall further and/or the prices in B will have to fall further in order to bring about the increased imports to A and the decreased exports from A which is necessary to equalize the balance of payments. Thus the "stable price level" in A is achieved at the expense of *greater fluctuation* in the exchange rates and in B's price level.

A further complication may be noted. If the restrictive measures adopted to bring about "stabilization" in A have the effect (as they may easily have) of raising the interest rate in A above that prevailing in B, this will tend to attract short-term capital from B to A thus increasing the flow of "hot money"[4] which A must "sterilize" in order to prevent a price rise. If this happens, the fall in the exchange rate and/or in B's prices which is necessary to equalize the balance of payments will be still greater.

Now let us suppose that, instead of A, it is country B (the country making the payment) which has a price stabilization policy. We remember that, according to the "rules of the game," B's currency should contract and its prices fall in order to restore the balance of payments. Under a stabilization policy, however, the monetary authorities would attempt to prevent this fall in prices and would deliberately expand the amount of money in circulation. The methods might be: (1) lowering the discount rate; (2) lowering reserve requirements; (3) purchasing government bonds in the open market; (4) issuing new paper money.

To the extent that the price decline is prevented, this source of stimulus to exports and discouragement of imports will not be present as it would be if B followed the "rules of the game." Consequently, it will be necessary for the exchange rate to fall still lower and/or the price level in A to rise still higher if the balance of payments is to be restored. Under these circumstances, a "stable" domestic price level in B is really "inflationary" when the international situation is considered.

Another complicating circumstance may be noted. Under our "rules," a country that is making greater foreign payments than it receives should contract its currency circulation. This (particularly if the discount rate is raised) will tend to cause a rise in the market rate of interest. Ordinarily, this will tend to be an inducement to the investment of funds by foreigners and the movement of these funds will contribute a part toward the restoration of the balance of pay-

---

[4] Imports of short-term capital which may cause inflation and then be withdrawn causing deflation.

ments. Just the reverse may occur if the country expands its currency when our "rules" require currency contraction. If people begin to fear that the expansion is a prelude to further inflation, there may be a "flight of capital" from the country. Under such circumstances we may say that the "money flows up hill" (that is, it flows in a direction opposite to that indicated by the longer trend), and temporarily the adverse balance of payments is increased. (Widespread misunderstanding has prevailed on this point. Even some finance ministers have argued that their inflation was occasioned by an "unfavorable" balance of payments, failing to see that the inflation itself was the prime cause of the continuing adverse balance.)

If *both* country *A* and country *B* are following a policy of domestic price stabilization, the full burden of correcting the balance of payments will fall upon the exchange rate. In consequence, the exchange rate must fall extremely low. It is quite probable that the rate may fall temporarily to a point far below that necessary to restore the balance. In our case (page 209) the banks in *A* were quite willing to buy exchange on *B* at rates only slightly lower than those previously prevailing, because they knew that two powerful factors (*A*'s price rise and *B*'s price decline) were operating to increase the future demand for foreign exchange. When the rate of exchange itself is the only factor which may be expected to cause increased imports to *A,* however, the banks either will not buy foreign exchange at all or they will buy only at rates so low that they feel assured they will not lose in carrying foreign balances for a long time.

Violently fluctuating exchange rates make it extremely difficult to carry on *both* import and export business. It becomes unwise to make commitments in terms of foreign currency even for the length of time required to ship goods, to say nothing of the time required to manufacture them. The export industries may then suffer from a severe amount of unemployment which will have an adverse effect on general business conditions throughout the country.

Exchange Stabilization

Now let us consider a situation in which neither country is attempting domestic price stabilization, but instead the exchange rate is held rigidly at a fixed point. This was roughly the case in prewar times between two countries on a full gold standard.[5] It is a mistake to say that the rate of exchange did not fluctuate in those times; it did fluctuate, but only within the relatively narrow limits set by the gold points. A fluctuation of 4 cents in the dollar-sterling rate of exchange, for example, amounted to only about one percent in the value of the pound.

Where rigid, or very narrowly fluctuating, exchange rates prevail, the full burden of corrective action must be borne by the price structures of the different countries. It is also urged by some writers that stable exchange rates tend to bring about the result that inflation or deflation in one country becomes "internationally contagious" and spreads to other countries. In general, it may be said that it is difficult to see how any country can reap the advantages of international trade without being subject, at least in some measure, to influences resulting from changing business conditions in the countries with which it trades. We can still concede, however, that exchange rates which are allowed to find their own level, without active regulation by the monetary authorities, will result in less disturbance to *prices* in other countries resulting from inflation or deflation by any one country.

[5] See Meyers, Albert L., *Elements of Modern Economics*, Ch. XX.

Exchange Stabilization Plus Price Stabilization in Both Countries

Now let us assume that both A and B are following a policy of stabilizing their domestic price levels and also that the exchange is being "pegged" at a fixed rate. Let us also assume that there is an excess flow of payments from B to A, due to the fact that the fixed prices in B are too high relatively to the fixed prices in A. Note that the excess flow of payments will tend to continue so long as the prices in the two countries are "frozen" (stabilized) at their artificial levels. There will be some difference in the mechanics, depending upon whether it is country A or country B which is exercising an active effort to peg the exchange rate.

If country A pegs the rate, it will do so by buying bills of exchange on B at a price above that which would prevail in a free market. Bills of exchange will also be sold at the same fixed price. Under our assumption of fixed price levels in the two countries (and with B's prices too high relatively to A's prices), the amount of bills of exchange which the A Government Exchange Stabilization Fund will have to purchase will always be in excess of the amount which can be sold at the pegged rate. Thus the stabilization fund will be taking a steady loss on its transactions, a loss which can never be recovered until something is done to decrease exports from A and/or to increase imports from B. That is, something must be done to increase the demand or to decrease the supply of bills of exchange. One possibility suggests itself: If A has had high tariffs, it may repeal or reduce them in order to encourage imports and so to stimulate the demand for exchange. We must not ignore the other complicating circumstances which will be present. Due to A's efforts to prevent a price rise, we have seen that the market rate of interest in A will tend to rise. At the same time, due to the exchange control, a unit of B's money will exchange for a greater number of units of A's money for the purpose of investment in A than if the rate of exchange were allowed to seek its own level. We thus have two influences, a higher interest rate and a higher exchange rate, both operating to cause capital movements from B to A. This will increase tremendously the amount of surplus foreign exchange which the Stabilization Fund will have to buy. Unless the Stabilization Fund is to go bankrupt, certain drastic measures, perhaps even in addition to tariff reductions, may be necessary, such as: (1) a prohibitive tax on capital imports, and (2) a prohibition of exports, and (3) refusal to allow tourists from B to enter the country.

Rather than adopt such drastic measures, country A would be quite likely to give up attempting to control domestic prices or to abandon exchange control, or to abandon both price control and exchange control. Note, however, that during the time the controls are in effect, the artificial difference in prices may stimulate the export industries in A to expand to a point which cannot be maintained when controls are relaxed. This expansion will tend to draw some resources away from their more usual employment in "domestic" industries. Thus we can have unwise expansion and maladjusted production even with, or perhaps we should say because of, a stable price level.

Now let us assume that it is B instead of A which is trying to control the exchange rate under the same circumstances (stable prices in both countries and an excess balance of payments from B to A, price level in B being held too high relatively to A's price level). In country B, the pegged price of bills of exchange drawn against A will be below the price which would prevail in a free market. The government will have to issue orders that all foreign exchange must be sold to the Stabilization Fund at the fixed price. Since this price for bills will be below that which importers could obtain by selling the bills of exchange directly to importers, there will be many attempts to evade the regulation and even "Black Bourses" (bootleg exchange markets) may be set up. Even more difficult to detect and stop will be the practice by exporters of collecting their debts in A and of investing the funds in A without resorting to exchange transactions. To ensure that the total available supply of foreign exchange passes through the hands of the fund at the fixed price will require a thorough policing and espionage of everyone likely to have foreign exchange transactions. (This is much the same as the situation which prevails in Germany at present.) Even if the exchange control authorities obtain possession of all available foreign exchange, they will not have enough to satisfy the needs of all those who would like to purchase exchange at the pegged rate. Consequently the exchange will have to be rationed and each buyer given a quota which he may purchase.[6] Since foreign sellers are not likely to be willing to give long term credits under these circumstances, rationing of exchange practically amounts to an import quota system. At first the quota basis may be set up as a simple percentage of past exchange requirements. This, however, will make a serious reduction in the imports of basic raw materials and the government will likely be driven into the practice of determining which imports are "essential" and which are "nonessential," exchange being issued only to importers of the "essential" goods. The country will then have to produce for itself, at higher costs, many of the goods which it formerly imported. Its resources will thus be economically misdirected. Note that the two chief stimuli to exports (a falling price level and a rising foreign exchange rate) have been deliberately foregone as a matter of policy. Consequently, the only hope of country B to restore the balance

---

[6] The success of the British Stabilization Fund without resort to quotas has been possible because the rate of exchange has *not* been pegged. The policy of the Board has not been to prevent normal movements of the exchange rate but rather to try to offset erratic fluctuations due to speculation and temporary panic. Even so, it was found necessary in May, 1939, to adopt the rather mild device of requesting British brokers not to quote prices on American securities.

of payments is through reduced imports. This means a lower standard of living for its people than would have prevailed had the exchange and price controls not been in effect.

General Aspects of Stabilization

The more naïve school of domestic price stabilizers is simply opposed to price declines and rather welcomes rises in the "general price level." The extreme form of this doctrine is found in the slogan, "Reflate prices to the 1926 level and then stabilize." More sophisticated advocates of stabilization are opposed to price rises, as well as price declines, from monetary causes, primarily because they believe that price rises induced by money and credit expansion are almost certain to result in drastic deflation. Even though we hold the latter viewpoint, we may still raise the question whether all changes in the price level occasioned by changes in international payments are of the same nature as changes caused by either deliberate or un-controlled monetary policy.

First, let us drop the assumption of only two countries trading with each other. This does no harm to any of the propositions we developed above. When we are examining conditions in country A, we now substitute "the rest of the world" wherever we formerly mentioned country B. Likewise, when we are examining conditions in B, "the rest of the world" becomes a synonym for country A. Both countries are now selling to, buying from, and making and receiving payments from, many other countries. Country A will now have an excess inflow of payments only when payments from the rest of the world exceed payments by A to the rest of the world. Country B will have an excess outflow of payments only when payments to the rest of the world exceed payments from the rest of the world. One important new circumstance is introduced: Each country's exports are now selling *in competition with similar products of other countries,* except for those few products on which the country may have a monopoly.

Now let us re-examine the situation in country *B* if it follows the rules of the game and allows its currency to contract and its prices to fall when it has an excess outflow of international payments. This procedure means a fall in costs and a fall in prices for its export goods. Since the country is in competition with other countries, we may raise the presumption that the elasticity of demand for most of its export goods is far greater than unity. Thus the fall in prices relatively to those of other countries will result in a great increase in volume of sales of export goods. (Other countries presumably will not be able to sell the same volume of goods at the lower prices as they formerly did because they have not had the *benefit* of a fall in costs due to a currency contraction.) The expansion in the export industries will call for a greatly increased volume of employment in those industries. This may not only offset other tendencies towards unemployment but, if the elasticity of demand for exports is great enough, it may re-employ many of those who previously happened to be out of work. Thus the chief bogeyman (deflationary unemployment) feared by opponents of a falling price level is not present in this situation. The beneficial effects of the falling price level may be seriously impaired, however, if the importing countries foolishly impose *new* higher tariffs in order to deprive themselves of the benefit of more goods at lower prices. This points to one advantage of "trade agreements" which bind duties at existing rates, or at specified maximum rates.

Now let us re-examine the situation in country *A*, assuming that it follows the rules of the game and allows its currency to expand when an excess inflow of foreign payments occurs. The chief danger that the stabilizers foresee is a temporary over-expansion of domestic industry which cannot be maintained when the flow of excess payments ceases or is reversed. We have seen that a simple attempt to prevent price rises may result in a continued inflow of foreign short-term investment funds. The "undesirable" expansion could be avoided more easily if the expanded purchasing power were *directed* to the purchase of imported goods. Insofar as the "new money" is spent for imported goods: (a) no temporary rise in domestic prices will take place, and (b) the balance of payments will tend to be restored by the increased demand for foreign exchange. The most appropriate means of accomplishing this end would be to empower the stabilization authority, *not* to sterilize foreign payments, but rather to make at least temporary tariff reductions whenever an excess inflow of payments occurs.

International Capital Movement and Foreign Investment

The type of foreign loan which results in the greatest advantage both to the country which makes the loan and to the country that receives it is a loan to improve the productive process in some product which the borrowing country is best fitted to produce. A good example of such an investment might be the building of a railroad in some Central American country which will lower the cost of transportation of bananas to the seacoast. The saving in cost will provide a means by which the Central American country can pay the interest on the loan at no sacrifice to itself and may very well be large enough to provide additional income above the interest charges. The people in the United States, on the other hand, will benefit by being able to obtain a greater quantity of bananas at a lower price than before. It is not necessary, of course, for the entire amount of the interest to be paid in bananas. As a result of the lower price, the Central American country may sell more bananas to England and then use bills of exchange on England as a means of interest payment. We may then use the English bills of exchange to obtain more good woolen cloth.

The type of foreign investment from which both the home and the foreign country profit least is the setting up of foreign "branch factories" behind a foreign tariff wall. Thus we put "protective" tariffs on Canadian lumber and paper and mineral products. In return, Canada puts a protective tariff on American automobiles. In consequence, we find Canadian branches of American automobile companies established just across the river from Detroit in Sarnia and Windsor, Ontario. Unit costs in the American factories are thus made higher than if the entire output were produced in them and costs in the Canadian branch factories are much higher because the smaller market does not permit full utilization of mass production methods. Capital and labor both in Canada and the United States are misdirected to less productive uses as a result of the mutual tariff wall.

Short-term foreign loans by a country which has an excess inflow of payments to a country which has a purely temporary (perhaps a seasonal) deficit in its balance of payments may be a means of avoiding unnecessary fluctuations in exchange rates and prices. Movements of capital from a country with a deficit balance of payments to a country with an excess inflow of payments are movements in the "wrong direction," usually representing a "flight of capital." Such movements can best be avoided by the discontinuance by the deficit country of the inflationary policies which cause the flight of capital. From the point of view of the country which receives the "fleeing capital," this is the type of payment about which the strongest argument for "sterilization" can be made. Since most of this capital will return to its own country as soon as the "scare" passes, it cannot be safely used as a basis of expansion by the country which gives it temporary custody.

Reciprocal Trade Agreements

Although it contains some elements of bilateralism, the reciprocal trade agreements program represents the first attempt at a return to sanity in American tariff policy in nearly twenty years. Under the program, this country negotiates treaties with other countries in which we give duty reductions on certain of their products in return for duty reductions on some of our exports to them.

Some curious features may be noted in the negotiation of these treaties. We are already bound by "most favored nation" treaties with many other countries whereby we are compelled to give them the same duty reductions as we give to any country under the new trade agreements. If we were not careful, each duty concession which we gave under the new treaties might seriously impair our bargaining power to negotiate other trade agreements with countries already on a "most favored nation" status. One way of avoiding this which the negotiators have used is to grant concessions on those products only of which the other country making the agreement is the principal supplier to us. In negotiating the British Trade Agreement, the Committee has gone even farther than this and introduced "price brackets" in order to avoid giving the same concessions to Japan as we are giving to England until Japan is also willing to make an agreement with us. Thus the duty was reduced on high-priced fishing rods, which England supplies, and no duty reduction was made on low-priced fishing rods, which come from Japan.

Protests Against the Trade Agreements

Each time the Trade Agreements Committee has a duty concession under consideration, the domestic manufacturers in the industry flock to Washington to protest against "the loss of invested capital" which they say will result and the trade union leaders trot dutifully along to protest against "the loss of jobs when American factories shut down." Let us consider the merit of these protests.

It is extremely unlikely that any real capital will be lost. Plant and equipment will continue to be operated so long as the price of the product is above marginal variable cost. Since few duties constitute more than 50 percent of the selling price of the product, it is extremely unlikely that even complete abolition of the duty would reduce the price below the variable cost level. Stockholders would lose dividends and bondholders might lose some part of their interest, but the plant would continue to be operated till it wore out. The loss to stock- and bondholders is offset by the gain to all consumers of the product. National income is not reduced, it is merely distributed differently.

How about labor? If plants are operated till they wear out, this will mean a period of ten or twenty years during which labor may shift into the expanding export industries which increase output as a result of tariff concessions gained from other countries. Meanwhile, the real income of all labor will be increasing as a result of the lower prices resulting from each tariff concession.

These results will follow even under the worst possible assumption, that is, that all firms are forced out of the industry in the long run as plant wears out. Far more likely, however, only the most inefficient firms will be forced out of competition and the others will continue to operate indefinitely at somewhat reduced profits.

The Gain from Trade Agreements

The unthinking observer will attempt to measure the gain from trade agreements solely in terms of increased exports. As a matter of fact, we will gain both from increased exports and increased imports; the greater gain will come through increased imports. Imports should increase more than exports in order to add to the real wealth and real income of the country. We are now "swapping" one $40 vacuum cleaner for about 100 pounds of sugar. Perhaps, when we have more agreements, we may be able to swap two vacuum cleaners for 250 pounds of sugar.

CHAPTER X
Problems of Organized Labor

SOME unions have as their avowed, or tacitly understood, purpose the overthrow of the capitalist system and its replacement by some other social and economic organization under which they think the position of labor will be better. Our interest in such unions is not in the union itself but rather in the economic plan which it advocates. We shall consider some of these plans in later chapters. Our present concern is with *business unionism,* that is, with labor organization which attempts to secure for itself better wages, hours, and working conditions within the framework of the capitalist system. It must not, however, be inferred that business unionism and revolutionary unionism are mutually exclusive classifications. Many unions which have started with revolutionary aims and which still pay at least lip service to their stated ideals have turned for all practical purposes into first-rate collective bargaining agencies. Other unions which are ostensibly business unions may actually be devoting most of their thought and effort towards changing the economic system. Almost invariably, as unions succeed in making gains for their members through business unionism, they tend to soft-pedal or lose sight of their revolutionary objectives.

It may be noted in passing that, in America, revolutionary ideals have not come spontaneously from the ranks of labor itself. They have come, rather, from "intellectuals" who have attempted to imbue the labor movement with their own zeal for reform. The utter failure of most intellectuals to understand the mind of labor is responsible for their lack of success. The average intellectual reasons somewhat in this fashion: "The present system is wrong. My plan will improve it. Who suffers most under the present system? Obviously it is the workers. Therefore they should embrace my program with open arms." Then he is bitterly disappointed when the election returns roll in. Actually the American worker is much more interested in personal advancement for himself or for his children. Free or cheap land, free public education, and a rapidly expanding industry have contributed to what Professor Perlman calls "opportunity consciousness." [1] Even though the statistical odds may have been against him, the worker has thought and *acted* as if opportunity for advancement were present for his children if not for himself. The naïve faith in "the value of education" is evidence of this. Where the worker has been motivated to group thought and action it has most often been in the interests of those in his own trade or craft or of fellow employees in the same factory or industry. Even then, such interests have centered mainly on "more benefits here and now." The "raise" in the pay envelope secured by business unionism is real and tangible as compared to vague hopes for a better status for labor under some other system a generation or two in the future. Consequently, we have the amusing statement by the intellectuals that "the American worker must be *taught* class consciousness." Class consciousness is a product of the environment and probably cannot be *taught*. If unemployment continues long and widespread or if our system fails to provide a better status for all labor and not simply for a few skilled trades, then we may expect class consciousness to arise by itself. Until then, it is

---

[1] Perlman, Selig, *A Theory of the Labor Movement,* The Macmillan Co., New York, 1928.

idle to expect an American worker to think and feel like a European worker who has been "born to his class" and who knows that his son will be born to the same class.

The Trade-Union or Craft Union

The trade-union or craft union is composed of the members of one particular skilled occupation. The large number of unions of this type is accounted for by the relative ease with which it can be organized. Workers in the same skilled trade can easily see the interests which they have in common and so may be persuaded to band together to protect and advance these common interests. The fact that a certain skill or training is involved makes it difficult for the employer to obtain strike-breakers in times of disputes and enhances the union bargaining power. If the training of apprentices is in the hands of union members, this may be used to prevent the development of nonunion competition in response to high wages. Only one, or at most a very few, wage rates need to be agreed upon by the members in order to present a common front to the employers. Wherever the workers in a skilled craft constitute only a small minority of an employer's total working force, an increase in their wages alone may result in only a small increase in total labor cost and consequently, such an employer may be persuaded fairly easily to make concessions rather than be forced to shut down his entire plant because of a strike by these "key men." Since the members of the union are generally on nearly the same intellectual level and have a common standard of living, internal friction due to jealousy is kept at a minimum.

Disadvantages of the Craft Union

The craft union is extremely vulnerable to technological changes in industry. New machines are often invented by which unskilled or semi-skilled workers can do the work formerly performed by skilled craftsmen. If a craft union attempts to prevent the introduction of the machines in present factories, competitive nonunion factories will be organized to use the machines.[2] High union wage rates in a particular craft may result in substitution of products or materials which have lower costs (substitution of poured concrete for brick or stone masonry, for example).

Another difficulty, which is partly the result of changing technology and partly inherent in the craft union type of organization, is that of jurisdictional disputes. A building contractor, for example, may have signed a contract with both the carpenters' union and the sheet-metal workers' union. He then gets a job erecting a building which has specifications calling for metal doors and doorframes. The carpenters' union insists that installing doorframes and hanging doors is carpenter work and should be done by them. The sheet-metal workers claim that the doors and frames are made out of sheet-metal and must be installed by their union. Each side threatens to strike if the work is given to the opposing union.

Strikes resulting from jurisdictional disputes have brought more discredit on the labor movement in the mind of the general public than any other single cause. When an employer signs a union contract, his labor troubles should be over for the duration of the contract so long as he keeps his side of the bargain in good faith. Note that in the long run, it is the union *officials* rather than the rank and file of the *membership* who have most at stake in a jurisdictional dispute. If the demand for sheet-metal work is increasing and the demand for carpentry decreasing, youths who are about to learn a trade may learn metal work rather than carpentry and even some of the carpenters may change their trade to that of sheet-metal work. If the number of union carpenters declines, however,

---

[2] See Meyers, Albert L., *Elements of Modern Economics,* p. 170, Prentice-Hall, Inc., New York, 1938.

the treasury of the carpenters' union will no longer be able to support union officials in "the style to which they have become accustomed." If there were but one industrial union embracing all building trades workers, the officials of such a union would not have such a personal stake in the result and would probably not tolerate a strike originating in a jurisdictional dispute between their own members.

In the past, organization upon trade or craft lines has left unorganized the vast majority of unskilled and semi-skilled labor. Consequently, as the craft unions raise wages, they are subject not only to the elasticity of substitution of capital for labor[3] but also to the elasticity of substitution of unskilled for skilled labor. (At least part of the saving in pre-fabricated houses results from the smaller amount of skilled labor which is required both in manufacture and in erection.)

The failure to organize the unskilled also accounts for the failure to organize a politically powerful labor party. It is true that the American Federation of Labor has always opposed the formation of such a party, but its attitude on this question might have been quite different if it had had twenty or thirty million members to vote instead of its two or three million skilled workers. Many of the reforms which the economic system has had to digest since 1933 might have come earlier and more gradually if labor had been better-organized politically in the past three or four decades.

Industrial Unionism

Industrial unions attempt to organize all workers in a given industry, regardless of their particular trade, occupation, or degree of skill. The industrial union is much better equipped to meet the problems of changing technology than is the craft union. Whether a job is performed by machine or by hand or by one trade or another, it still may be done by an industrial

---

[3] *Ibid.*, p. 170.

union member. As the industrial union may have a much larger membership than a craft union, it may be able to support its officials and pay for office expense upon the basis of a much smaller contribution per member. To the extent that it is able to organize an entire industry, it may be better able to prevent nonunion competition. If the union is able to call a strike of the employer's entire working force, skilled as well as unskilled, he is not apt to be able to run the plant with strike-breakers. With larger membership, the industrial unions will have greater political strength than the craft unions.

Disadvantages of Industrial Unionism

We have said that the industrial union is better equipped to handle jurisdictional disputes due to trade or craft differences. Such disputes center around the *definition* of the work of a trade or craft. As industrial unionism expands, it will begin to encounter jurisdictional disputes based upon the *definition of an industry*. Several possible bases for demarcation of the borderline between one industrial union and another may be suggested, but each is open to objections:

(1) Require that all those working for the same employer belong to the same union. In the case of the United States Steel Corporation, this would include mineworkers, who might more properly belong to a mineworkers' union, structural steel erectors, who should belong to a building trades industrial union, and railroad trainmen and seamen, who might be placed more appropriately in railroad and shipping unions.

(2) Require all workers making the same product to belong to the same union. In the case of electric refrigerators, such a union would include only part of the employees of General Motors, Nash-Kelvinator, General Electric Company, and only part of the employees of many kitchen equipment manufacturers.

(3) Require all workers using the same material to belong to the same union. In the case of leather, this would result in a conflict between the jurisdictions of a shoe and leather workers' union, an automobile workers' union, and a furniture and upholstery workers' union.

(4) Make the union co-extensive with any employers' or manufacturers' association in a particular field, for the purpose of presenting a united front in bargaining with such an association. Many manufacturers, however, who produce a variety of products, are members of more than one association. This basis would, in many cases, cut across all three of the other types of classification.

Two principles are involved in the selection of the proper basis of industrial union organization: (1) As far as possible, different employers should be kept on the same competitive basis in hiring and using union men to make products which are sold in competition with each other. (2) To secure solidarity, all workers in one factory should, as far as possible, belong to one union. As may be seen from the preceding discussion, even these two principles are not mutually exclusive.

No scheme of classification will be able to work without modifications in individual cases as questions arise. This suggests the need of a strong central organization governing all industrial unions which will have the power to make and *enforce* somewhat arbitrary decisions as to which union shall have the right to organize any particular group of workers whose status is in question. This will work more smoothly the more any one of our four bases is adhered to as the *primary* basis of classification, from which exceptions will be made in particular cases. The greatest danger of conflict lies in the possibility of the rapid organization of several different industrial unions, each with a different primary basis for membership. Whether the C.I.O. will be found capable of meeting these problems remains to be seen. The dismal failure of the

A. F. of L. to solve these questions accounts, in the main, for the growth of industrial unionism outside of, rather than within, the Federation.

Another very weighty problem which confronts each industrial union is the determination of *different* wage scales for workers of different skills within the union membership. So far this problem has been side-stepped by the newer industrial unions through the expedient of using the existing wage scales and simply demanding a 5 or 10 percent increase in pay for all workers. This dodge will not work forever. A great increase in demand for airplanes, for example, may result in an increased demand for toolmakers by the airplane industry. Then, unless toolmakers in the automobile industry are paid higher wages, they will shift to the airplane industry and automobile factories would have to close from lack of these skilled men. The automobile factories, however, will not be able to pay increases to all employees. Consequently, the automobile workers union will have to negotiate wage increases for the toolmakers but *not* for other employees. It is even quite conceivable that the automobile industry may already be paying as high a *total wage cost* as it can afford unless output and employment are reduced. In such circumstances, if the union wishes to keep all its members employed, it will have to negotiate wage *increases* for the toolmakers and wage *decreases* for other workers. Another circumstance which will force the union to consider wage differentials is the introduction of a new machine. Running the new machine is a new job and a new wage rate will have to be determined for it. If the wage on the new job is set too high in relation to the amount of skill required, other union members may become dissatisfied. If the wage is set too low, workers on the new job will be discontented and the machine may be introduced much more rapidly than necessary owing to the added incentive of lower wage cost. This does not imply that these problems are insoluble. (The Amalgamated Clothing Workers have done a first-rate job along these lines.) It does indicate, however, that if industrial unionism is to avoid the perils of internal dissention, it must have leaders with a sound economic knowledge of the business with which they are dealing and with sufficient statesmanship to make the rank and file of the workers accept their ideas. Leaders must be capable of saying "No" to unwarranted wage increases and of ordering wage reductions when necessary.

Union Wage Policy

In the early stages of their organization, most unions take the attitude that they are "fighting the battle of labor against exploitation by unscrupulous employers," and there are no doubt many situations in which this may represent the facts of the case. Because this attitude has a certain amount of dramatic appeal to the public it is also usually the favorite pose even of officials of a well-established union when they are being quoted by the press.

However, once the union has won its struggle for recognition and has become the bargaining agent for its members, it is actually in the *business of selling labor*.[4] Whether the union itself recognizes the situation or not, it is actually in much the same situation as a monopolist attempting to sell his product. The union may fix the price of labor, but it will then be the conditions of demand which determine the number of men who will be employed at that price.

In most cases, the demand for labor is a derived demand. Employers do not generally hire labor for its own sake but rather because the labor is capable of making some product which the public will buy. Thus the demand for labor is derived from the demand for the product. In any case, where it is possible to vary the proportions of capital and labor which

---

[4] See Schlicter, Sumner, *American Economic Review*, March 1939, pp. 121-137.

are used in making a product, the demand for labor, in the long run, will be more elastic than the demand for the product itself.

A source of possible confusion which may prevent the union from perceiving clearly the full implications of its wage policy is the fact that the short-period demand for a certain type of labor may be fairly inelastic while the long-run demand for the same labor is extremely elastic. The building trades offer a good example of this. Assume that a certain contractor has signed a contract to build a large apartment house. Such a contract usually provides a bonus if the building is completed ahead of the agreed date and a penalty for delayed completion. The contractor, therefore, is in a position where he may agree to considerable wage increases without cutting down his working force. Indeed, after a brief strike is settled, he may even hire more men than before in order to complete the job on time. He is in a position where he may have to forego his profits, or even take a small loss, in order to avoid a greater loss. On all future contracts, however, this contractor and all others dealing with the union will regard the new high wage scale as given cost data in setting their bids. The cost of building apartments and hotels may then be so high that it will be impossible to make a profit from their rents. No hotels or apartments will be built at such costs, and the vast majority of the building trades workers will then find themselves unemployed.

Only in the event that the elasticity of demand for a given type of labor is *less than unity* will it be possible for the entire group to benefit by a wage high enough to result in some unemployment. Under this circumstance, it might then be possible to assess dues upon those who are employed and pay out of work benefits to those who are unemployed. In any case, where the elasticity of demand for labor is greater than unity, total wages paid out will be less at a high wage than at a low wage. In such circumstances, any wage high enough to result in unemployment means a net loss to the union membership considered as a group. If all wages were pooled and then divided equally among the membership, both employed and unemployed, the effects would be apparent to everyone. In actual practice, the majority who remain employed will gain at the expense of the minority who are unable to find work.

There may be cases in which an industry is composed of a large number of efficient employers and a few very inefficient ones, who manage to stay in business because the general wage level in the industry is low. In such circumstances, a higher union wage level imposed on all employers would drive the inefficient ones out of competition. If the other employers were all operating under conditions of decreasing costs, they might then be able to absorb (even at the higher wage) all the employees who are laid off by the firms which fail. Cases like these are among the few in which minimum wage laws may benefit labor as a whole.

The position of the union official with respect to the wage problem is by no means a happy one. He may happen to understand the economics of the situation without being able to enforce his policies. Let us suppose that the wage scale is the highest which can prevail for the time being without resulting in serious unemployment. A rival for the office may then make political use of the situation, telling the members, "What has this fellow done for us? We haven't had a raise in two years. Put me in office and I'll see that we get action." The official is then faced with a situation where he must either convince the membership that the present wage is better policy than a higher one, or yield to pressure and fight for a higher wage which he believes will be injurious to the union's best interests, or lose his office to the rival who will fight for the higher wage.

Hours of Labor

Historically, we have witnessed the somewhat startling phenomenon of increased productivity per worker with a shorter working day. Not all of this increased productivity can be traced to the shorter day since new machinery and new methods have been introduced in many instances. There have, however, been many experiments in which, with the same machinery and methods, the length of the working day has been reduced from twelve to ten hours, or from ten to eight hours, with an actual increase in total output from the same labor force. Wherever increased productivity results from a decrease in hours, there is a clear gain both to the employer and to the worker.

We have probably approached the limits of such gains in many industries. Productivity *per hour* might still be increased through a shorter day, but it hardly seems reasonable to expect that a man will produce more in six hours than in seven or eight hours. Several factors are at work. The increased productivity of the eight-hour day over the twelve-hour day is largely accounted for by the proper amount of rest given by the eight-hour day. Once a worker has sufficient time to get the rest he needs, this source of possible increased productivity tends to be exhausted. It is also well-known that even in short working days the first and last hours are the least productive due to "getting into the swing" and "getting ready to stop." If the day is shortened from eight to six hours, these two hours become one-third of the total working time and productivity in the other hours would have to increase considerably to make up for them as well as for the two-hour decrease in the length of the day. It may still be the case, however, that many industries will find productivity increased by a reduction from a six-day forty-four-hour week to a five-day forty-hour week.

In many labor disputes we must be careful to distinguish between the demand for an actual shorter working day and a shorter "basic day." The latter is usually a demand for higher wages in disguise. The workers do not care to work shorter hours in such a case, but they want the overtime wage rates to begin at an earlier hour. Workers have sometimes struck for a shorter "basic day" and then have been very much disappointed when the employer shortened the length of the actual working day. One argument can be offered for the short basic day. It may be a means of making the employer pay higher wage rates in rush times when he can afford to do so, without compelling him to pay the same rate when work is slack. This will be the case, however, only when the actual day is the same length as the basic day in the slack seasons.

"Share the Work"

The shorter working week has recently been advocated as a means of relieving unemployment. It is open to serious question in this respect. In most cases, the employer cannot afford to pay the same wage for a shorter week, unless productivity is as great in the shorter week as in the longer one. If the productivity is as great, he will require no additions to his present working force to produce the same amount of product. If wages per week are reduced in proportion to the reduction in working time, this becomes a method of sharing the unemployment. If the week is reduced from forty to thirty hours, and the wage from $40 to $30, we may say that all workers who were formerly employed at forty hours are now 25 percent unemployed. However, it is by no means certain that in such a case the employer would hire 25 percent more men to make up for the reduced hours.

There are several reasons for this: In some cases the employer may be producing for stock in order to keep his working force employed. Such an employer would not be motivated to take on more workers by a reduction in hours. For every employer, the hiring of added men means an increase in expense for workmen's compensation insurance and an increase in payroll taxes for social security. If this happens to result in higher unit costs, the operating force will not be increased by a full 25 percent. The possible effect of shifts in demand may also affect the final result. Assume that WPA workers now receiving $20 a week are employed at $30 per week as a result of the shorter week. This represents an increase of $10 per week in their "purchasing power." Against this, we have a drop of $10 per week in the purchasing power of the workers who were already employed and whose wages decline from $40 to $30. The increase in demand of the first group will be concentrated mostly on "necessities," while the decreased demand of the second group will be mainly in the field of "comforts" and "luxuries." Whether total employment resulting from these opposite changes will increase, decrease, or remain unchanged, is difficult to prophesy.

Working Rules

Different unions have different working rules, varying from a few short and simple regulations to a long and complex document. We shall consider only some of the most common. As a union achieves a high wage scale, there is a tendency on the part of the employer to substitute lower-paid labor for union members wherever possible. Many union rules are drafted in an attempt to defeat this practice. For example, a rule may specify the number of apprentices or helpers which may be hired for each union man on the job. Other rules may specify very carefully the type of work which must be done by master craftsmen and that which may be done by apprentices or helpers. (A carpenter's helper may drive nails but must not use a saw, plane, or chisel.)

Another group of rules may deal with restriction of output: That is, that which constitutes a "day's work" is specified and no union member may exceed this performance. The original argument offered for such regulations is that they are designed to prevent the driving or "sweating" of workmen by the employer. In many cases, however, the amount of the "day's work" has been steadily reduced through other motives.

Both apprenticeship rules and restriction of output are usually the result of a very common fallacy in union reasoning, namely, the assumption that there is a fixed amount of work to be done. The idea is then that if each man does less work, or if the work is confined to master craftsmen as far as possible, there will be more jobs for union men. This idea is valid only if the demand for the product is *perfectly inelastic*. With any considerable amount of elasticity of demand for the product (as is more often the case in reality), these rules may have the effect of *decreasing* the employment of both union men and helpers. An example of this case may be helpful. Let us assume two different sets of cost figures for a five-room house, as follows:

	CASE I		CASE II
3 Union men	$1,500	6 Union men	$3,000
9 Helpers	900	6 Helpers	600
Materials	1,600	Materials	1,600
Total cost	$4,000	Total cost	$5,200

If conditions of demand for these houses are such that 300 of them would be bought at $4,000 but only 100 at $5,200, the employment situation would then be:

	CASE I		CASE II
Union men employed	900	Union men employed	600
Helpers employed	2,700	Helpers employed	600
Total employment	3,600	Total employment	1,200

Now let us assume that instead of requiring a ratio of 1 union man to 1 helper, Case I is altered by cutting the union "day's work" in half. The cost situation would then be:

CASE III

6 Union men	$3,000
9 Helpers	900
Materials	1,600
Total cost	$5,500

If the demand is such that 90 houses will be bought at $5,500, the employment situation will then be:

CASE III

Union men employed	540
Helpers employed	810
Total employment	1,350

We have, of course, picked a situation of very elastic demand (although it may be a close approximation to the facts). The point to be emphasized is that the union cannot count on a change in working rules to "increase the number of jobs" unless it is actually certain that the demand for the product is *extremely inelastic*. Again we see the necessity for the union to recognize that it is in the business of selling labor-power and that it must pursue a wise price policy in its own self-interest.

The National Labor Relations Board

Under the act establishing the National Labor Relations Board, an employer is compelled to engage in collective bargaining with a union chosen by his employees. Thus the "right to bargain collectively" has now acquired legal status. The employers who have gone to such violent lengths in opposing union organization are probably more responsible for the passage of this act than any other single cause. If it does nothing else, the act should tend to reduce the number of strikes where union recognition is the main issue.

The ultimate benefit to labor as a result of this act depends not so much upon the decisions rendered by the Board as it does upon the ability to organize competent business unions (either craft or industrial) in the previously unorganized fields.

Unions in the past have been the products of a slow and steady growth which has given them a chance to develop competent officials and to understand the necessity for a strong union discipline. There is grave danger that the new unions which have been established by mushroom growth will prove so irresponsible that public reaction will start the pendulum swinging the other way again just as it did after the experience with the War Labor Board.

CHAPTER XI

Social Security

THE PROBLEMS of provision for industrial accidents, unemployment, old age, sickness, death of the breadwinner of a family, and care for mothers may be grouped under the general head of the problem of social security. In the days when society was characterized by the self-sufficing, or nearly self-sufficing, farm family, some of these problems did not exist and the others were handled in a more or less competent fashion by the family group itself, supplemented at times by the contributions of private charity. In more recent times, changing industrial and social organization has (1) rendered the worker dependent on a money wage as practically the sole source of income, (2) reduced the size of the family and scattered it geographically, (3) abolished, or severely curtailed, child labor as a possible source of additional family income, and (4) resulted in periodic widespread unemployment. Unemployment, in addition to being a problem itself, has rendered the worker less able to meet from his own income the other problems enumerated in the first sentence. Private charity, although greatly expanded, has been unable to meet the added burden through lack of funds, inefficient administration, and because of the natural reluctance on the part of many people to accept charity. Many private charities are also confined in scope by the conditions of the gift.

Workmen's Compensation

Before the passage of workmen's compensation acts, and even in occupations not yet covered by the acts, the workman could recover damages only in those cases of industrial accident which could be proved to be the result of the employer's own negligence. Negligence on the part of an employer is exceedingly difficult to prove under the common law, particularly as several defenses are open to the employer:

(1) The doctrine of contributory negligence. Under this doctrine, if a worker is himself negligent in the slightest degree, he cannot receive damages no matter how great the negligence of the employer. Thus, an employer might leave dangerous gears entirely uncovered, but if a workman wore baggy overalls which caught in the gears, he might be adjudged guilty of contributory negligence and refused damages.

(2) The assumption of risk. Under this doctrine of common law, the worker is presumed to assume the "ordinary risks of his occupation" as a condition of employment. Thus, the risk of being burned in handling molten steel in a steel plant would be considered one of the ordinary risks of the employment and no damages would be paid even if the accident were the result of an employer's negligence.

(3) The fellow servant doctrine. Under this doctrine, if the accident is the result of another employee's negligence, the employer is held to be not responsible.

As if these obstacles were not enough, the fact remains that the employer has generally been able to hire better legal talent than the workman. Some employers would also threaten to discharge any workman who brought suit and any other employee who testified in his favor. For all practical purposes, the odds against the worker probably exceeded 100 to 1, and he would either be content with no damages or be happy to sign away his claim for perhaps $50.

Where workmen's compensation laws are in effect, the general practice is to make the employer responsible for "any accident arising out of or in the course of the employment." No proof of negligence is required. All that must be shown is that the accident occurred on the job. Where questions have arisen, the courts have generally been extremely liberal in interpreting these acts to the employee's benefit. The American Association for Labor Legislation has drawn up a set of standard provisions which should be included in the best type of workmen's compensation law. Some of the most important points may be briefly summarized:

(1) Payment of all medical and hospital costs by the employer.

(2) Payment for loss of working time due to accident at a rate not to exceed two-thirds of the regular wage. (Full payment is not recommended, in order to avoid malingering.)

(3) No compensation should be paid for a period of not less than three nor more than seven days at the beginning of the disability. (The purpose is to cut down administrative and insurance expense on a large number of petty claims which result in no serious loss to the worker.)

(4) Compensation for total disability. The disabled workman should receive during disability 66 2/3 percent of wages, compensation not to be more than $25 or less than $8 a week, unless his wages are less than $8 a week, in which case compensation should be the full amount of wages. If he is a minor, he should, after reaching twenty-one, receive 66 2/3 percent of the wages of able-bodied men in the occupation group to which he belonged.

(5) Compensation for partial disability. The workman who is only partially disabled should receive a percentage of his wages, proportioned to the degree of physical disability (taking into account age and occupation), and subject to readjustment only on account of changes in extent of disability

(maximum and minimum payments to be the same as under total disability).

(6) Compensation for death.

(a) Funeral expenses. The employer should be required to pay a sum not exceeding $150 for funeral expenses, in addition to any other compensation.

(b) Compensation for widow or widower. If living with the decedent at the time of death, or if dependent, they should be granted 35 percent of the worker's wages till death or remarriage, with a lump sum on remarriage equal to two years' compensation.

(c) Compensation for widow or widower and children. In addition to (b), 15 percent should be allowed for each child under 18, not to exceed a total of 66 2/3 percent for all dependents. Compensation on account of a child should cease when it dies, marries, or reaches the age of 18.

(d) Compensation for children with no surviving parent. Twenty-five percent for one child under 18, and 15 percent for each additional child, to be divided equally among them and not to exceed a total of 66 2/3 percent. Compensation to cease in the same manner as under (c).

(e) Compensation for other dependents. Should be the same as under (d) except that such compensation should be paid only during dependency.

(7) Employments to be included. All employments should be included, only excepting those of casual workers in the service of employers who have no regularly employed workers.

(8) Injuries to be included. Compensation should be provided for all personal injuries in the course of employment, and for death resulting therefrom within six years, but no compensation should be paid where the injury is occasioned by the willful intention of the employee to bring about the injury or death of himself or of another. The act should include *occupational diseases* which, when contracted in the course

of the employment, should be considered personal injuries for which compensation is payable.

(9) Other remedies. To avoid needless and wasteful lawsuits, no other claims for damages should be allowed to the worker. If the employer has been criminally negligent, he can be prosecuted by the state under other laws.

(10) Methods of insurance. Employers may:

(a) Maintain their own insurance fund subject to approval of the Accident Board or the state insurance authority.

(b) Insure in a State Insurance Fund managed by the Accident Board upon the same principles and subject to the same general requirements as those governing Mutual Insurance Associations.

(c) Insure in a mutual or stock insurance company which is subject to strict regulation by the state insurance authority.

(11) Organization of the Accident Board. The board should consist of three or five members appointed by the Governor with the consent of the upper house of the legislature, and should have power to employ necessary assistants. Its members should be required to devote their entire time to its work. The entire cost of administration of the Accident Board should be paid out of a state appropriation.

(12) Procedure. Provision should be made for the determination of all claims for compensation, either by the Accident Board, or if the number of claims is large, by one member of the Board or an authorized deputy. A decision by a member or deputy should be conclusive, unless appeal is taken to the entire Accident Board within a specified time. Appeals from decrees of the Accident Board should not be allowed, except on questions of law, in which case they should be carried direct to the highest court.

(13) Reports of accidents. The Board should be required to use the Standard Accident Reporting Blank of the Ameri-

can Association for Labor Legislation, which is now in use for about half the industrial population of the country and requires full and accurate reports of all industrial accidents as a basis for computation of future insurance rates and future safety regulations to decrease or prevent accidents.

(14) Rehabilitation. Restored earning power is of more importance than is the distress relieved. The administrative board should therefore be authorized to encourage, to co-operate with, or to conduct enterprises for the re-education and rehabilitation of injured persons.

The reader may be interested in comparing his own state workmen's compensation law with this set of standards. The most common defect to be found will be the exclusion of many classes of employees from the benefits of the act. Typical classes often excluded are: employees of small firms, agricultural workers, domestic servants, and employees of religious institutions. If there is any justification for workmen's compensation, there is no justification for these exclusions. The fact that accidents occur less frequently in some occupations than in others is no justification. Insurance rates are extremely low for occupations with low accident experience. The few employees who do happen to be injured or killed in the excluded occupations are just as injured and just as dead as those who come under the provisions of the act. In general, the greater the number of workmen protected, the lower the insurance rates can be made.

Many arguments are offered in favor of workmen's compensation, some of them on ethical and some on economic grounds. It is argued that injuries to workmen should be a cost assumed by the employer just as much as depreciation and wear and tear of capital equipment. Most workmen either are too improvident or earn wages too low to enable them to care for themselves out of savings or even by means of individual accident insurance policies. Hazardous occupations often do not pay wages sufficiently higher than less hazardous occupations to compensate for the degree of risk involved, since workers either do not realize the risk or are overly optimistic. If compensation is not provided, the burden of caring for the injured and their families will fall on the community. It is argued that it is more equitable to place this burden upon the employer and/or the purchasers of the product who have the benefit of the services of the labor involved.

The strongest argument for compulsory workmen's compensation is that it tends to reduce the number of accidents. When each employer knows that each accident means a definite cost to him (either in the form of a deduction from his own accident reserve fund or in the form of higher insurance premiums), he has a financial incentive to reduce accidents. Under the old Factory Inspection Laws, an employer would often try the effects of a ten-dollar bill in producing astigmatism in the factory inspector. Where workmen's compensation laws are in effect, an employer often hires a safety engineer to find danger spots and to try to eradicate them. A conspicuous example of what may be done to reduce industrial accidents has been given us in the construction of the Chrysler building. Previous to this time it had been the almost normal experience that one life was lost for each story of a building above eleven stories. A careful study was made of these accidents and the chief cause was discovered to be that of tripping over tools or materials left in the workers' way. The engineers then made a schedule providing that no material was to be moved to any floor until it was ready to be used immediately. They also provided for the immediate removal of all waste material and the picking up of all tools not in use. The result was that this building, the tallest in the world when completed, was built without a single loss of life and without a single accident resulting in permanent disability. Other industries have been able to show equally remarkable records when scientific safety methods have been employed. In recent safety contests, some factories employing thousands of men have gone as long as two or three years without a single loss-of-time accident.

It must not be assumed that the employer actually bears the full cost of workmen's compensation. The passage of workmen's compensation laws, or their application to a new group, acts exactly in the same manner as the imposition of a new tax. (See Chapter III.) In some cases the insurance cost, or part of it, may be shifted forward to the consumer, and in other cases the cost may be shifted back to the worker. Sometimes the employer may have to bear all or part of the cost himself. This consideration, however, does not materially weaken the arguments for workmen's compensation. If people demand products which are produced by hazardous methods (such as radium watch dials or highly explosive materials), it may be argued that they should be made to bear the added cost of insurance for workers. Even where the cost of insurance is shifted backward to the worker, he is probably better protected at lower cost to himself than could be achieved by any other means.

Unemployment Insurance

Some writers claim that unemployment insurance is exactly analogous to workmen's compensation insurance, and the plans for insurance which they propose offer many close parallels to some of the provisions of compensation insurance. We may note at the outset, however, certain fundamental differences which make unemployment insurance a problem that must be considered on its own merits and which may suggest a somewhat different procedure:

(1) The amount of unemployment that may occur in any one year is not subject to prediction within acceptable limits of actuarial accuracy.

(2) Unemployment is well known to occur in large waves rather than evenly over a period of time. Points (1) and (2) both involve serious qualifications of the principles of fire or accident insurance. Fundamentally, fire and accident insurance involve the principle of paying current losses out of current premiums, plus the maintenance of a reasonable reserve fund to meet "unforeseen" contingencies. Unemployment, however, since it is characterized by wide and unpredictable fluctuations, would require either (a) the establishment of huge reserves relative to total insurance in force, or (b) ability to borrow to meet benefit payments in excess of receipts, or (c) periodic gifts to the fund by the government. While (b) and (c) are not necessarily poor solutions for the problem, they are distinctly outside the realm of insurance on an actuarial basis.

(3) While industrial accidents are usually capable of reduction by active effort on the part of the employer, unemployment is a matter which is largely beyond the individual employer's control. If there are any fixed costs, the employer already has a financial incentive to continue in operation if price of the product is above minimum variable costs. Even assuming that the full cost of unemployment insurance was actually borne by the employer, the ability to save all of a 6 percent payroll tax (by maintaining full employment) might be sufficient to compensate for conditions which would otherwise indicate the layoff of about 6 percent of the working force. When conditions are such that least loss will be incurred by running the factory at half or quarter of ordinary output, the possible saving on unemployment insurance becomes negligible as a stimulus to greater employment.

(4) In unemployment insurance on a national scale, the alternate accumulation and disbursement of sums running into billions of dollars constitutes a monetary problem which does not exist in the case of fire and accident insurance. Consider

the difficulties if unemployment insurance were handled on the same basis as private companies handle fire or accident insurance. In times of nearly full employment there would be huge amounts of premiums to be invested. The use of these funds to buy securities in the open market would tend to drive securities prices still higher than those in a "bull" market which ordinarily accompanies expanding employment. Then when unemployment came, in order to pay out the benefits, large blocks of these securities would have to be dumped on an already declining market. The possible losses which would be incurred might easily be so great that it would be better to hold the funds as hoarded cash. Furthermore, the marketing of the securities in times of recession might easily contribute to a state of panic which would increase unemployment still further.

(5) Any attempt to base unemployment insurance premiums upon risk experience will tend to place the heaviest burdens of added cost upon industries which may be least able to bear them. Thus, public utility companies and others which have a very steady volume of business may easily be able to guarantee their workers a minimum of, say, 48 weeks' work a year and so avoid all payments. Other industries, where the demand for the product fluctuates more, would be saddled with heavy costs. This might be desirable if the employer could readily reduce unemployment, but we have already seen that this possibility is sharply limited.

The Real Nature of Unemployment Insurance

The above discussion would lead us to conclude that unemployment insurance can hardly be called insurance in the ordinary sense of the term. What is it then? Properly speaking it more nearly approaches the status of systematic unemployment relief. As such, there are many arguments in its favor: (1) It tends to treat all unemployed workers (who are covered by the plan) on an equal basis. (2) It removes the stigma of charity from the benefit payments. (To further this end it is probably better to keep on calling it "insurance," even though the term is inaccurate.) (3) It gives us a means of keeping an accurate count of the unemployed which is currently up to date and may be used as a means of guiding other government policies. (4) If used on a national scale, it may be a better means of distributing the burden of caring for the unemployed than throwing the burden on the local community. (5) Regardless of the plan of raising the funds, contributions to the fund are apt to be more equitable than those of private charity.

Coverage of Unemployment Insurance

Unemployment insurance cannot be considered separately from other forms of relief. The indigent who are not cared for by unemployment benefits will constitute a "residual relief load" which must be cared for by other means. If the Federal Government "turns the relief problem back to the states" as some people now advocate, there will be a heavy burden of "residual relief" for the state and local communities to handle. If unemployment benefits are to constitute the "first line of defense," this suggests that as many occupations and as many people as possible be covered by unemployment insurance. When a local community is suffering from heavy unemployment, the possibilities of raising revenue locally from real estate taxes, income taxes, or even sales taxes, are seriously curtailed. The imposition of a heavy residual relief burden, if unemployment insurance coverage is unduly restricted, will thus tend to fall on the local communities at times when they are least able to bear such a burden. The present Social Security Act probably provides too many exemptions. In particular, the exemption of employers with less than eight employees permits evasion by some industries which might properly be included in the plan. For example, some gasoline companies and chain stores have already adopted the expedient of "leasing" the units to the man who was formerly the hired manager. Thus all the stores and gas stations having less than eight employees in the individual units are exempted from the plan, although the total number of such employees may run into the thousands.

Somewhat the same general criticism may be offered against the arbitrary limitation of the length of the benefit periods. (The Social Security Act places a limit of twelve weeks.) The general theory of such limitation is to keep the plan "solvent," that is, to pay benefits only from payroll taxes and workers contributions. Considered in terms of the total relief load, however, such solvency is only technical. Those workers who happen to be out of work longer than the alloted period are simply given into the care of some other agency. The time limitation is no guarantee against malingering, and this problem can be better handled by other means.

Amount of Benefits

Almost every consideration dictates that the size of the unemployment benefit should closely approximate a bare sub-sistence level. This will be the best guarantee against "loafing on the dole" and the strongest inducement for a man to hunt a job for himself rather than to wait until one is offered him. It also makes it possible for the funds to cover a wider number of cases and to reduce the burden of residual relief. If a sub-sistence standard is adopted, it should, of course, take into account the number of dependents on the worker. Some advocates of large benefits base their argument on the "main-tenance of consumer purchasing power." The consumer pur-chasing power theory is itself open to question, but even if it were valid, when the total amount of funds is limited, consumer purchasing power cannot be enhanced by giving higher benefits to fewer people rather than small benefits and wide coverage.

Methods of Raising Funds

Most economists seem to be agreed that either all or a great part of a payroll tax for unemployment insurance will be eventually shifted to the worker. Since this is a tax which varies not with output, but with the amount of labor used and the amount of wages paid, it does seem logical that the tax will be shifted to the worker. (See Chapter III.) If this is substantially true, there is much to be said in favor of having the worker pay such a tax directly rather than through a "concealed" wage reduction; direct payment by the worker helps to maintain the idea of insurance rather than charity. If the workers realize the share they are paying, there might be a tendency to reduce political pressure for higher benefits. There also might be motivation to bring social pressure against those individuals who are known to be malingering.

Workers' contributions alone, whether made directly or in the form of a payroll tax on the employee, will not be sufficient to support an unemployment benefit program unless there is a long period of full, or nearly full, employment before a depression occurs. The contributions will be still less adequate to meet an emergency if they are segregated in the funds of the several states, and within the states are still further segregated by industries or individual firms (a practice allowed by the Social Security Act). Two alternatives are thus left open to the government if the unemployment relief problem is to be adequately handled: (1) It may supplement the unemployment funds out of general revenue or by borrowing in periods of depression. (2) It may provide other agencies such as PWA, WPA and the like to care for the residual relief load. The second alternative is the one to which we are apparently committed by present legislation.

There is much to be said for a national system of unemployment insurance, plus alternative (1). If insurance were on a national basis, it would promote more mobility of labor. (Under the present Social Security Act there is danger that workers will have to remain within a particular state or even in the employment of a particular firm in order to be eligible for benefits.) It would also permit a more even distribution of the costs and a closer balancing of receipts and payments, and there would be the possibility of continuing unemployment benefits for longer periods of time in individual cases and localities than is possible under a segregated system. The supplementing of the funds by Federal borrowing in periods of severe depression would permit the further extension of unemployment benefits rather than make necessary so extensive a resort to other forms of relief. If sound public works projects are available, they can be used to take workers from the unemployment insurance roster. If not, continuation of unemployment benefits will certainly be less expensive (and perhaps no more demoralizing) than "made work" projects.

Unemployment Provisions of the Social Security Act

The Social Security Act (Public No. 271, 74th Congress) does not itself provide a system of unemployment insurance but gives aid to those states which do set up such systems, and (in effect) penalizes those which do not. The method is the imposition of a Federal tax (to be paid exclusively by employers) of 1 percent of all wages and salaries in 1936, 2 percent in 1937, and 3 percent for all subsequent years. In states where there are unemployment insurance systems approved by the *Social Security Board,* the employer may claim an exemption from the federal tax of the full amount paid to the state system up to nine-tenths of the amount of the federal tax. Therefore, in states which do not have approved laws, employers will still have to pay the tax but the states will be receiving none of the funds to help with their unemployment relief problems.

Certain exemptions are made. Employers who have employed fewer than eight workers are exempted regardless of the nature of the firm. In addition, exemptions are provided for: (1) agriculture; (2) domestic servants in a private home; (3) shipping on the navigable waters of the United States; (4) services of members of the immediate family, except children over 21; (5) employees of the Federal Government or its agencies; (6) employees of a state government or its subdivisions; (7) nonprofit agencies carried on for religious, charitable, scientific, literary, and educational purposes.

Certain minimum standards to which state laws must conform to receive approval are provided:

(1) Benefits to the unemployed eligibles must be paid through public employment offices in the state or through such other agencies as the state may approve. (This is the wisest provision in the act.)

(2) No payments may be made until two years after the state plan has been established.

(3) All funds received by the states shall be deposited with the Secretary of the Treasury to their credit in the Unemployment Trust Fund.

(4) All funds withdrawn by the states from the trust fund must be expended in the payment of unemployment compensation.

(5) The states must make such reports in such form and containing such information as the Board may require.

(6) Compensation shall not be denied under the state law to any otherwise eligible individual for refusing to accept new work under any of the following conditions: (a) If the position offered is vacant due directly to a strike, lockout, or other labor dispute; (b) if the wages, hours, or other conditions of the work offered are substantially less favorable to the indi-

vidual than those prevailing for similar work in the locality; (c) if, as a condition of being employed, the individual would be required to join a company union or to refrain from joining any bona fide labor organization.

Additional credits. Where permitted by the state law, an employer may claim a credit up to 90 percent of the Federal tax, in lieu of contributing to a state fund, by: (a) establishing his own unemployment reserve fund under approved conditions, (b) joining with others in the establishment of a reserve fund for an industry or local group of employers, (c) guaranteeing thirty hours of wages for forty calendar weeks (or more, with one weekly hour deducted for each added week guaranteed) in each twelve months.

So long as they conform to the minimum requirements of the act, the states are thus allowed a considerable amount of freedom in developing their own plans for unemployment insurance. After the plan has been in effect for a while, the comparative experience with different plans will probably lead to greater uniformity among the state plans than exists at present. One achievement of the law is that it prevents any industries covered within any state from profiting competitively against other states by not having unemployment insurance or by having plans which are seriously substandard as compared with the others.

Old-Age Pensions

A growing need for some form of care for the indigent aged has become apparent. In the past such care has been provided by the local or county poorhouses plus some pensions or cash relief provided by some few states or local authorities. Most state laws have also attempted to compel close relatives to care for aged dependents when they were financially able to do so. In times of prolonged depression, however, the latter alternative has been of little help since large numbers of unemployed

workers have been unable to care for themselves, to say nothing of other dependents.

The Social Security Act provides that the Federal Government will match state contributions for old-age pensions dollar
for dollar up to a maximum of $15 per month contributed by
the Federal Government. In other words, of all pensions
totaling $30 or less, the Federal and state governments will
each pay half. On pensions of more than $30, the Federal
Government will pay $15 and the state will pay the balance.
The same plan is also made available to local and county
governments (some state constitutions specifically place relief
in the hands of the local authorities), but such local plans
must be under the supervision of a state authority which is, in
turn, responsible to the Social Security Board. In order to
qualify for these pensions, the recipient must be shown to be
in actual need; other sources of income may result in a reduction of the amount of pension granted.

Old-Age Insurance and Annuities

A sharp distinction must be kept in mind between old-age
pensions and old-age insurance and annuities. The former
are solely a form of relief and are granted on the basis of age
and need, without regard to previous occupation. The annuities, on the contrary, are paid solely on the basis of past
contributions to the fund and without regard to the wealth of
the individual. (He must, however, leave gainful employment
in order to start receiving the annuity.) The entire administration of insurance and annuities is in the hands of the
Federal Government.

The taxes for old-age insurance are levied on all employments
except those specifically excluded. The exemptions are about
the same as those listed for unemployment insurance, except
that establishments with less than eight workers are not exempt
and no tax is levied on the amount of any individual wage

which exceeds $3,000. As provided in the original act, the schedule of payments is as follows:

PERCENT OF TAX ON ALL WAGES AND
SALARIES OR PART THEREOF WHICH
IS $3,000 PER YEAR OR LESS

Year	Payment by Employer	Payment by Employee
1937–1939	1.0%	1.0%
1940–1942	1.5%	1.5%
1943–1945	2.0%	2.0%
1946–1948	2.5%	2.5%
1949 and after	3.0%	3.0%

This scheme of collections will mean that estimated receipts plus interest will exceed disbursements for most of the earlier years by such an amount that the reserve fund will reach an estimated maximum of 47 billion dollars in 1980. Since the funds must be invested in Federal Government bonds which yield 3 percent (the Treasury to issue special bonds for this purpose if necessary), interest payments will have to come out of the general government funds. The interest, or at least a part of it, is thus a "concealed subsidy." If the Treasury does not spend the proceeds from the sale of the bonds to the fund, the effect is deflationary. If it does spend the funds, either new taxes or new borrowing will have to be used to repay the money when the annuity payments begin to exceed the payroll taxes. To avoid this, an amendment has been proposed in Congress which would "freeze" the taxes at 1.5 percent per worker and employer until such time as the taxes are actually needed to pay out the annuities.

The annuity payments under the fund are based on the total amount of wages which have been taxed to provide the income for the fund. On income which has been received under the plan (and on which the payroll tax has been paid), the monthly annuity is to be 1/2 of one percent on the first $3,000 of income, 1/12 of one percent on the next $42,000 and 1/24 of one percent on all over $42,000, but the maximum

monthly annuity shall not exceed $85. If the insured worker
dies before he reaches the age of 65, his estate shall receive a
sum equal to 3 1/2 percent of the income on which annuities
are calculated. If he dies after age 65 and the total annuities
which he received while living do not equal 3 1/2 percent of
the insured income, his estate shall receive the difference between the total payments he did receive and the sum represented by such 3 1/2 percent.

Other Grants

In addition to unemployment insurance and old-age pensions, the Social Security Act provides for grants to the states
for care of dependent children, for mothers' pensions (mater-
nal and infant care), for crippled children, for rehabilitation
work, and for public health services. Some of these features
require state contribution and others do not, but in no case is
it necessary for the state to match the Federal contribution
dollar for dollar.

General Aspects of Social Security

Most of the arguments for social security legislation rest
upon ethical or humanitarian grounds which we need not
question here. The most important economic question is,
"How much social security benefits can we afford?" With
very little exception, all social security benefits are paid to
people who are not working and who therefore are not producing any wealth for the community. We are already approaching the limits of returns from the "soak the rich policy"
to support present forms of Federal, state, and local expenditure.
It follows that the costs of the social security program will fall
mainly on those who are employed in the middle and lower
income classes. Only a few provisions (such as those for
public health and child care) offer any possibilities of increasing the productive power of future generations. The provision

against any gainful employment for those drawing old-age annuities prevents them from making any contribution to material national wealth. (This provision was intended to make jobs for younger workers and might be withdrawn if we reach full employment.) As time passes, the whole net effect of the legislation will be to increase the proportion of national money income which is spent on consumption. In the case of the old-age insurance, present money-spending on consumption is decreased in favor of greater spending in the future when the annuities are received. Much more important than money, however, is the question of goods. If less goods are consumed now, will there be more goods available for future consumption? We could produce more goods now and save them till later, but this is not advisable as we do not know what forms of goods will be in demand in the future. Raw materials can be saved for future generations by not consuming them now, but this does not apply in the case of labor. The only way in which present labor-power can be saved for the use of future generations is to use the labor now in the construction of tools, machinery, buildings and other capital equipment which may be used to increase the productive capacity of labor in the future. In times like the present, when there is a deficiency of private investment for these purposes, it follows that there is a grave responsibility for the government to invest the receipts from payroll taxes in ways which will tend to increase the future productive capacity of the nation rather than to fritter away the labor-power in "made work" projects. Either this must involve more "government competition with private business" or means must be found by which the government can make loans to private business for the purpose of expanding capital equipment. Some people may not like either of these alternatives, but we cannot tell labor to take a vacation and then expect to find any product of labor when the vacation is over.

Even with government investment in capital improvement, we still have the question of how many people we can support in idleness while the others work. There is no easy or definite answer to such a question. The implication is rather that we should wait until the present legislation has had a chance to demonstrate some of its effects before adding further commitments to be fulfilled in the future.

CHAPTER XII

Economic Planning in a Socialist State

THE present chapter is not an attempt to "evaluate" socialism. It merely represents an effort to analyze the problems which would confront a planning board trying to organize an economic system based on socialist standards of welfare
and conforming to socialist principles. Any innuendos either
in favor of or against socialism are the reader's own, and are
not intentionally the author's.

In recent years socialism has come to have almost as many
different meanings as there are different individuals who attempt to explain its doctrines. As a starting point for our purposes, the best definition is the one given by Professor Pigou[1]:
"A socialized *industry* is one in which the material instruments
of production are owned by a public authority or voluntary
association and operated, not with a view to profit by sale to
other people, but for the direct service of those whom the
authority or association represents. A socialized *system* is
one the *main part* of whose productive resources are engaged
in socialized industries." Further, Professor Pigou points out
that while socialism abolishes *profits* (in the sense of buying or
hiring resources of production and selling the product at a
price greater than cost), it need not abolish the *profit motive*
if the latter term is used simply as a synonym for the motive of
monetary gain.

---

[1] Pigou, A.C., *Socialism Versus Capitalism,* p. 2, Macmillan & Co., Ltd., London,
1937. Reprinted by permission of the Macmillan Company.

A planned society is not necessarily a socialist society.[2] A scheme of central planning could be devised which would operate to yield its greatest benefits to a small aristocracy, to all native whites, to the leaders of a communist or fascist party, or to any other controlling group. While in theory a socialist society might get along without much central planning, operating simply as a collection of individually socialized industries, most contemporary socialists lay great stress on planning as an important feature of such a society.

The concept of planning cannot be dissociated from the end or purpose such planning is expected to achieve. The vaguer Utopians tell us that such planning should be for the "common welfare" and fail to give us any very definite standards of their concept of this ambiguous term. It is possible, of course, to decide the standards of common welfare upon the basis of a majority vote. It is entirely within the realm of possibility, however, that under such a system the voting of the majority (or of an effectively organized voting minority) might result in as much, or nearly as much, exploitation of minority groups as exists in our present much-maligned system. Some more definite statements of the socialist welfare formula have been: "From each according to his ability, to each according to his need," "Equal distribution of income," and recently the more sophisticated, "The most equal distribution of income that is consistent with the greatest social net product." It is not our purpose here to question the wisdom of these welfare concepts. We are more concerned with the problems of the Socialist Central Planning Board which is entrusted with the task of effectuating them.

The basic problems confronting such a board are: (1) How much of each good shall be produced? (2) How are the resources of production to be allocated for the production of these

---

[2] See Mackenzie, Findlay, *Planned Society: Yesterday, Today, Tomorrow,* Prentice-Hall, Inc., New York, 1937.

goods? (3) How can the efficiency of any given production unit be measured? (4) How much of the resources of production shall be devoted to the production of goods for present consumption and how much to goods for future consumption (capital goods)?

If equal, or nearly equal, incomes are to be established, the present proportions in which goods are manufactured will hardly be more than a point of departure from which the board may start its calculations. Steam yachts, mink coats, and other articles of "conspicuous consumption" would be definitely out of the picture for home consumption. (It still might be desirable to produce some of this type of goods for export if other countries are capitalistic: caviar and sables are important articles of export from Russia.) In place of these goods there would need to be a tremendous expansion in some of the more common articles of consumption. How shall the various quantities of these goods be determined?

Assume that the board should happen to make a fairly good statistical estimate of the total amount of each good required. There is still the problem of distributing these goods. Rationing does not seem to be an adequate solution for the problem. Of some goods there would not even be one apiece to go around (automobiles for example). Even for other goods which might be more plentiful, rationing would not achieve the greatest possible satisfaction for each individual. One might prefer to have an additional suit of clothes rather than more shirts and shoes, while another would prefer to have more books or phonograph records. Surely the Socialists who are so critical of inefficiency in our present system would not ask us to return to the crudities of barter to correct the faults of rationing. It would seem that some sort of money and price system would not only be more efficient but also, through allowing greater freedom of choice, would result in a greater total satisfaction. Goods that were scarce relative to the demand for them could be priced high and other goods, of which there was a greater quantity available, could be priced low. The buyers' responses to these prices would then serve as a guide to expansion or contraction of production of various goods in subsequent periods. The chief criticism of capitalist price structure from a welfare point of view is that it reflects differences in incomes as much as or more than it does differences in desire for the product. With a more nearly equal distribution of income it would seem that the prices which people were willing to pay would be a fairly accurate indication of the desire for the product.

Even with a price system the problem is by no means simple. In addition to the desire for each good, the prices set should take account of the social cost involved in its production. The social cost of production of any unit of a good will be the amount of the most valuable alternative product that could be produced with the same resources. Since the socialist system is presumably ruling out profits, equilibrium for an industry would be established at the point where average revenue is equal to average social cost.

The magnitude of the task of the planning board is occasioned both by the number of prices which must be set and by the fact that these must be set with reference to each other, that is, there must be a general equilibrium solution. Under capitalism the individual firm is more or less able to accept the demand curve for its product as given data (possibly to be altered by advertising); the cost elements are also given data for the vast majority of firms. With our planning board, however, the prices which it sets for all other products will be an important element in determining the demand for any one product; the prices set for other products will be the basis for imputing the value of labor and capital used in their production. This value of labor and capital will then, in turn, be the cost data upon which the output and price of any single commodity must be adjusted. To solve the problem at one fell swoop would require the solution of thousands of simultaneous equations (possibly with the number of unknowns exceeding the number of equations). Even if the socialized state were a static state, the ideal solution could be reached only after a long process of trial and error. The Socialists, however, are insistent that socialism will not be a bar to technological progress so that these problems must be solved not for a static, but for a dynamic state. The solution to the pricing problem and the balance between the production of different goods is admittedly faulty under capitalism. There is little ground for arguing that socialism would improve upon it. According to Professor Pigou, "What is needed to improve on it, is not will, but knowledge. The relevant knowledge is of a sort that we do not at present possess, and the eventual winning of which is no more likely under the one system than under the other."[3]

Allocation of Resources

The allocation of resources is, of course, dependent upon the decision of the relative quantities of goods to be produced. However, certain other problems are also present. The allocation of labor possibly presents more difficulties than any other factor. Workers may be allowed their own choice of occupation as far as is practicable, but it is still extremely unlikely that the number of workers who desired to enter any particular occupation would exactly correspond to the required number. If equal wages are to be the rule, excess numbers would have to be weeded out of the overcrowded occupations by some arbitrary decree and workers would have to be forced into the employments where there was a deficient labor supply by similarly coercive means. It appears that the only way to avoid such arbitrary action would be to pay higher wages in the understaffed occupations and lower wages for those in which the labor supply was in excess. Whether this would be too

---

[3] Pigou, A. C., *Socialism Versus Capitalism*, p. 44.

much of a compromise with the doctrine of equal incomes is still a matter for debate among Socialists.

Certain occupations also require a much longer period of training than others. The state will have to decide which individuals are to be selected for such training. For some occupations this selection may be done much better under socialism than under capitalism. Previous school records may be made the basis for selection without the qualification of family wealth to cover the expense of education which exists in capitalistic societies. There is still bound to be a considerable margin of error, however; the mere fact that a boy makes an "A" in beginning chemistry is no positive proof that he will be a competent physician or surgeon.

The costs of training suggest an additional element in general cost calculations. Those industries which are given highly trained workers must be charged with the cost of training not only the workers actually used but also a proper *pro rata* share of the cost of training, or partial training, of other individuals who have been "tried and found wanting." If equal wages are to be paid to all workers, those who are selected for higher technical training should be paid, while they are studying in the technical school (in addition to free tuition), a wage equal to that which they might otherwise be earning. If higher wages are to be paid for the more highly trained occupations, simply giving tuition and living expenses during the training period may constitute an adequate recompense and an adequate inducement. Regardless of which system is used, the social cost of training (which, in addition to the cost of running the school, consists of the loss of otherwise possible productive services of students during the training period) will be about the same.

Unless some such form of cost accounting is used to charge the various industries with the cost of training workers assigned to them, the calculations of the planning board are apt to fall into serious error. Those industries which ordinarily employ a greater proportion of skilled and trained men might easily be found to be turning out a greater value product than are other industries employing a similar number of less skilled workers. This might lead to false judgments as to the relative efficiency of management in the two types of industries. Worse still, it might lead the planning board to divert a greater amount of labor into the skilled and trained occupations than would be warranted by a proper balancing of properly calculated social cost and social product.

The allocation of resources other than labor may not be quite so difficult (assuming that the problem of determining the right proportions of consumers' goods has been solved). The same price may be charged for raw materials to all industries which use them so that efficiency comparisons on this basis will not necessarily be distorted. Other serious considerations are present, however. If the industries are willing to take more than the present output at the established price, should the output of the mines be expanded to accommodate the demand, or should the price of the materials be raised so as to exclude the least valuable uses? The decision here rests on the relative merits of conservation of resources *versus* present satisfaction of consumers' wants. The price cannot be set simply to cover the costs of extraction but must take some account of the "depletion" involved in using up exhaustible natural resources. In the case of lumber the solution is fairly easy. The "harvest" can be confined to mature timber and reforestation can be practiced to assure a fairly even annual supply. In agriculture the best soil conserving practices can be adopted and a price sufficient to cover the costs of these practices may be sufficient to guarantee against soil depletion. For irreplaceable mineral resources the board has no such easy solution. Under capitalism the scarcest of these resources are generally under a considerable degree of monopolistic control. The element of monopoly profit in their price has a considerable tendency to check what may be too rapid consumption. Under socialism the only check will be the wisdom of the board in weighing the relative merits of the claims of present and future generations to the use of the resources.

Measurement of Efficiency

We have already mentioned some of the general problems of efficiency measurement but there are some particular problems which deserve special consideration. In the competitive parts of a capitalist economy at least a rough method is provided in the comparison of results of different firms which operate under more or less similar conditions. Also, wherever competition is effective there are strong tendencies toward increased efficiency, regardless of whether or not any efforts are made to measure efficiency. Competition for the best land tends to force it into its most valuable uses (most valuable from a capitalistic viewpoint, of course). Competition for the use of the most efficient laborers' services may result in wages which are roughly proportional to the differences in efficiency. Most important of all, the process of bankruptcy is continually at work to weed out the least efficient managers. It is one of the most pertinent criticisms of monopoly that these forces either do not operate, or operate much less strongly under monopoly than they do under competition.

In a socialist economy, although monopoly prices may perhaps not be charged, each industry will constitute a monopoly from the viewpoint of operation and management. It follows that if the capacity of managers is to be measured so that the inefficient ones may be removed and replaced, there must be some method of measuring the potential productive capacity of the resources with which they are supplied. A part of the problem with respect to labor might be solved by the adoption of the piece-work system of wages wherever applicable. (In addition to the actual wage, a system of family allowances might be made to give additional compensation out of general state funds to workers with dependents.) If some such system is not used, and in places where piece-work is not applicable, some form of "accounting labor cost" must be adopted which will charge the manager who is given highly efficient workers with a higher labor cost than the manager to whom less efficient workers may be assigned. Much the same principle applies to other resources. It would be obviously unfair to expect the manager of a collective farm in Montana to produce the same yield of corn as is obtainable in Iowa or northern Illinois. In accounting, some consideration must be given to the element of economic rent even in a socialist economy.

Some form of reasonably accurate cost accounting must be devised, not only to measure the efficiency of management but also to be used as a guide in the proper allocation of resources. There are some jobs which are best adapted to take full advantage of the most efficient workers' capacities. In other jobs individual differences in labor efficiency may be only a negligible factor in affecting total output. Obviously, if greatest production is to be achieved, the efficient workmen must be placed in those positions where their superior efficiency will have the greatest opportunity to affect the output.

Note that in the measurement of efficiency for the purpose of allocation of resources, the relevant criterion must be economic efficiency rather than mere technological efficiency. Thus a given piece of land might be capable of producing a bale of cotton to the acre as compared to a national average of only half a bale. The same land might be capable of producing only 20 bushels of corn to the acre as compared to a national average of 25 bushels. If the national economy was in more pressing need for corn than it was for cotton, however, it might be advisable to use this land for corn rather than for cotton.

A very serious problem of efficiency measurement presents

itself where one industry is producing semi-finished products which are turned over to other industries for further fabrication or for incorporation as parts in some other product. If the price set for the semi-finished product is too high, the efficiency of the primary producer will be made to appear greater than it actually is, whereas the other industries which use the product will be made to appear less efficient than they really are. If the price is set too low, the comparison will be unfair in the opposite direction.

Balance Between Capital Goods and Consumers' Goods

Our planning board will have several types of decisions to make with respect to capital. It must decide whether the existing capital equipment is to be reduced, maintained, or expanded. Even on that portion which represents maintenance, it must be decided whether capital shall be apportioned among industries in the same ratio as it has been in the past or whether the capital equipment of some industries should be expanded and that of others contracted. If it is decided to expand the total capital equipment of the nation, the decision must be made as to how this equipment is to be allocated among the old industries and what part is to be devoted to the establishment of new industries, if any. The rate of capital replacement must also be determined: Should old machines be used until they are worn out or should they be replaced by newer types of machines as fast as new ones are invented?

Perhaps the best approach to these problems is to work from the particular to the general. If the principle of social cost is to be followed, each industry should be charged for the maintenance of the capital which it uses. Such a charge may properly be made a part of the price of the product. It does not necessarily follow that maintenance charges must be used to replace capital in the particular industry; changes in "demand" may indicate that capital in this particular industry should be reduced while in some others it is being expanded. The maintenance charge is necessary in all industries, however, to prevent an *involuntary* reduction in the total amount of capital equipment of society and to keep a proper cost accounting basis. If it should actually be decided that the total amount of capital in existence was too large, then the maintenance charges of all industries could be reduced by a flat percentage representing the desired amount of decrease.

In addition to the maintenance charges, some account must be taken of the fact that labor and other resources, if not used to make capital goods, could be used to make consumers' goods by more direct processes. This brings us back to the general question of the desirability of present goods *versus* future goods, or in other words, to the question of a social rate of interest. The question here is whether this decision is to be made on an individual or a group basis. One method might be the dependence on individual voluntary savings to provide capital. Such saving might be induced by setting a rate of interest to be paid. Immediately, however, we run into some difficulties. If socialism prohibits inequalities of income due to inherited wealth, if it provides completely free public education, and if it reduces unemployment and cares for the aged and infirm, many of the motives for saving which exist in a capitalist society will no longer be present. Practically the only motive left for saving is that provided by the interest rate itself, that is, by the prospect of the increased amount of goods to be consumed by the same individual in the not-too-distant future. It seems almost certain that, to induce any considerable amount of saving, this rate would have to be extremely high.

An interest rate does not solve the problem. It merely allows individuals to save or not as they see fit and to govern their savings by the amount of the interest rate as it appeals to them. The decision is still up to the planning board. If it thinks that a large accumulation of capital is desirable, it will set a high interest rate; if not, it will set a low one.

It is not necessary for the socialist state to pay interest in order to obtain capital equipment. (Strict Marxist theory regards interest with horror as an "unjustified" return.) The state could simply assign workers and resources arbitrarily to the industries producing capital goods. Payment of money wages to the workers would enable them to buy their share of consumers' goods in competition with other workers. The net effect is a form of "forced saving" quite similar to that resulting from the use of created bank credit under capitalism.

Even though there is no such thing as a market rate of interest in the socialist state, some concept closely similar to it is necessary for figuring social cost and for the allocation of capital goods to various industries. When any industry receives capital goods (either for addition to total capital or for replacement), it means that the community has had to go without the present consumption of such consumers' goods as might have been produced if the labor and resources had not been used to make these capital goods. Therefore, capital should be put to only those uses in which it can yield a return in social value which will be sufficient to compensate for the postponement of consumption as well as for the cost of production of the capital goods. This compensation for the postponement of consumption is really a social rate of interest. Thus, although the board does not pay a rate of interest, it is compelled to charge one for proper accounting purposes. If saving is not voluntary on the part of individuals, the state must operate on the theory that the planning board is a better judge of the relative merits of present *versus* future consumption than the people are themselves.

Contrary to the opinion of many critics of socialism, there appears to be more danger that arbitrary decisions of a planning board will result in too-rapid expansion of capital equipment rather than that the expansion will be too slow. Engineers and technical experts in the various industries will always be eager to adopt new machinery which, by purely engineering standards, is more efficient than the old machines with which they are working. The Russian experiment is confirming evidence of this. Workers have been asked to "pull in their belts" for one Five-Year Plan after another in order to industrialize the country at what most observers believe to be too rapid a rate. (In part this was due to the fear of not being able to obtain goods from capitalist countries. In this the Russians displayed their ignorance of the businessman's psychology; a communist dollar sounds as sweet to him when it is ringing in the cash register as any other dollar.) In order for new machinery to replace old machinery or to be made as an addition to total capital, the net gain in value of product added by the new machine must be sufficient to compensate for the postponement of consumption as well as for the other costs involved.

We still have not solved the problem of what should be the amount of the social rate of interest. We have not found a proper welfare standard for balancing the merits of present consumption against future consumption. One possible method might be to put the question to a popular vote, but this might easily lead to too small an accumulation of capital. People might vote to feed and clothe and house themselves well at the possible expense of provision for future generations. The Socialist would, of course, answer that the difference in human nature under socialism would militate against this. This, however, is an argument which the economist is not competent to answer.

CHAPTER XIII

Economic Planning in a Totalitarian State

THE IMMEDIATE difficulty in discussing totalitarian planning is to find a proper statement of its objectives so that the planning may be analyzed in the light of possible attainment of the desired goals.[1] In all the pronouncements of the leaders of these states we find the avowed aim of "aggrandizement of the state" or "welfare of the state"; for example, "nothing outside or above the state, nothing against the state, everything within the state, everything for the state."[2] It is difficult for most of us, however, to grasp a concept of the "welfare of the state" which is avowedly different from the "general welfare" of the individuals who compose the state. We know how hard it is to measure or even to define "general welfare" in the ordinary sense of the term; how much more difficult, then, to frame a concept of the "welfare" of an abstract creature called the state in whose advancement even the identity of the individual is supposed to be lost.

A few possible explanations offer themselves. First, for the vague concept of the "welfare of the state" we might substitute "the development of the state as an efficient engine for waging war." Such a statement would hardly be inconsistent either with the statements or the actions of Hitler and Musso-

---

[1] See Mackenzie, Findlay, *Planned Society: Yesterday, Today, Tomorrow,* Ch. XXIII, Prentice-Hall, Inc., New York, 1937.

[2] Sturgo, M. Luigi, "The Totalitarian State," *Social Research,* May 1936, pp. 222-235.

lini. It might be said further that such a concept involves the ability to wage a war of aggression rather than the mere defense of the state. Warfare, however, would seem to be the antithesis of welfare, even for this nebulous creature called the state. Even expenditures for defense consume, rather than create, national wealth and are regarded by most people simply as a necessary evil. It seems to be fairly well established also that no nation has made a net profit on any territory acquired by war in recent years. The "bloodless victories" of Germany over Austria and Czecho-Slovakia may appear to be exceptions to this. If it turns out to be necessary to maintain any large military force to keep these countries subjugated, however, it may prove that Germany could have made more by trading with these countries than by technically owning them.

There is one peculiar psychological basis for a military "welfare" concept: Some individuals may derive great pride in being citizens of a powerful state which is respected or feared by other nations. The theory behind this is that membership in a "glorious" group is a compensation for an individual inferiority complex. Much the same phenomenon can be observed in college fraternity life and in supposedly more adult fraternal organizations. The individual who wastes the most time bragging about his fraternity or his club is usually the one with the fewest personal attributes of which he can be proud as an individual. We cannot dismiss this attitude too lightly. The question is, though, how many people are so constructed that the satisfaction of this vanity will compensate for the lack of satisfaction of more material wants? How much butter and bratwurst will the German be willing to give up in exchange for bullets and bayonets?

There is also another angle to the military "welfare" concept. Some individuals are so constructed mentally that they do not like to make decisions for themselves. For these people, the regimentation of their lives under an army type of discipline where most of the decisions are made for them, plus a reasonable amount of security, may offer an attractive rather than an unattractive mode of existence. Even though these people may recoil from making decisions themselves, a considerable part of their happiness will depend upon how well the central authority succeeds in making decisions which are pleasing to them. Again we have the question of what proportion of the population is of this mental type. On the basis of these two aspects of military "welfare" we have a curious paradox. The "all glorious state" is best adapted to the welfare of a nation of weaklings and mental misfits.

Another possible explanation presents itself. The "welfare of the state" may be simply a smoke screen to cover the exploitation of the rest of the people for the benefit of a certain favored group (the Nazi leadership in Germany, the Communist party members in Russia). The fact that party membership is limited, although all totalitarian states have one-party governments and will tolerate no other parties, lends substance to this interpretation. The claim of "acting in the best interests of the nation" is always considered good political strategy in any country. It is, moreover, a comparatively easy process of reasoning for those in power to convince themselves that what is good for them personally is good for the nation as a whole. The chief difference between democracies and dictatorships in this respect is that democracies provide a ready means of "turning the rascals out" when the decisions resulting from this form of mental astigmatism are in fact offensive to the majority of the people.

A distinction must be drawn here between totalitarianism as it exists in Russia and its manifestations in Italy and Germany. Stalin claims repeatedly that the present techniques are simply a temporary expedient designed to prepare the people and the country for its ultimate goal of pure Marxist socialism. It is somewhat difficult, however, to reconcile this claim with the purges of the "Old Bolsheviks" whose principle offense is apparently a more strict adherence to Marxist doctrine than that practiced by the Communist party under the Stalin dictatorship. The longer the change to a pure social democracy is delayed, however, the less likely is the possibility that it will be achieved by anything short of a revolutionary overthrow of the present leadership. Fascist totalitarianism, on the other hand, makes the subjugation of the individual to the state a matter of avowed and permanent policy. Judged by actions rather than by avowed claims, the difference between the two forms is apparently steadily diminishing. Fascism[3] started as the avowed protector of capitalism and private property. The devices of exchange control, compulsory cartellization, price-fixing, conscription of labor and similar measures have, however, left little semblance of capitalism as it exists in a free market and have meant much more impairment of the rights of private property than most other countries have exercised even in war time. Russia, on her side, starting from a strictly communist ideology, has modified this with differential wages, various forms of private property, and other characteristically capitalist devices. We shall devote no further particular attention to Russia. To the extent that she tries to operate on socialist lines, the preceding chapter gives an analysis of her problem. If she turns towards fascism, as she may possibly do, the present chapter will be more applicable.

We still have not settled upon a statement of the fascist objective. In spite of other interpretations which may be placed upon both the words and actions of leaders in the fascist states, let us consider as their objective "the development of the state as an efficient engine for waging war." We have the authority of Mussolini himself in considering this to be the fascist aim:

---

[3] The terms "fascism" and "fascist" as used in this chapter are intended to designate the systems prevailing in both Italy and Germany.

And above all, Fascism, the more it considers and observes the future and the development of humanity quite apart from political considerations of the moment, believes neither in the possibility nor the utility of perpetual peace. It thus repudiates the doctrine of Pacifism—born of a renunciation of the struggle and an act of cowardice in the face of sacrifice. War alone brings up to its highest tension all human energy and puts the stamp of nobility upon the peoples who have the courage to meet it. All other trials are substitutes, which never really put men into the position where they have to make the great decision—the alternative of life or death. Thus a doctrine which is founded upon this harmful postulate of peace is hostile to Fascism. . . .

. . . But here again Fascism repudiates the conception of 'economic' happiness, to be realized by Socialism and, as it were, at a given moment in economic evolution to assure to everyone the maximum of well-being. Fascism denies the materialist conception of happiness as a possibility, and abandons it to its inventors, the economists of the first half of the nineteenth century: that is to say, Fascism denies the validity of the equation, well-being equals happiness, which would reduce men to the level of animals, caring for one thing only—to be fat and well-fed —and would thus degrade humanity to a purely physical existence.[4]

Judged as a system of preparing the state for war, the fascist plan offers many advantages. The rigid discipline which prevails during peacetime means that no very great change in governmental controls will have to take place when a war actually occurs. Giving preference to "essential industries of war" in obtaining labor and raw materials during peacetimes tends to lessen the shock and confusion to the economic and industrial system in changing from a peacetime to a wartime basis. Roads, railroads and other forms of transport are constructed and operated, not with a view to maximum economic service in time of peace, but rather with a view to maximum strategic importance in time of war. The maintenance of a very large standing army plus a trained reserve, together with carefully rehearsed mobilization plans, allows the state to bring

---

[4] Benito Mussolini, "The Political and Social Doctrine of Fascism," in Mackenzie, Findlay, *Planned Society: Yesterday, Today, Tomorrow,* Prentice-Hall, Inc., New York, 1937, pp. 803-805.

the maximum possible number of men under arms in the minimum length of time.

The technique of exchange controls plus subsidization of domestic production in essential industries tends to make the fascist state as nearly self-sufficient as national resources and national genius in inventing substitute goods will permit. Another advantage must be conceded to the fascist economics of warfare. In a free market the attempt to expand the production of munitions by such great amounts would naturally lead to large increases in wages and prices of raw materials for the munitions industries. The fascist state is not troubled in this manner. It controls the labor unions and forbids them to ask for wage increases. It may set maximum prices on domestically produced raw materials. If the raw materials are imported, it may prevent "nonessential" industries from bidding competitively for them by denying them the necessary foreign exchange with which to make purchases. If not enough labor offers itself at the fixed wage rates, the state conscripts labor to work on desired military projects. Where the state can command it does not have to induce.

Currency inflation (carefully concealed as far as possible by exchange controls), together with the ability to fix maximum prices for certain goods, provides for a tremendous amount of what might properly be called "extra-budgetary taxation"; or we might call it "forced saving" for military purposes. If a free market were maintained, the attempt to raise the necessary funds for military expenditures by direct taxation might be sufficient to arouse the open hostility of even so phlegmatic an individual as the average German.

On the basis of the above considerations we must concede that the fascist system is magnificently designed for preparation for a "quick short war." Even on the basis of war efficiency, particularly if the war is to be a long one, we may raise some questions concerning the efficacy of fascist organization. The morale of the people is considered to be an extremely important element by all of the experts in the art of war. To what extent will the lowered standard of living (made necessary by the devotion of so much of the country's resources for military purposes) be a contributory factor to reduced wartime morale? Simply to maintain themselves in power and to facilitate the acceptance of what would otherwise be unpopular decrees, the fascist leaders have made a greater use of propaganda and appeals to patriotism than has ever been witnessed in a peacetime state. Will not the too-often repeated use of this instrument have dulled its edge so that actual wartime propaganda will be ineffective? As the peacetime benefits of fascist organization become increasingly and obviously confined to party members, and more particularly to party leaders, will not the resulting dissatisfaction tend to make a poor basis for national unity in time of war?

We must now turn to an appraisal of fascism as a program for peacetime economic planning. In spite of the lofty disdain which Mussolini and Hitler profess for the material things of life (speaking themselves with full stomachs), the average Italian and the average German are probably still concerned with the standard of living which the regime gives to them. In judging the ability of fascism to increase national wealth or national income or to provide a higher peacetime standard of living, we may be unfair to fascist leaders who specifically disavow such ends. In deciding whether to adopt fascism for America, however, it might be perfectly in order to postulate some such criteria. We do not need to fight an offensive war; preparation for defense is sufficient. Therefore, the question as far as we are concerned is: What has the technique of fascist control to offer in the way of solution for our peacetime economic problems?

At the very outset it must be conceded that a dictatorship is much better adapted for comprehensive central planning than is a constitutional democracy. The plan can be worked out as a consistent whole and need not suffer the amount of compromises which are necessary to get legislation adopted by a democratic legislature. While the plan is in operation the only political compromises which need to be made are the minimum necessary to prevent a revolution. Perhaps this means only the maintenance of a sufficiently large police force, and keeping the police themselves contented. All this implies, however, is that the dictatorship has power; it is not implied that it has the requisite knowledge to make the best plan or to administer it.

The minute that we advocate departure from the judgments of a free market in establishing economic values, we are postulating that the central authority has a better knowledge of what is best for the common welfare than have the people themselves. We found in the preceding chapter some of the difficulties which this entails. The Socialists are at least able to offer the claim that unequal distribution tends to distort the pricing process. Fascism is the avowed "protector of capitalism" and so cannot promise equal incomes. Perhaps the fascist system aims simply to give us a "better" distribution of income rather than equal incomes. If so, what standards are there to determine how such income should be apportioned?

Fascism has, of course, offered us no plan of income distribution. The only obvious policy along these lines has been the attempt to "preserve small business." Planning for this purpose, however, involves a negation of, rather than an increase of, economic efficiency. Insofar as small businesses are efficient, unless they are actively hindered, they will survive by themselves or grow into larger businesses which may be still more efficient. The retention of inefficient small business may involve considerable waste of national resources. The use of the cartel system for this purpose, with fixed prices and production quotas, may prevent the weeding-out of inefficient business firms even in industries where the typical firm would continue to be small in a free market. (On this basis, anti-chain store and resale price maintenance legislation might be considered fascist measures.)

One of the achievements of fascism that has attracted widest attention has been its apparent ability to reduce unemployment. What are the reasons for this reduction? They are: (1) The tremendous increase of expenditure for armaments and military purposes. This reduces rather than increases national wealth. (2) The maintenance of a large standing army. These men are consuming rather than producing wealth. (Whatever useful work is performed by the WPA and the CCC is a net gain as contrasted with this, yet we count them among the unemployed.) (3) The prevention of imports through exchange controls, resulting in great expansion of certain domestic industries and particularly of domestic agriculture. This has meant the diversion of labor into occupations where it is less efficient. The statement of Hitler that Germany must "export or die" is a tacit admission of this. The sum total of these measures simply shows that Germany has produced a smaller quantity of goods with more labor than would have been the case if this labor were efficiently applied. She has not solved the unemployment problem; in one sense she has merely spread partial unemployment among all workers. One other factor has operated to reduce unemployment: Through state control of trade-unions it has been possible to prevent money wages from rising with the cost of living, thus reducing real wages.

This last point offers food for thought for the American labor movement. If American unions are unable to set wages at which it is economically possible to hire most of their members, there is some danger that "It can happen here." Many students of the problem are convinced that the rise of Hitler in Germany was primarily a reaction against the too-rapid advance of the German labor movement.

Another Viewpoint on Fascism

We have been under considerable difficulty in the analysis of fascism, perhaps because fascism cannot be considered as an economic system in the same sense as socialism or capitalism. In one sense, fascism may be regarded merely as the extreme expression of economic nationalism. If this interpretation is accepted as correct, then external rather than internal conditions are chiefly responsible for the rise of fascism in Italy and Germany. The Smoot-Hawley tariff in the United States, high tariffs and import quotas in France, high tariffs in the new countries created by the Versailles Treaty, and the system of Empire Preference in the British Empire, deprived Germany and Italy of their most important foreign markets. In consequence, they have been forced to become much more self-sufficient than would be the case under more intelligent economic conditions of international trade. These two countries are not equipped with the natural resources to practice self-sufficiency so as to achieve a standard of living appropriate to a modern industrial nation. Hence the emphasis on war preparations, either as a serious intention for war of conquest or as a bluff to obtain the desired ends.

CHAPTER XIV

Economic Planning in a Capitalistic Democracy

THE BEST approach to our problem is through a definition of capitalism. That of Professor Pigou[1] can hardly be improved upon: "A capitalist *industry* is one in which the material instruments of production are owned or hired by private persons and are operated at their orders with a view to selling at a profit the goods or services that they help to produce. A capitalist *economy,* or capitalist system is one the *main part* of whose productive resources is engaged in capitalist industries."

Immediately some people will object that the very idea of central planning is inconsistent with capitalism unless it becomes fascist planning, and inconsistent with democracy unless it becomes socialist planning. This does not necessarily follow, although the avoidance of these two horns of the dilemma must necessarily limit the field within which planning may be considered both capitalistic and democratic. The avoidance of socialism and fascism must be found both in the statement of the ends to be achieved by planning and in the techniques for achieving those ends.

We might choose as a statement for such ends, "the elimination or minimization of business cycle fluctuations," or "the fullest possible utilization of resources." Note that we say

---

[1] Pigou, A. C., *Socialism Versus Capitalism,* p. 1, Macmillan & Co., Ltd., London, 1937. Reprinted by permission of the Macmillan Company.

nothing directly about welfare or the distribution of income. There can be little doubt, however, that the attainment of these ends would increase the material "well-being" of the nation. Also, success in eliminating the business cycle and in keeping resources more fully employed would undoubtedly increase the incomes of most of the low income groups. The relative share in national income received by the lower income groups might very likely increase. There can be little doubt that their absolute real income would be greatly enhanced.

Most of the chapter will be devoted to a consideration of possible techniques although we might well precede this by a statement of some general principles which these techniques must follow if the "pitfalls" of fascism and socialism are to be avoided. (1) Consumers must be considered to be the best judges of what is best for their own individual welfare as expressed by their demand for goods and services in a free market. Such choices may be influenced by education or propaganda but they may not be coerced, either by rationing of goods or by arbitrary control of allocation of productive resources. (2) Some goods or services, whose widespread or general consumption is considered to be "socially desirable" by a democratic decision, may be provided by the state either without charge or at prices lower than those which would be charged by private industry. (These are really "islands of socialism in a sea of capitalism." If the islands become too numerous, we have a socialist continent with capitalist lakes.) [2] (3) The amount of individual saving must be left to the individual as influenced by the rate of interest and such other personal considerations as may happen to determine his choice between present and future consumption. (4) The *direction* of investment (other than that made by the state) must be determined by the competition of various opportunities for profit to obtain the supply of available capital at prevailing interest

---

[2] *Ibid.*, p. 10.

rates. This does not prevent the state from attempting to control either the interest rate or the total quantity of money, or both, in an attempt to equate the rate of investment with the rate of saving. (If, however, the bulk of direct investment is made by the state rather than by private individuals or private institutions, the socialist islands again threaten to become a mainland.) (5) Competition must be relied upon to establish prices as far as possible. Where competition does not exist or is not practicable, price regulation may be necessary. The goal of such price regulation must be prevention of monopolistic restriction of output rather than the elimination of profits.

We might summarize these points by saying that their general implication is that the technique of planning should be along the lines of "making capitalism work the way it is supposed to work." The primary function of the state thus becomes the determination and enforcement of "the rules of the game." The state becomes an active participant itself only in those cases where the rules will not work. We shall now attempt to discover what techniques of planning are possible within these rather narrow limits.

Provision of Information

No scheme of planning, whether capitalist or otherwise, can promise much without adequate data on which to base decisions. While tremendous improvements have been made in the amount and quality of both government and private business statistics in the last twenty years, we have only begun to scratch the surface in accumulating data for the solution, or even for the intelligent discussion of many economic problems. Many theories of the cause of business cycles, for example, center around some phase of saving, investment, or the rate of capital goods production, yet the available data permit only the rashest kind of wild guesses as to quantitative changes in these factors. Even on unemployment, the reduction of which is one of the avowed ends of most planning schemes, our most adequate data up till now has been that of censuses which are out of date by the time they are compiled and published. As soon as various state unemployment insurance plans come into operation, we may have accurate monthly or weekly information concerning the number of unemployed *who are eligible for benefit payments*. It will still require some inspired statistical guessing to estimate *total unemployment* on the basis of this partial sample. For banking, our best data includes only reporting member banks of the Federal Reserve System and does not cover large numbers of nonmember state and private banks.

Even though nothing further were done in the way of planning, the provision of more adequate information might enable individual businesses and industries to plan their own operations better. A few economists have even predicated a theory of business cycles upon errors in the decisions of businessmen which are based on lack of information. Even though other economists dispute this as a primary causal theory, they would doubtless agree that the possession of better information might be an important element in lessening the amplitude of business fluctuations. Adequate information all along the line from primary producer to ultimate consumer as to inventories and volume of sales should help to prevent accumulation of such large excess inventories as have existed in the past. Smaller excess inventories will tend both to lessen the amount of price decline in depression and to shorten the length of time which is necessary to reduce them. In addition to this, if primary producers have adequate information that dealers' stocks are getting low in relation to the volume of sales, it may appear to be a safe procedure to increase production in anticipation of increased sales. This practice would tend to bring recovery earlier than might be expected in the absence of such information.

Businessmen might bear this in mind when tempted to grumble about the work of filling out reports for the government. On its part, the government might do well to accept the recommendations and to further the work of the Central Statistical Board to avoid needless duplication in such reports. This might then be made the basis of obtaining more information at the same cost to the businessman and to the government.

Definition of the Fields of Various Types of Competition and Monopoly

In place of the present half-enforcement, or sporadic enforcement, of the anti-trust laws, the government might formulate a definite policy on the nature of competition or monopoly which appears to be best suited to each industry. (See Chapter VIII.) Under the present unsettled policy, no large firm which is in a dominant position in an industry can feel sure that it may expand its capital equipment and its output without running afoul of the anti-trust laws. New firms, on the other hand, may be deterred from entering the industry through fear of possible expansion on the part of the large firm. While such fears may be of negligible importance in times of prosperity and lax enforcement, they may be a contributing element in deterring new capital investment in times of depression when it is most needed.

In a field such as this where there are so many conflicting interests, and where changes in technology may alter the entire nature of an industry, no one would be so foolhardy as to suggest an absolutely rigid plan, which would not be subject to alteration in the light of experience. This does not mean, however, that this is a question that can be dumped in the lap of some administrative board trusted to act on its own discretion. Uncertainty as to the probable decisions of such a board might be as great or greater than present uncertainty as to the degree of lethargy in the Federal Trade Commission and the

Department of Justice and the uncertainty as to the probable attitude of the courts. It would seem, nevertheless, that we should be able to formulate some statements of general policy on this question which might be a much more definite guide for business action than we now have. If a more definite policy is not formulated, the request of businessmen that plans for combination be approved or disapproved by the Department of Justice before they are adopted does not seem to be unreasonable.

Definition of the Fields of Public and Private Enterprise

This is another question which is not strictly so much one of planning as it is one of statement of policy. The production and distribution of electric power is the most conspicuous example of the lack of such a policy at present. The obvious difficulty is the lack of a definite majority political opinion on either side of the question of public ownership. The advocates of public ownership are not strong enough to force the general adoption of their policy, while their opponents are not strong enough to prevent piecemeal adoption. The unfortunate result is that neither public nor private investment is as great as it might be, for an expanding industry, if a definite policy were determined upon. It is idle to hope that private interest will give up without a struggle, nor do the advocates of public ownership give any signs of relaxing their efforts. A compromise might be effected, however, on the basis of limitation of territory for each of the two forms of ownership. Such a compromise need not be the permanent solution, but if it is to be effective it must be for a sufficient length of time to permit reasonably safe investment in durable capital equipment.

Co-ordination of Government Activities

Before a government can exercise much claim to wisdom in planning for general business activity, it would seem reasonable to expect that the various activities of the government itself should at least be designed so as not to work at cross purposes with each other. The Treasury Department cannot have one monetary policy and the Federal Reserve Board another. The State Department cannot have one foreign trade policy and the Commerce Department another. The Interior Department cannot have one conservation policy and the Agriculture Department another. This is not a criticism of these departments or agencies. They must administer the laws which are given to them. The fault lies in the passage of one piece of legislation after another with little regard to the completed whole into which they are expected to fit.

Fundamentally, the difficulty lies in the problem of determining what is in the interest of the nation as a whole and then in making that interest politically articulate. The only economic interest which all of us have in common is that we are all consumers. As such, we are obviously all benefited by a greater total output of goods at lower prices. Unfortunately, each of us is more concerned about his own individual income as a producer. A 10 percent increase in my own wages or profits will more than offset a 20 percent increase in prices of any group of goods that comprises anything less than half of my total expenditures. Consequently, those of us who are faced with foreign competition lobby for a tariff on our product. Those of us who are small retailers lobby for anti-chain store laws. Those of us who are interested in shipping lobby for ship subsidies or for laws preferential to our own ships. Those of us who are butter producers lobby for a tax on oleomargarine. Each of these types of legislation, and many others are a bit of *governmental favoritism* which benefits one group as producers *at the expense of all the rest of the nation as consumers.* If all measures of this sort were up for consideration at one time and the effects of each of them on the prices we pay were to be clearly shown, opposition might become active and effective. Instead of this, the measures are introduced slowly over a period of time. The people who can see their direct interest in them are active in bringing pressure on the legislature for their passage. The rest of us sit idly by, perhaps not even realizing that one chip after another is being whittled from our real income. Later on, after one measure after another has gone into effect, we begin to wonder what makes "the high cost of living," why "the farmer receives so small a percent of the retail price of his product," and why "labor is unable to buy the goods which it produces." We have already reached the point where new special benefits to certain groups of producers (to farmers, for example) are advocated and enacted on the grounds of attempted remedy for the inequities created by old special benefits. This system will not work universally. Most of these special benefits tend to divert labor and capital into industries where they are less efficient than if they were allocated in an unsubsidized market. So long as resources are continued in employment in these less productive uses, *total national real income must be less than the possible maximum.* The only real remedy is the *removal* of the special benefits so that resources may be put to better uses. Short of this, "equality" can only be achieved by making everyone take an equal loss as his share of the reduced national income caused by misdirection of resources through tariffs and subsidies.

It may be objected that the removal of special privilege is an extremely difficult political feat. Granted. If we cannot accomplish this task, however, it would seem to be idle to talk of economic planning in a capitalist democracy. Any system of planning which contemplates the continuance permanently of special political privileges is not likely to stop short of fascism unless it happens to be overthrown by social revolution.

The inefficient producer, who is protected in his inefficiency by a tariff or subsidy, is in a rather poor position to point the finger of scorn at the inefficiency of socialism.

Monetary Planning

This is one field in which at least a policy, if not planning itself, is practically forced upon us.[3] Paradoxically, if we judge by results, even the absence of a policy is itself a policy; that is, if the government exercises no control over the quantity of bank credit, it is really following the policy of leaving control of the effective quantity of money to the discretion of the banks themselves.

So pervasive is the influence of money upon all forms of economic activity that a successful solution of the monetary problem might obviate the necessity for the more elaborate and detailed schemes of planning in many other fields. If we could manage money properly, we could probably eliminate the business cycle with the least possible amount of "government interference in business."

A statement of the goal for monetary policy is much easier to make than a statement of the means for its attainment. We may develop standards for a monetary policy by considering the situation which exists in a barter economy, where the supply of any one commodity constitutes a demand for all other commodities. Under barter I cannot sell (swap) the goods which I possess without taking my payment in other goods. Thus, such a thing as general overproduction is impossible. There may be too great a quantity of one good and not enough of another, so that one product may have a low exchange value in terms of the other, but people with the scarce goods cannot dispose of them without taking the other goods in exchange.

---

[3] Henry C. Simons, "Rules vs. Authorities in Monetary Policy," in Mackenzie, Findlay, *Planned Society: Yesterday, Today, Tomorrow*, p. 463, Prentice-Hall, Inc., New York, 1937.

One concept of a "perfect" monetary system is that it should leave the above situation unchanged. In other words, money should be so managed that the only cause for changes in the prices of goods will be changes in their relative production and changes in desire or taste for them. *Money itself* should exert no independent influence upon prices. Professor Hayek and other economists call this the concept of *neutral money*.

As our economic system is organized, changes in the quantity of money cause changes in the *relative* prices of different goods because we do not all have the quantity of money in our pockets, or in our bank accounts, changed at the same time and in the same proportion.[4] Monetary changes make their effects felt first at one point in the system and later on at other points. If the prices which constitute selling prices for any business firm rise faster as a result of an increase in money circulation than the prices which constitute its costs, that firm will be motivated to expand its output. To do this, it will borrow from a banking system which *creates money* for the firm to use in the form of a credit to the firm's checking account. This new money will help to increase prices elsewhere. As long as there is unemployed labor and resources, selling prices for many firms will tend to rise more rapidly than costs. When resources become more fully employed, costs will tend to catch up with selling prices. Meanwhile, the capital goods industries will have expanded output, not because there is an increased demand for capital goods due to increased saving but rather because of the fact that other firms are trying to take advantage of an increased *monetary* demand for their goods. As soon as the money increase stops, demand for capital goods will fall off immediately. As workers are discharged from capital goods industries, demand for consumers' goods will de-

---

[4] Meyers, Albert L., *Elements of Modern Economics*, Chs. XVIII and XX, Prentice-Hall, Inc., New York, 1938.

crease. As bank loans are repaid and not renewed, demand in terms of money for other goods will decrease and we are in a "vicious spiral of deflation."

To prevent this whole process by monetary control, we would have to keep the effective quantity of money constant. Another way to express this is to say that we must keep the amount of money equal to the "money work to be done." In any period, the amount of money which can be used for making payments is the quantity of total cash and bank credit in existence, multiplied by its average velocity of circulation (the average number of times it changes hands). The "money work to be done" consists of the total amount of payments which must be made. This work would be increased, for example, if a farmer, who had previously paid his hired men in farm produce, now started to pay them in cash. It would be decreased if one firm, which formerly bought materials from another, should merge with the other firm.

At present we have only roughly accurate estimates of the quantity of money and still rougher estimates of the velocity of circulation. Concerning the "money work to be done," it might be difficult even to hazard a guess as to the direction in which it is changing. Perfectly neutral money, therefore, is practically an impossible achievement.

While perfect control may be an impossibility, we may easily prevent the amount of expansion and contraction which we have at present. One step toward this would be to require the banks to maintain a 100 percent reserve ratio against demand deposits. In other words, the banks would not be allowed to create money on their own account, but would be reduced to the status of middlemen who would collect cash savings and lend them out again. To be effective, however, this might have to be supplemented by measures designed to prevent the creation of other money substitutes by business firms themselves.

Less drastic but perhaps less effective controls may be found in the full use of the powers of the Federal Reserve Board, plus variations in government fiscal policy with respect to taxation and borrowing. (See Chapter IV.) Even this would seem to require that all banks be compelled to become members of the Federal Reserve System.

Conclusion

The difficulties which we have found in connection with all forms of planning are mostly traceable to deficiencies in our knowledge. Whatever may happen to be our political, social, or economic philosophy, we are challenged with the necessity of improving upon it. As yet no one has all the answers. There is plenty of room for you to contribute.

Index